Separatism
and Women's
Community

DANA R. SHUGAR

Separatism and Women's Community

University of Nebraska Press, Lincoln and London

Library of Congress Cataloging in
Publication Data. Shugar, Dana R., 1961–
Separatism and women's community /
Dana R. Shugar.   p.   cm. Includes biblio-
graphical references (p.) and index.
ISBN 0-8032-4244-1 (cloth: alk. paper)
1. Feminist theory – United States.
2. Feminism – United States.
3. Radicalism – United States.
4. Lesbianism – United States.
I. Title. HQ1190.5.U6s58   1995
305.42 – dc20   94-32900 CIP

To Carla:

for our pasts,
present,
and future

CONTENTS

ACKNOWLEDGMENTS

When I began this project, the social climate was such that I received repeated cautions against undertaking such a 'controversial' topic as a graduate student/assistant professor. What a difference five years can make! I can never be grateful enough for the diligent, unwavering sociopolitical activism that has made this study not only acceptable but also sought after.

More specifically, I am indebted to many people who provided support, encouragement, and offers to read various drafts during the early stages of my research. For her unshakable faith in this project, support, and willingness to read any draft at any stage, I owe my deepest gratitude to my partner, Carla Marcus. For their advice and good humor, I thank the members of my feminist dissertation group: Janet Delwiche, Janet Kaufman, Joyce Meier, Mary Metzger, and Nancy Reincke. I am very grateful for the courage, support, and sheer hard work of my thesis advisor, Adalaide Morris, and my committee members: Florence Boos, Susan Birrell, Kathleen Diffley, and Mary Lou Emery. I also wish to thank Dorothy Parkander and my parents, Samuel and Shirley Shugar, for their love and support throughout the dissertation process. Several people willingly shared information and ideas about feminist utopias and separatist collectives: Diane Crowder, Mary Lynn Broe, Steely, and Quinn. Further, without the courage and stories of the women of OWLS and of separatist collectives throughout the Midwest, my understanding of our lives would be far less than it is today. And without the invaluable resource of the Lesbian Herstory Archives, this project would have been impossible. Finally, the initial stages of my research were made possible in part through an Alumni Dissertation Travel Award granted by the Department of English at the University of Iowa.

x

Further thanks are due to those who aided the process of transforming my dissertation into a finished book. For reading drafts of my abstract and helping me through the initial stages of publication, I wish to thank Mary Cappello, Bernice Lott, and Mary Ellen Reilly. Mary Cappello, Greta Cohen, and Mathilda Hills generously and insightfully provided editorial advice for the book's interstices. I also am indebted to Frances Bartkowski, Greta Cohen, and Marcia Anderson for their help with choosing a publisher for the work. I am very grateful for the overall support and encouragement from my colleagues and friends in the Women's Studies Program and the Department of English at the University of Rhode Island. URI's Department of English provided further aid in the form of course load reductions and financial support for my graduate assistant, Diane Wellins Moul. Diane deserves special thanks for her meticulous efforts to correct the quotations, citations, bibliography, and index of this work.

Finally, I can never repay the kindness, encouragement, and attention given me by both Joan Nestle and the women of the Bloodroot collective: Selma Miriam, Noel Furie, and Betsey Beaver; together, they have shown me what community and its conflicts are all about. I acknowledge their struggle and offer this study in hopes that our conflicts will become one part of, rather than the end of, our community. (Note: All names found within the Interstices are real except in three cases in which I was unable to locate the individuals to request permission.)

The Community Work
of Separatist Discourse

INTRODUCTION

Perhaps nothing is more out of fashion in feminist critical theory today than the discourse of lesbian separatism. Because separatism (that is, the belief that women must and should separate from men politically and personally in order to accomplish the goals of a feminist revolution) and cultural feminism both strive to create or codify a female culture, many contemporary feminist scholars often conflate the two.[1] This conflation has led to a dismissal of separatism as essentialist, unappealing for a large number of women, politically naive or ineffective, and morally oppressive, especially on issues that concern the representations of women's sexual desire.[2] Yet the energy scholars spend on all sides of the debate over separatism clearly indicates that separatism continues to be important to feminists engaged in a wide range of theories and practice.

The purpose of this study is to begin to move beyond the debate of the legitimacy or effectiveness of separatist discourse to a more useful examination of the functions such texts play in the creation and continuation of feminist communities. To do so, I examine the community work of three historically specific moments in American separatist discourse: separatist theory of the late 1960s through the 1970s, historical narratives of separatist collectives, and separatist utopian novels. By 'community work' I mean the ways in which these texts interact with the social order of feminist communities to participate, through discourse, in the movement for the sociopolitical changes demanded by radical-feminist agendas. I define 'radical feminism' as the beliefs that women are oppressed as a class in patriarchy, that patriarchy is a geographically and historically vast social system of sexism, and that only the complete destruction of this patriarchal system – not reformist measures or the destruction of a few of its aspects – will liberate women. My use of community work thus concerns what optimistically could be called the utopian nature of separatist discourse; that is, the ways it attempts to envision a better world and advocates action toward the achievement of that world.[3]

Though the recent critical focus on cultural feminism (which includes, besides separatism, aspects of lesbian and radical feminism) may indeed point to the influence this diverse coalition of feminisms has on current feminist theory, it often dismisses or ignores the effects separatism has on a variety of women's lives. For example, Frances Bartkowski's refusal to discuss Sally Miller Gearhart's separatist novel *The Wanderground* in her carefully considered work, *Feminist Utopias,* on the basis that it is essentialist and thus, as she implies, doubtfully feminist (Bartkowski 167), obscures the point that for many feminists of the late 1970s, *The Wanderground* not only shaped but was shaped by their experiences in separatist collectives. If the essentialism of the book is detrimental for one feminist, what in the text compelled so many others? What, in short, made *The Wanderground* a 'feminist supernovel' (Roberts 74), as it has been called by its more enthusiastic reviewers? To dismiss the novel based on a facet that may have been part of its appeal blocks an important understanding of the ways that such rhetoric works among feminist communities.

But 'essentialism,' though perhaps the most frequent charge levied against separatism, is not the only critique of the discourse today. In her recent book, *Daring to Be Bad: Radical Feminism in America, 1967–1975,* feminist historian Alice Echols clearly expresses her dismay over the rise of separatist practice in radical feminism. For Echols separatism was a phenomenon of feminist excess, as the rhetoric she uses to describe radical-feminist group Cell 16's movement toward separatism indicates:

Certainly, Cell 16 with their program of celibacy, separatism, and karate seemed the quintessential radical women's liberation group. Cell 16's political perspective became well known within the movement because the group published one of the very earliest radical feminist journals, *No More Fun and Games* – a title that captures all too well the essence of the group's message. . . . For Cell 16 the problem was women's diffidence and their dependence upon men, and the solution lay in women's 'unconditioning' themselves by taking off the accumulated emotional and physical flab that kept them enthralled to men. (158–60)

Stereotypic feminists 'without a sense of humor,' the members of Cell 16 appear here as women who promoted their feminism by means of a modified physical fitness plan. The tone and structure of this passage reveal that, for Echols, the zeal with which radical-feminist groups practiced their politics functioned mostly to hide the ineffectiveness of their activism.

But Echols's attention to the variety and scope of radical feminism reveals what her sarcasm might wish to refute: as a political program and practice, separatism once appealed to many heterosexual and lesbian feminists alike. Indeed, Echols's research indicates that at one time or another during their existence, most radical feminist groups experimented with some form of separatist practice and contributed to the significant number of separatist tracts. Through an examination of the community work of separatist theory, we can begin to realize the different ways separatist discourse compelled these women and to understand the unique value such texts held that was unavailable in the larger realm of feminist theory.

More problematic for me than the charges of essentialism or political ineffectiveness are the instances of racism or classism in separatist discourse. Position papers such as the Combahee River Collective's 'A Black Feminist Statement' or the discussion of separatism found in Beverly and Barbara Smith's essay 'Across the Kitchen Table: A Sister-to-Sister Dialogue' clearly illuminate the struggles over social constructions of race, class, and sexual orientation that raged in separatist circles from the early 1970s on. Yet even these critiques tend to ignore evidence that oppressions based on social constructions of difference were actively engaged and fought in separatist theory and practice long before they became of issue in other white feminist groups. To overlook such an interesting paradox obscures the complex rhetorical processes that led separatists both to struggle with progressive issues picked up only years later by other feminist communities and to reinscribe the very dichotomies that helped to generate the rhetoric and practice of oppression in the first place. My analysis of the community work of separatist discourse, then, examines the ideologies that both encouraged and made impossible a radical, effective critique of social constructions of difference.

The desire to denounce separatism within feminism has led to other, perhaps more minor problems for feminist communities as well. More so in the past but to a certain extent even today, separatist discourse motivates a significant segment of activist, grass-roots feminist practice. This contention may appear implausible until we recall the structures of battered women's shelters, women's health-care centers, rape crisis lines, women's political groups, women's historical archives, and to a lesser extent feminist journals and the women's music industry. Although these institutions may not explicitly subscribe to separatist politics, their philosophies and practice clearly are influenced by separatist theory. To ignore or minimize that relationship not only denies a rich area of study for academicians, it also may contribute to the perceived and unnecessary split between feminist scholars and community activists.

Yet, clearly, the examination of the community work of separatist discourse, as in any study of cultural phenomena, is influenced by my interests today as well as by past events. And while it is certainly possible to conduct such an analysis without entirely agreeing with separatist thought, I do so from a position that is neither neutral nor uninvolved. My claim is not that I offer a historically or theoretically more unbiased view than others who have discussed separatist texts, but that the history and analysis I construct here ultimately provide an understanding of the motivation, appeal, and interactive potentials this discourse has had on its community of readers.[4]

To be explicit about my own motivations, then: this project began out of continued interest – that of my own and my students – in separatist utopian novels such as *The Wanderground*. Despite quite valid critiques of the essentialism, naiveté, and probable political ineffectiveness of separatist texts, these utopias continue to intrigue new and seasoned feminist readers in ways that are unaccounted for by current critical consensus. Further, the portrayals of lesbianism in these works compel me because of their very material impact on the ways many lesbians once chose (or continue to choose) to live our lives. Current critiques of cultural feminism fail to illuminate both the attraction of this discourse and the influence it had on many women at a very specific sociopolitical moment in American history.

As I began to look more closely at these novels and their discursive counterparts in theory and historical narrative, I found wide gaps between contemporary critical accounts of separatism and the self-perceptions of separatists. These gaps became of further importance because I have come to see connections between early separatist constructions of gender and sexuality and today's vehement debates among feminists over representations of women's sexual desire. That these debates divide feminists who might ally to fight the programs of their common antagonists disturbs me deeply. Thus, the task of analyzing the community work of separatism interests me not only for its historical constructions of gender and sexuality but also because I find this particular discourse to be an important, little-acknowledged component of contemporary feminist theory.[5] To that end, I intersperse several short, autobiographical narratives (interstices) throughout the body of the text of my experiences in and with separatist collectives. This inclusion is intended both to explore the connections between community debates of the past with those today and to begin to situate myself relative to the questions and concerns of separatism in general.

I have suggested that there are three primary sites of separatist discourse crucial to this study: theory, historical narrative, and utopian fiction. These three sites are important because they most clearly map out the creation, growth, and conflicts of separatist groups over a range of discursive formations. In general, the discourse of feminist separatism attempted to envision and create a community of women dedicated to the destruction of patriarchal society through (though not always exclusively so) the practice of separatism itself. Each literary form, however, acted in different ways within the social order of the separatist communities it helped to create.

The genre of separatist theory includes a variety of works by women who identified with the radical-feminist, lesbian-feminist, and lesbian-separatist movements of the 1960s and 1970s. To define 'separatism' and discuss its effects, I will discuss texts by radical-feminist authors such as Shulamith Firestone, Robin Morgan, Ti-Grace Atkinson, and the Redstockings, along with those of self-identified separatist authors such as Julia Penelope, Anna Lee, Sidney Spinster, and the Gutter Dyke Collective. Such an examination demonstrates that while the radical-feminist movement of the 1960s may have been the genesis of modern feminist-separatist politics (which only later became seen as exclusively lesbian), separatist practice – especially among lesbians – existed long before the advent of contemporary feminism in this country.

This combination of a politicized call for separatism with an extant model of separatist practice produced a unique cultural phenomenon, one that was to change what it meant to be a 'woman,' a 'lesbian,' and a 'feminist.' As we will see, the community work of separatist theory was most effective in its solidification of the ideology of sexism as the basis of all other oppressions. Thus, the need for women to bond with one another, regardless of their differences in economic status, race, age, physical ability, or sexual orientation, became paramount for many separatists. At the same time, separatists effectively used the rhetorical strategies of the lesbian-feminist movement to posit separatist practice as proof of one's feminist commitment.

The discursive call to separatism was most often put into practice through participation in collective living and business arrangements. This phenomenon occurred across the nation: living collectives generally were rurally located; collective businesses usually operated in the larger metropolitan areas. The movement toward collectivity was both ideologically and materially motivated: separatist women sought out means of supporting themselves in ways that were compatible with their politics.

Yet, as we might expect today, the lack of attention paid to social constructions of differences among women in separatist ideology (even while many separatists worked diligently on these issues within their own lives) took a heavy toll on the collectives themselves. The expectation of a durable bond between women based on gender was scarce comfort when women began to point out each other's racist, homophobic, classist, or ageist behaviors, and little in separatist theory prepared collective members for the extremely difficult task of the resolution of their differences. Thus, collective narratives such as Joyce Cheney's *Lesbian Land* or Michal Brody's *Are We There Yet?* followed a common pattern: what began as an exciting, activist movement to destroy women's oppression through the creation of separatist communities all too often ended in disillusion and dissolution as collective members confronted the evidence of their own oppressive behaviors. While the stated intent of these narratives was in part to illustrate the exhilarating possibilities of living out separatist politics, the texts worked more within their communities to discourage future attempts to create collectives.

By the mid-1970s it seemed apparent to many women that the dreams of separatist politics and practice – at least as they pertained to collectives – became highly questionable in light of women's experiences. I argue that the next discursive step for feminists who refused to give up the goal of female community came in the sudden interest in separatist utopian fiction.[6] Why utopian fiction? Part of the answer lies in the genre's popular form: for many readers, feminist fantasy provided a vision of the 'good life' beyond the feminist revolution.[7] But an analysis of the community work of these novels provides another way to understand the appeal of separatist utopias. As discussed in the third section of this study, separatist utopias sought to interrupt the fragmentation of feminist communities through the vision of processes that neutralized the destructive conflicts over social constructions of difference. In other words, the community work of separatist utopian discourse comes not in the simple creation of separate communities for women but in their visions of such communities that could safely navigate the dangerous clashes of identity differences.

I illustrate this reading through a detailed analysis of two separatist novels: Sally Miller Gearhart's *The Wanderground* (Persephone Press, 1978), a text written, in part, from authorial experiences with rural lesbian-separatist collectives, and Suzy McKee Charnas's *Motherlines* (Berkley-Putnam, 1978), a book written by a heterosexual, nonseparatist feminist. I point out these authors' social identities to demonstrate that separatist discourse influenced (even as it was created by) lesbian and heterosexual, separatist and nonseparatist women alike. Finally, the community work of separatist utopian fiction was of importance to the relationship between separatist and nonseparatist feminist communities as well.

To read separatist discourse in light of its community work is to value these texts not because they have some inherent worth as literary 'masterpieces' but because at a specific historical moment they provided their readers with means both to envision and to attain goals defined by the community from which the texts came. As I have mentioned, however, the effects of separatist discourse have been felt long past their immediate applications to the radical- and lesbian-feminist movements of the 1960s and 1970s. In the conclusion of this study, I take up the question of the influence of separatism on contemporary feminist theory and explore the community work – acknowledged and unacknowledged – this discourse continues to perform in feminist thought and practice today.

The Development of Separatist Theory and Ideologies of Female Community

PART ONE

Radical Feminism and the Safe Space
of Female Community

One

The advent of the radical-feminist movement within women's liberation promoted a new and different sense of the term 'community.'[1] Merriam-Webster's definition of community, for example, includes communities defined by their geopolitical boundaries, as in a state or commonwealth; by their geography, such as that of the Staten Island area of New York City; by their legal or economic status, as in a class identity or business community; by common interests, concerns, or social activities, as in a religious or cultural community; or by common professional interests, such as that of the academic community. The importance of these delineations lies in their reliance on facets other than those broadly biological; characteristics of race or ethnicity, for example, are communal only when crossed with geographic, economic, or shared social concerns.

With its theoretical formulation of women's status in patriarchal society, however, radical feminism utilized a definition of community that did not easily fit any of the word's common usages. The purpose of this chapter is not only to define what community meant for radical feminists but also to analyze the effects these definitions had on feminist politics, practice, and the creation of women's communities. As we shall see, the concept of community in radical feminism was so tightly bound to the concept of separatism that for many radical feminists separatism itself was synonymous with the creation of a politicized female community. Yet as I will discuss in subsequent chapters, heterosexual radical feminists often felt threatened by the growing numbers of lesbians attracted to the movement's sense of community and to its separatist politics. The tensions produced by radical feminism's ideological appeal to lesbians, coupled with the hostility lesbians often faced from heterosexual feminists, affected both the politics and practice of community within radical feminism.

3

4

For women in geographically scattered radical-feminist groups, the exchange of ideas and theories on their status in society could not be accomplished solely through oral communication or small-group discussions. Thus the publication and distribution of theory through books, pamphlets, newspapers, and journals became important not only to the spread of radical-feminist thought but also to the recognition and status of those groups who became most influential in the formulation of radical-feminist theory. In short, those with the capability to distribute their materials nationally often became recognized leaders in the movement.

This phenomenon helps to explain today's formulation of the history of radical feminism as predominantly based on literature published by groups from the East and, to a lesser extent, West coasts. For example, Alice Echols's historical account, *Daring to Be Bad: Radical Feminism in America, 1967–1975*, defends its heavy reliance on literature from East Coast groups with the assertion that 'these were the groups that made significant theoretical contributions' (20); but Echols also admits that

New York groups in particular benefited enormously from the presence of eager media. Their easy access to the media not only helped them to get their ideas out, but also gave them a special consciousness about themselves. The very title of New York Radical Women's 1968 publication, *Notes from the First Year* . . . reflected a certain awareness of their place in history. (20–21)

While availability of written material certainly affects our understanding of radical feminism in historical and literary projects today, it also affected national conceptions of the movement during its most active period. And while short essays, pamphlets, and position papers were important in these formulations, the printing or reprinting of these essays in anthologies or single-author books clearly had the edge in exposure, frequency of access, and length of availability in stores or from the publisher.

Thus even though radical feminism was formulated through a variety of written and oral discourses throughout the United States, only relatively few books and journals attained and maintained national recognition. The following brief descriptions are intended as an introduction to some of the most influential radical-feminist works. Again, these works are by no means the only ones published – or even available today – on radical feminism. Nor do I want to claim that they are the best representations of that movement. They are, however, those that became popular among women during the early stages of radical feminism and continue to influence our understandings of the concepts of female community envisioned by that movement.[2]

One of the earliest published books on radical-feminist theory was Shulamith Firestone's *The Dialectic of Sex* (1970). Before *Dialectic* was published, Firestone had been instrumental in the publication of *Notes from the First Year* and co-edited *Notes from the Second Year,* journals that detailed the theories of a radical-feminist group called the New York Radical Women, co-founded by Firestone and Pam Allen in 1967. Firestone, whose leftist background included work in Students for a Democratic Society (SDS), moved on from the New York Radical Feminists to the staunchly radical group Redstockings. By the time *Dialectic* was published, Firestone was a seasoned activist and instrumental theorist in the women's liberation movement. *Dialectic* explores the origins of American feminism and utilizes a combination of recast Marxist and Freudian theory to analyze sexism and racism in American society. Firestone's theoretical framework allowed her to provide new paradigms for the conceptualization of gender and race. But as we will see, her use of Marxist and Freudian theories to explain homosexuality did more to reinscribe homophobic mainstream ideologies than it did to challenge them.

Published the same year as *Dialectic* by a woman no less active or charismatic than Firestone, Robin Morgan's *Sisterhood Is Powerful: An Anthology of Writings from the Women's Liberation Movement* (1970) celebrated radical feminism through an extensive collection of essays on women's involvement in a variety of subjects: housework, child care, labor, race, class, prostitution, the church, and the law. Unlike Firestone, Morgan does not hesitate to claim the genesis of radical feminism to be women's discontent and ill treatment in leftist movements of the early 1960s. Morgan came to radical feminism from the Left (specifically, the antiwar movement) and spent many years as an activist before she joined women's liberation. She was also, not unhelpfully, an editor at Grove Press.

Three years after the debut of *Dialectic* and *Sisterhood Is Powerful,* Anne Koedt, Ellen Levine, and Anita Rapone edited *Radical Feminism* (1973), an anthology that collected many of the essays from the three years of *Notes. Radical Feminism* was quite deliberate in its choice of essays and avoided the so-called prowoman strain of Redstockings' theory.[3] Anne Koedt co-founded the New York Radical Feminists with Firestone; *Radical Feminism* contains some of the classic essays from the movement, including Koedt's 'The Myth of the Vaginal Orgasm.' *Radical Feminism* also reprinted Radicalesbians' 'Woman Identified Woman,' an essay that, as I will explain in chapter 2, became a key text of the lesbian-feminist movement.

In 1974, Ti-Grace Atkinson's *Amazon Odyssey* was published by Link Books. Though a relative latecomer, Atkinson's book is perhaps better remembered than many of its predecessors. That may be due in part to Atkinson's quasi-celebrity status: originally groomed by Betty Friedan for the leadership of New York's NOW chapter, Atkinson very publicly defected to found the Feminists (1970), another New York radical-feminist group. Atkinson went on consistently to define the cutting edge of radical feminism and was, as one historian has described her, determined to be 'the most radical of all radical feminists' (Echols 167). *Amazon Odyssey* collects Atkinson's essays that range in topics from her discontent in and resignation from NOW to her changing views on lesbianism and feminism.

Though it was one of the last books published on early radical feminism, Sara Evans's *Personal Politics* (1979) concentrates primarily on the events that led up to the beginning of the movement. Evans's account is an academic examination of the issues that compelled women to agitate for liberation as well as the difficulties they faced in the initiation of the modern feminist movement. Her description ends with the events of 1968, little more than twelve months after the first radical-feminist groups began to form. But her text is a valuable inscription of the issues that influenced the movement and is written by a woman who became a member of the Westside Group, a Chicago-based, leftist-identified group to which Firestone herself had once belonged.[4]

While the accounts of these authors vary in their emphasis on and approach to feminist theory, they all tend to posit the following, generalized version of the history of the women's liberation movement. White, economically secure women participated heavily in the various protest movements of the 1960s. For them, at least, activism had been all but dead since the 1930s and 1940s, when many joined the communist, socialist, and trade labor movements that swept the country. The 1960s renewed the hunger for social reform and encouraged many middle-and upper-class white women to join the struggle for freedom that had continued in the lives of women of color and poor white women for decades. Noting that most white women active in the early civil rights movement were southerners who came to activism through the church, Sara Evans recalls:

The longing for a new purpose in American society was becoming intense. For at least some young Christians in the South, the opportunity to act upon their faith and passionate concern would be welcome as a great relief. Moreover, through conferences and meetings a small group in the South had begun to develop contacts with black students unlike any they had previously known. For deeply religious southern whites the discovery on a personal level that black people were human beings, 'just like us,' was an often startling and moving experience. (32–33)

But as I will explain, the divisions or differences implied in Evans's description – white versus black, human versus nonhuman – were to have serious consequences for women, especially as they attempted to forge a cohesive women's liberation movement.

While white southern Christians began to feel the pull toward activism, middle-class white women throughout the country grew increasingly dissatisfied with the narrow roles available to them. Their general malaise was given voice especially by Betty Friedan in *The Feminine Mystique* (1963), who felt that social expectations for white, middle-class women stifled their mostly college-educated minds as well as constrained their physical activities. The combination of dissatisfaction with their lives and active participation in the social movements of the 1960s produced a heightened awareness of the anatomy of oppression for these women, an awareness that rather quickly led to the formulation of radical- (and other) feminist analyses.

Whites in general, and white women in particular, held a precarious position in the civil rights movement even before the interest in black separatism became strong. Joan Nestle, a Jewish activist who later co-founded the Lesbian Herstory Archives, recalls the realization of her peripheral role upon her arrival at Selma to do voter registration work:

Once on the ground, we were greeted by Jim Bevel, his head covered by an embroidered skullcap, his clear direct eyes looking straight at us, the small group of Northern do-gooders. He said, 'I hope you will be there when we come to New York.' We knew immediately we were no more than what we are, still part of the killing problem, and he treated us as if we were tourists who had signed up for some offbeat adventure vacation. His gait and the lines around his eyes told us that for him this was a war he could not walk away from: he would make do with whatever troops he had. (Nestle 54)

Nestle's voter registration work, though, seems an uncommon memory for many white women in the Movement.[5] Often, white women characterized their experiences as auxiliary to that of the activism of white and black men, as well as sexual conquests for both (Echols 25–30). While men burned draft cards and risked jail, women felt confined to 'Say[ing] Yes To Guys Who Say No!' White women who joined the Movement in order to accomplish tangible change – or, as Firestone charged, in order to fight vicariously for their own freedom through the struggles of others (Firestone 123–124) – were often sorely disappointed.

Yet attempts by women to address their status within the Movement were frequently met with silence, if not outright derision or harassment. Echols feels that the changes men perceived women's liberation demanded made them at best hesitant to support the women's movement: 'Movement men were not anxious to divest themselves of male privilege. The fight against male supremacy was considerably less abstract than the struggle against racism, in which white radicals could win points by reciting Panther rhetoric. Fighting sexism required that men make tangible changes in their lives, such as sharing the housework' (135). But whether men refused to confront their own behaviors or whether they felt that a Marxist revolution would liberate everyone, they paid little attention to women's increasing concerns. Repeatedly unsuccessful attempts by white women to focus the Movement on sexism caused many to break away from leftist groups altogether. And when recognition finally came from the Left, it was perceived by many women as too little, too late:

During the '70s, sectors of the nonsectarian left did begin to acknowledge the validity of at least some feminist claims. However, for many women the change came much too late. Repeated encounters with antagonistic or indifferent Movement men persuaded many women like Marge Piercy and Robin Morgan, who had been politicos, that they would have to go outside the left to build a women's movement. (Echols 135).

White women's growing dissatisfaction with social expectations, the perception of their peripheral roles within the Left, and the analyses of oppression they learned from their leftist training encouraged them to analyze and organize around what they understood to be their own oppression as women. Thus many accounts such as Firestone's or Morgan's cast leftist activism of the 1960s as the catalyst, and sometimes the genesis, of radical feminism.

In the introduction to *Sisterhood Is Powerful,* Robin Morgan wrote:

The current women's movement was begun largely, although not completely, by women who had been active in the civil-rights movement, in the anti-war movement, in student movements, and in the Left generally. There's something contagious about demanding freedom, especially where women, who comprise the oldest oppressed group on the face of the planet, are concerned. Thinking we were involved in the struggle to build a new society, it was a slowly dawning and depressing realization that we were doing the same work and playing the same roles *in* the Movement as out of it: typing the speeches men delivered, making coffee but not policy, being accessories to the men whose politics would supposedly replace the Old Order. But whose New Order? Not ours, certainly. (xx)

Morgan's characterization of women's impetus toward feminism embodies several concepts that were to become vital to radical feminist theory and its vision of female community. First, Morgan's assertion that 'women . . . comprise the oldest oppressed group on the face of the planet' encompasses two important theoretical aspects. Thoroughly trained in Marxist analyses of the nature of class oppression, early radical feminists began to understand women's existence in patriarchy as similar to that of the existence of the working class under capitalism: as an oppressed, socially defined group. This view of women as an oppressed class became one of the definitive theories of radical feminism and was almost universally adopted by radical feminists as that which was unique to their social analysis. Bonnie Kreps, for example, utilizes this argument in her differential definition of radical feminism:

Broadly speaking, the [women's liberation] movement can be divided into three areas: (1) The largely economically oriented (usually Marxist) segment which sees liberation for women as part of a socialist revolution; (2) liberal groups like the National Organization of Women. This segment . . . is working for some kind of integration of women into the main fabric of society; and (3) radical feminism, which chooses to concentrate exclusively on the oppression of women *as women* (and not as workers, students, etc.). This segment therefore concentrates its analysis on institutions like love, marriage, sex, masculinity and femininity. It would be opposed specifically and centrally to sexism, rather than capitalism (thus differing from Marxists), and would not be particularly concerned with 'equal rights,' 'equal pay for equal work,' and other major concerns of the NOW segment. (238–39)

The radical-feminist position on the status of women posited by Kreps and Morgan was, of course, predated by two earlier movements: the definition of (at least one group of) women as oppressed was the basis of the suffrage movements in the United States and Britain; the definition of a group of people from diverse cultures, races, geographies, and histories as a social class was proceeded by the American Left's use of Marxism in its explanation of world economics. And, in part, radical feminists designed their formulation of women's experience so that it could carry as much weight in the Left as did the category of economic class. Thus, the conception of 'woman' as a social category became instrumental in the formulation of a theory of women's oppression.

A second emphasis in Morgan's statement on women's oppression is an aspect that was to become one of radical feminism's most significant theoretical contributions to the discourse of feminist theory. Morgan calls women the *oldest* oppressed group on earth, a characterization that was meant both to challenge the Left's analysis of the primacy of class oppression and to answer opponents who tended to trivialize or ignore the issue of women's oppression. Faced with increasing pressure from Movement men to drop the divisive issues of women's liberation, early radical feminists began to insist that gender oppression was the original oppressive division in human society; that is, sexism, rather than racism or classism, was the primary contradiction. And as the primary contradiction, sexism within radical feminist theory became the paradigm of all other oppression. Morgan uses just such an analysis later in her introduction:

How, we are asked, *can you talk about the comparatively insignificant oppression of women, when set beside the issues of racism and imperialism?*
    This is a male-supremacist question. Not only because of its arrogance, but because of its ignorance. First, it dares to weigh and compute human suffering, and it places oppressed groups in competition with each other. . . . Second, the question fails to even minimally grasp the profoundly radical analysis beginning to emerge from revolutionary feminism: that capitalism, imperialism, and racism are *symptoms* of male supremacy – sexism. (xxxiv)

And in her analysis of the nature of the biological family, Shulamith Firestone utilizes Marxist theory to claim that oppression rooted in the biological differences between men and women is the basis for all oppression: 'the natural reproductive difference between the sexes led directly to the first division of labor based on sex, which is at the origins of all further division into economic and cultural classes and is possibly at the root of *all* caste (discrimination based on sex and other biologically determined characteristics such as race, age, etc.)' (9). It is important to remember that Firestone, like Morgan, quickly cast sexism as fundamentally more oppressive than (especially) classism in part out of the perceived need to respond to the Left's trivialization of women's experience. But radical feminism's use of sexism as the primary contradiction was, of course, ironic in its very continuation of the prioritization of oppression and in its refusal to recognize the symbiotic nature of any form of oppression. As I will discuss in later chapters, radical-feminist conceptions of sexism as the primary contradiction fostered severe consequences for the very communities the theory helped to create.

Given her analysis of women's oppression within the framework of sexism as the primary contradiction, the fact that Morgan proceeds to totalize women's experience within society is perhaps to be expected. Her characterization of women as 'doing the same work and playing the same roles *in* the Movement as out of it' posits a certain segment of white women's experience as both normal and normative, a description that quickly was challenged by African-American women. Cynthia Washington, a project director for the Student Nonviolent Coordinating Committee (SNCC), cast African-American women's involvement in the civil rights movement in strikingly different terms:

During the fall of 1964, I had a conversation with Casey Hayden about the role of women in SNCC. She complained that all the women got to do was type, that their role was limited to office work no matter where they were. What she said didn't make any particular sense to me because, at the time, I had my own project in Bolivar County, Miss. A number of other black women also directed their own projects. What Casey and other white women seemed to want was an opportunity to prove they could do something other than office work. I assumed that if they could do something else, they'd probably be doing that. (15)

What Washington says she did not recognize at that time, however, was the stake black men, white men, and the media had in discouraging the formation of community among African-American and white feminists. As Jill Lewis, co-author with Gloria I. Joseph of *Common Differences: Conflicts in Black and White Feminist Perspectives,* indicates, the differences in the treatment of white and black women in the women's liberation movement were exacerbated by many Movement men and the media in order to keep the women's liberation movement socially less influential than the New Left (43). But whether conceptual or actual divisions occurred due to media distortion, racism, mistrust, male agitation against women's coalitions, or any combination thereof, it is evident that even early on radical feminism faced significant skepticism over its conceptions of women's oppression and especially of its vision of all women as a social class or community.

The final important facet of Morgan's analysis comes in her delineation of a 'New' versus an 'Old' order. Her suggestion here is that, for women, the new order envisioned by the American Left was nothing more than the old order under new management. Morgan implies that this order holds nothing new for women, much less carries the ability to accomplish revolutionary change. Behind her implication lies one final aspect of radical feminist theory on women's oppression: the suggestion that for women, Marxism – like liberal feminism – is merely a reformist measure. Radical feminists often were the strongest voice in the critique of the inadequacy of an economic revolution for the eradication of sexism, in part again because they felt the urgent need to position themselves against criticism of their movement from the Left. In fact, much of Firestone's *Dialectic of Sex* suggests that Marxism only explores the symptoms of sexism – not its causes – and that basic 'biological' divisions of labor formulated the economic mechanisms that Marx proceeded to analyze. Thus radical feminists argued that only radical feminism, in its call for the elimination of the root of sexism, could accomplish revolutionary change.

Begun as a reply to the minimalization of women's concerns by the Left, the concepts of women's shared oppression and sexism as the primary contradiction quickly became the crucial analysis and comprehensive theory shared by most radical-feminist groups. These concepts further helped to create a redefinition of the term 'community' itself: through the assertion that women were bound together solely on the basis of a shared oppression, radical feminists defined a community that had in common none of the geographic, historic, legal, or political aspects traditionally associated with the meanings of community. But for early radical feminists, this focus on sexism as the primary contradiction still did not mean they abandoned leftist concerns. Rather, they understood themselves, as Irene Peslikis stated, to be 'attacking the left from the left' (Echols 81) and always had assumed an anticapitalist/

antiracist analysis within their feminism. Yet as women who had little experience in the Left joined radical-feminist groups during the 1970s, the radical-feminist analysis of sexism and female community began to lose its connection to its origins and increasingly became theorized outside most leftist contexts.

13

The theory of sexism as the primary contradiction, coupled with the phenomenon of outside pressure to drop agitation on the behalf of women, also encouraged the development of separatist practice and politics within radical feminism. When women first began to discuss the issue of sexism within the Movement, they sought and encouraged open dialogue with Movement men. But as their attempts were continually thwarted, women began to demand and create separate spaces where they could meet without the presence of male anger and interference. Sara Evans describes one such scenario that occurred during an SDS conference:

When the women's workshop convened it included both men and women, but it gradually broke down into three or more subgroups. . . . The men and women remaining in the lounge of the Student Union began to argue about whether there was an actual 'problem.' . . . For a number of the women it seemed clear that the discussion was futile unless it included both men and women. Soon there was a mixed group at one end of the lounge and an all-female group at the other. . . . Some of the men followed the women who separated off, demanding to be allowed to participate. . . . Heather Tobias had come committed to talking with both women and men, but when she felt it was impossible, she left with [an all-female] group that included Sara Murphy, New York regional coordinator, and Nanci Hollander Gitlin. (162–63)

Such experiences encouraged radical women to develop separatist strategies wherein their own needs might finally be heard and addressed. In essence, the entire radical-feminist movement might be thought of as separatist in that women felt it necessary to separate from the Left in order to address their own oppression. Here, however, women took the issue of separatism one step further with their separation from leftist men. And as women participated in consciousness-raising groups centered on the issue of sexism, it became apparent to many that reformatory measures (usually promoted by liberal-feminist groups) would never eliminate sex roles and therefore never change the fundamental imbalance of power they felt to be the crux of sexism in their lives.

Some radical-feminist groups thus developed theories of separatism as a political act through which women could deny their energy to men and thereby increase women's collective strength. A group called the Radical Feminists #28, for example, saw separatism and the gain of women's power as crucial to human survival as well as to the creation of a new civilization:

We need power for women, not fairy tales and knights in shining armor. We have only to gain by separatism. We shall gain freedom, independence, and power and we shall give hope to the human species. We will no longer allow men to drain our energies. We will no longer have to beg male power for legitimacy. We will have strength and power because we will refuse to let men call the shots. We will challenge them on every level of their society and they will be forced to justify their power or support our separation. It is as simple as that. Left alone to their masculine exploits the patriarchs will completely destroy human life in only a matter of years. Our liberation and the liberation of our mother earth is at stake. We owe feminist rebellion to our daughters and their daughters. Ours is not a struggle for reform within an oppressive culture; ours is a struggle for an entirely new civilization. (Radical Feminists #28 2)

Though Radical Feminists #28's claims for separatism may appear inflated to us today, it is important to note that to women who were just beginning to sense the power of such actions as the Miss America Pageant protest (New York, 1968), separatism seemed to be the strongest move they could make toward that power. Further, though in the 1990s we usually think of feminist separatists only in terms of lesbian separatism, early separatism was not determined by sexual orientation or even by lesbian-feminist theory. In fact, calls for separation from men were made before lesbians began to take radical feminism to task for its homophobia – and certainly before lesbian separatism developed its own political analysis for action.

Finally, at this stage in the development of separatist theory, separatism became a method by which to form female community through solidarity. Firestone called the isolation of women from each other because of marriage 'on some levels [women's] worst disadvantage' (43); other radical feminists stressed that separatism was effective because it was a collective, not individual, endeavor:

Separatism is power for women. Separatism is a new reality. It is a political force that gives women the option of showing their man the door and throwing his baggage out behind him. Separatism is women united in our own self-interest. It is the only way to freedom.

Separatism does not mean women individually leaving men and fending for themselves. It means women fighting together in a political, economic, and social struggle for power. Organizing a revolutionary movement is a central aspect of separatism. Without the movement, separatism offers us no alternatives to powerlessness. Likewise, power for women will come only if we leave men. Separatism is an essential aspect of Feminist Revolution. (Radical Feminists #28 1)

While this statement claims a strong place for the act of separation within feminism, it nonetheless indicates that for early radical feminists, separatism was only one method by which radical feminism might achieve its goals, one (essential) aspect of a broader feminist revolution. The value of separatism for them comes in the united community of women it could create: a safe community that would lead to the only viable feminist 'freedom.' Consequently, many newly formed radical-feminist groups chose separatism as their path to activism while older, nonseparatist groups began to move toward separatist practice. For example, the Feminists (an early New York radical-feminist group) voted in 1969 to limit the number of women who lived with men to one-third the group's total membership. By 1971, all married women were excluded from the group (Echols 176–82).

Radical feminism's vision of female community, positioned in concert with or synonymous to separatism, thus was developed as a defensive measure against criticisms from leftist and mainstream opponents. Because it included only women, female community through separatism was perceived as a safe space wherein women could join to plan revolutionary action. Such a perception, of course, implied that women would not harm one another as they had been harmed in male-dominated, mainstream society. The community work of these theories therefore came in the value they placed on the strength of women's bonds with one another, bonds that would, presumably, surmount all other differences that existed among women.

Of course, more than one woman attracted to the radical feminist assertions of the unity of women quickly discovered that 'all women' did not necessarily include her. In particular, early radical-feminist theoretical discourse on lesbians and their place within the movement left many lesbians wondering how inclusive a radical-feminist women's community would be. While most radical-feminist groups did not reject lesbians or lesbianism as had the National Organization for Women, the equation of lesbianism solely with sexuality in radical-feminist theory left many lesbians with the same uneasiness they felt within liberal-feminist groups such as NOW. Further, such theoretical equations in NOW led to openly homophobic, discriminatory actions against its lesbian members. Allowed only to work behind the scenes or within positions of power if they stayed closeted, lesbians became more and more subject to lesbian baiting within NOW during the mid-1960s. Heterosexual feminists at the same time felt ever-vulnerable to charges of lesbianism from their opponents; Betty Friedan, founder of NOW, called lesbians within NOW the 'lavender menace' and termed the issue of lesbianism a 'lavender herring' for the organization.

In 1969, antagonism toward lesbians in NOW heightened when the New York chapter attempted to silence then–newsletter editor Rita Mae Brown on the issue of lesbianism (Abbot and Love 111). Brown and two other women resigned from NOW in 1970 and formed a radical-feminist group that, as I discuss in chapter 2, became instrumental in the formulation of lesbian-feminist theory. Meanwhile, homophobia and lesbian baiting within NOW grew and culminated in the infamous purges of lesbians during the winter and spring of 1971 (Abbot and Love 27). Lesbians who were not expelled outright began to leave NOW in large numbers; many joined newly formed radical-feminist groups.

Yet radical-feminist uneasiness over issues of sexuality in general (Echols's study details the avoidance of or even refusal in radical-feminist theory to approach constructively most issues of sexuality) made even these groups less than hospitable for many lesbians. Further, radical-feminist discourse on the topic of lesbianism produced a surprising number of articles that seemed bent more on the preservation of the status quo than they were on the promotion of a 'radical' understanding. For example, though she left NOW in disagreement with its conservative governmental practices, Ti-Grace Atkinson approached NOW's position on lesbians in her early radical-feminist essays. In a 1970 speech entitled 'Lesbianism and Feminism,' Atkinson claimed:

> . . . lesbianism is totally dependent, as a concept as well as an activity, on male supremacy. This fact, alone, should make a feminist nervous.
>
> . . . lesbianism is based ideologically on the very premise of male oppression: the dynamic of sexual intercourse.
>
> . . . Because lesbianism involves role-playing and, more important, because

it is based on the primary assumption of male oppression, that is, sex, lesbian-ism reinforces the sex class system.

. . . The price of self-respect for oppressed people is to adopt the role of the Oppressor, and, thus, ultimately, toward oneself.

Lesbians, in that one paradoxical sense, become their own Oppressors. (*Amazon Odyssey* 85–88)

The comparison of lesbianism to male supremacy was, of course, nothing new to lesbians, though perhaps early lesbian feminists were dismayed to hear it from women who insisted on the primacy of women's commitments to one another. In essence, Atkinson's portrayal attempted to write lesbianism out of the women's movement: lesbians were, by her description, men rather than women – if not in actuality then certainly in behavior, mind-set, and social outlook. And as 'men,' lesbians were less than welcome in a 'woman's' movement.

Atkinson's declaration, and others such as Firestone's that claimed lesbianism to be 'limited' or 'sick' and stated that lesbians often 'believed they were men' (Firestone 65–66), made it clear to many lesbians that radical feminism's conceptions of women's oppression spoke on behalf of only a specific group of women. But unlike feminists of color who often disengaged themselves from the women's liberation movement or formed feminist coalitions specifically dedicated to the issues of racism,[6] many white lesbians agitated within the framework of radical feminism in order to make it more receptive to – and active for – lesbians in general. In so doing, lesbian feminists were to posit new definitions of what it meant to be a woman, lesbian, and feminist and did so in such a way as to change irrevocably the concept of female community within feminism. Those redefinitions, as well as the effects they had on the politics and practice of separatism and the reformation of women's community, are the subjects of the next chapter.

17

BLOODROOT ONE

I bake bread at Bloodroot in Bridgeport, Conn. and cook a few other things there too. In my spare time I take photos of things I see and want to talk about. This series of Lesbian Lovers is the result of, and, for me, an antidote to the current proliferation of pornography and s+m. I began taking these pictures after seeing a so-called 'lesbian' 'erotic' video which had no similarity at all to my experience of lesbian sexuality. These photos are, in part, a healing – of damage done by that video and by all pornography which clouds our Vision of our Selves. They are also a celebration of the beauty and power of us as we make love with each other. – Noel Furie

Though we had to attend Columbia University's graduation in May 1989, New York hotels were too expensive for our graduate-school budgets. We thrilled at the find of a far more appealing alternative: the Bloodroot, Connecticut's version of a separatist business (and quasi-residential) collective. The collective runs a small B&B perfectly located on the coast, an acclaimed vegetarian restaurant next door, and the only women's bookstore beyond Yale-permeated New Haven. 'A community,' we joked, 'away from community.' And the welcome we received seemed to support our sentiment.

As soon as we had finished unpacking, Lori, the proprietor, knocked on our door and announced, 'The restaurant's open tonight, if you want to come for dinner.'

'Thanks,' Carla said. 'We'll be over in a bit.'

Because we had registered at the B&B, the women of the collective knew we were from Iowa. But Iowa is removed from Connecticut by more than geography; it hadn't occurred to me that anyone in the restaurant might have connections with the state. Yet after we had eaten, a member of the collective approached us, introduced herself as Noel, and asked:

'You're from Iowa City?'

'Yes,' I said. 'Would you like to sit down with us?'

'I'd love to, thanks. Do you know *Common Lives?*'

Common Lives/Lesbian Lives, a diverse journal of lesbian fiction, poetry, essays, and photography established in 1981, is produced by a collective in Iowa City. I did, indeed, know of it. 'I've been a contributing editor for the last few months,' I replied.

'Really?! I'm the one who took the pictures in volume twenty!' Noel exclaimed.

Volume twenty in any other context of the journal's history would be unremarkable except for 'the pictures.' They depicted women making love and were taken of, as I came to realize, members and friends of the Bloodroot. *Common Lives* published the pictures as representations of lesbian-feminist erotica. But the University of Iowa took issue with the photos; it refused to publish the volume although it had, in the past, published explicit images of heterosexuality. *Common Lives* brought suit. Two and a half years later we reached a settlement whereby the university agreed to publish three issues free of charge. The settlement and our celebration had been announced in an issue the season before Carla and I arrived in Connecticut.

'Did you see the announcement?' I asked.

'Yes – it was great! Too bad you couldn't get them to acknowledge any fault, though.'

'They refused . . . but the agreement to free publication amounts to the same thing, don't you think? We felt that the settlement was at least implicit recognition of their homophobia, and printing the statement, I hope, said as much to the community.'

'Well, *I* certainly was happy to see it,' Noel replied. 'And it's important that we are able to represent our own sexuality.' I agreed; we talked a few moments longer about our elation over the victory. As she rose to go, however, she hesitated for a moment, frowned, and said:

'By the way, I was very upset over a couple of articles in the last issue.'

'Really?' I asked, puzzled by her sudden anger. 'Which ones?'

'The two s&m pieces. And several friends said they had some bad reactions to them because they didn't know what they were getting into. I don't think *Common Lives* should be printing such woman-hating stuff. In fact, we've talked about not selling the magazine in the bookstore because of it.'

'Yeah?' I stammered, quite at a loss for any articulate reply. 'Well . . . thanks . . . I'll relay the message,' I finished lamely. She gave me a sincere smile and walked away.

Beyond Sexuality: Woman-Identification and New Definitions for Women's Community

Two

Long before the advent of radical feminism, lesbians sought out and created community amongst themselves and, at times, with gay men. But the protest movements of the 1960s and the influence of radical-feminist thought changed what community meant for many lesbians and sparked the creation of a specifically lesbian-feminist political analysis and activism. This chapter explores the history of lesbian community from the 1950s through the early 1970s as it was created and shared via written discourse. Through feminism, lesbians created new, politicized definitions for our lives and communities.[1] These definitions in turn changed what it meant to live one's life as a lesbian, feminist, and separatist and provided a new definition of activism within which separatist women sought to live and work. Thus, any analysis of the community work of separatist discourse would be incomplete without an examination of the theories of lesbian feminism and, subsequently, lesbian separatism. Again, however, this chapter presents not a comprehensive account of lesbian-feminist history but an account of the major forces within radical feminism that contributed to the formulation of specific lesbian-feminist theories of female community. These theories, in particular the critique of heterosexual ideology, in turn became those that separatists used as the cornerstone of their written analyses and lived ideologies.

Though what lesbian community means to lesbians has changed since the 1950s, the practice of naming ourselves in community with one another is long-standing. Deborah Wolf, in her study of the San Francisco lesbian community of the 1970s, argues that a sense of community began when gays and lesbians defined themselves as a minority group rather than as individual, isolated deviants (51).[2] Anthropologists in this country recognized the existence of a lesbian and gay community as early as 1961, when Evelyn Hooker argued that 'if one is permitted to use the term [community] to refer to an aggregate of persons engaging in common activities, sharing common interests, and having a feeling of sociopsychological unity with variations in the degree to which persons have these characteristics . . . then it is completely germane to homosexuals' (quoted in Wolf 73). However, women's sense of lesbian community before the 1950s remained fairly localized. Communities tended to exist as small pockets rather than as national or even statewide identifications; in other words, one's 'community' was often bound by geography as well as by its social status as a sexual minority (and this remains true to a certain degree even today). But in 1955 Phyllis Lyon and Del Martin co-founded the Daughters of Bilitis (DOB) and subsequently published the *Ladder*, the first major, long-lived lesbian journal in the United States.[3] For a great number of lesbians, the *Ladder* was their link to a suddenly broadened lesbian community. Joan Nestle, co-founder of the Lesbian Herstory Archives, calls the journal 'the most sustaining Lesbian cultural creation of this period' and remembers 'desperately search[ing]' for it in her working-class neighborhood newsstands (Nestle 109n). Wolf further describes early reactions to the *Ladder*'s publication:

Apparently there was a real need for such a publication, for mail began pouring in from lesbians who used the staff to make contact with other lesbians. Throughout its career, an important function of the organization has been to answer this mail and to try to be available to these women by telephone. Many lesbians over the years have come to San Francisco only because they knew about the Daughters of Bilitis from reading the *Ladder*. To many other lesbians who remained isolated, the *Ladder* was their only link with other lesbians and, as such, served as an important outlet for them. (52–53)

In the case of the *Ladder*, it seems that while the need for a sense of community existed among lesbians prior to its publication, the journal was a crucial element in the vocalization of that need and, subsequently, in the characterization and formation of that community.

Both DOB and the *Ladder* have been examined as primary markers of lesbian culture and as examples of the ways lesbian conceptions of self and community changed between the 1950s through the 1970s. Rose Weitz demonstrates the shift from the assimilationist stance taken in the *Ladder* during the 1950s, presented through the advice to lesbians to look and act as much like heterosexual women as possible in order to win social tolerance, to the far more radical position of the 1970s, in which authors demanded recognition and acceptance of lesbianism in whatever ways lesbians chose to define it.

More compelling for this study, however, is Weitz's discussion of the *Ladder*'s shift in loyalties from the homophile movement (predominantly led by gay men) to the feminist movement. During the 1950s, the primary mark of lesbian community for lesbians was homosexuality (e.g., based on the sex of one's partner as opposed to specific sexual practices) rather than biological femaleness. Put more simply, when everything from the vice squad to the McCarthy trials engaged in legal gay bashing, both gays and lesbians knew the authorities were not too particular about the victim's gender; bonds between gay men and lesbians often developed because of social threats based on their shared minority status. Slowly, though, the *Ladder* began to identify lesbian community as different from gay community in its functions and goals because of gender differences. As early as October 1966 the *Ladder* announced:

Certain changes in editorial policy are anticipated. To date emphasis has been on Lesbians' role in the homophile movement. Her identity as woman in our society has not yet been explored in depth. It is often stated in explaining 'Who is a Lesbian?' that she is a human being first, a woman second, and a Lesbian only thirdly. The third aspect has been expounded at length. Now it is time to step up the *Ladder* to the second rung. (Quoted in Weitz 241)

Indeed, Weitz finds that identification with the women's movement became so strong for the *Ladder* that very little attention was paid to the Stonewall uprising of 1969, a protest which is now popularly known as the beginning of the gay pride movement in the United States. For the readers of and contributors to the *Ladder,* then, the 1950s and early 1960s was a period of identification with heterosexual women and gay men. These identifications were shaped both by and for the *Ladder*'s audience and began to change only as lesbians became aware of and active in the protest movements of the 1960s.

But even these early steps toward feminism began to divide the lesbian community in ways that were to be exacerbated by lesbian feminism's definitions of lesbian sexuality. Often portrayed by lesbian feminists as those who simply lived out oppressive imitations of heterosexuality, lesbians who identified themselves as butch or femme during the 1950s recently have become both the authors and subjects of studies that strive to redefine their lives. In her essay 'Butch-Femme Relationships: Sexual Courage in the 1950s,' Joan Nestle argues that butch-femme couples neither imitated nor attempted to recreate heterosexual marriages. Rather, she finds a feminist activism in butch-femme visibility that allowed these lesbians both to support themselves and to be recognized within the lesbian community:

I believe . . . that many pre-Stonewall Lesbians were feminists, but the primary way this feminism – this autonomy of sexual and social identities – was expressed, was precisely in the form of sexual adventuring that now appears so oppressive. If butch-femme represented an erotically autonomous world, it also symbolized many other forms of independence. Most of the women I knew in the Sea Colony [a lesbian bar in Greenwich Village] were working women who either had never married or who had left their husbands and were thus responsible for their own economic survival. . . . Their feminism was not an articulated theory; it was a lived set of options based on erotic choices.

None of the butch women I was with, and this included a passing woman, ever presented themselves to me as men; they did announce themselves as tabooed women who were willing to identify their passion for other women by wearing clothes that symbolized the taking of responsibility. Part of this responsibility was sexual expertise. In the 1950s this courage to feel comfortable with arousing another woman became a political act. (Nestle 105, 100)

Though Weitz's and Nestle's studies seem to focus on two fairly disparate facets of lesbian existence in the US, the conception of lesbianism implied in both is remarkably similar.[4] Whether proponents of the *Ladder*'s assimilationist stance or openly rebellious adventurers in butch-femme couples, lesbians before the late 1960s identified with lesbian community as a *sexual* minority: as women who had sex with other women. Further, community arguments through channels such as letters to the *Ladder* seem to have occurred primarily over the visible expression of desire, not whether that desire was in and of itself immoral or, conversely, valuable. Yet that which makes Weitz's study possible and Nestle's necessary – lesbian feminism – strove to define lesbianism as germane to more than women's sexuality. In the process lesbian feminists, like the *Ladder* before them, created new conceptions of being for women and, especially within women's attempts to practice separatism, new ways of living their lives. And as we will see, these conceptions broadened the definition of what it meant to be a lesbian in such a way as to create quite a different sense of lesbian community from those that preceded it.

To insist, however, as Alice Echols and others have, that lesbian feminism developed solely out of radical feminism is to obscure facets of lesbian history such as those summarized above. While lesbian feminists both utilized and formulated much of radical feminist theory, lesbian pride and the genesis of the lesbian-feminist critique of heterosexuality began in much the same ways radical feminism did: through participation in the protest movements of the early 1960s. Weitz argues, for example, that mid-1960s contributors to the *Ladder* took their cue from the civil rights movement when they urged lesbians to fight against discrimination in the law and employment (240). Wolf notes that even the publication of the *Ladder* itself as a statement of lesbian consciousness and community 'helped to pave the way for the more militant and far-reaching demands of the liberation movements in the following decade' (48–49).

Further, despite the *Ladder*'s cursory treatment of the Stonewall uprising, Stonewall did become an important marker of a specifically gay/lesbian resistance and pride for many lesbians. Stonewall is a Greenwich Village dance bar where, in June 1969, lesbians and gays finally fought back against the constant harassment and raids by the city's police force. Begun when a lesbian resisted arrest, the riots at the bar lasted three days while gays and lesbians fended off police with help and support from area neighbors (Marcus 51). Stonewall gave birth to the Gay Liberation Front, one of the first specifically gay-rights groups to form in the United States.

Thus because of their heavy involvement in the newly emerging gay/lesbian rights movement as well as the feminist movement, it is perhaps more accurate to say that lesbians began to develop politicized definitions of lesbianism simultaneous to and in concert with the development of radical feminism. The oppression experienced by lesbians as women and as members of a sexual minority, however, gave many lesbians an affinity to radical feminism even long before radical feminism openly addressed the issue of lesbianism. Both the compelling ideologies they found within radical feminism and the hostility many experienced from heterosexual feminists urged lesbians to forge the creation of lesbian feminism and, as I will discuss in the next chapter, lesbian separatism. Yet like the radical-feminist theories on which they heavily depended, the theories that recreated lesbian community eventually alienated many lesbians who found themselves outside the new definitions.

For lesbians drawn to the radical-feminist movement, the constant homophobia they faced had to be addressed if radical feminism was to remain a viable social and political critique. During the late 1960s, lesbians began to agitate within radical-feminist groups in order to confront the movement on its homophobia. Many essays, position papers, and journal articles dedicated to the issue were published, but one – written shortly after Ti-Grace Atkinson's 'Lesbianism and Feminism' (February 1970) – made its mark in such a way as to remain today the definitive theoretical discourse on early lesbian feminism and its conception of female community.

In May 1970, a newly formed lesbian-feminist group, the Lavender Menace, chose the Second Congress to Unite Women as the place to confront the women's movement on its own homophobia. As soon as the entertainment portion of the evening ended, the lights in the auditorium went out. When they were relit, nearly twenty women stood at the front, 'Lavender Menace' stenciled on their T-shirts. They pre-empted the rest of the evening's activities and proceeded to facilitate a speak-out and discussion on homophobia in feminism. Though they had placed women sympathetic to their action in the audience, these 'plants' were unnecessary; when the Menace opened the microphone and asked women to come forward to speak, dozens thronged to the stage. It was at this action that then little-known author Kate Millett declared her alliance with lesbians and spoke of her own bisexuality. At the same time, unknown to the members of Lavender Menace, three lesbian groups from California held panels at the Second Congress meeting. Lesbians thus began to demand the recognition of their presence and work within women's liberation (Abbot and Love 113–16).

Lavender Menace's impact reached far beyond the congress, however. In preparation for the congress and during its aftermath, the Menace – later renamed Radicalesbians – wrote and widely distributed 'Woman Identified Woman,' their position paper on lesbianism. The essay contained five basic sections: a definition of homosexuality, an analysis of society's derogatory views of lesbianism, the place of lesbianism within feminism, an analysis of women's dependency upon men, and a call to all women to begin the creation of a new sense of what it meant to be a woman.[5]

As the title 'Woman Identified Woman' suggests, this discursive rep-

26

resentation of lesbianism was in part an attempt to push the social definition of lesbianism away from sexuality and toward a constructed
identity that had far more to do with a sociopolitical critique than it did
with what one did in bed. Thus a lesbian was a woman who 'acts in accordance with her inner compulsion to be a more complete and freer
human being than her society . . . cares to allow her. . . . She is forced
to evolve her own life pattern, often living much of her life alone, learning usually much earlier than her 'straight' . . . sisters about the essential aloneness of life (which the myth of marriage obscures) and about
the reality of illusions' (Radicalesbians 240–41). This redefinition of
lesbianism resonated on several levels within the early radical-feminist
movement, in part because it effectively utilized characterizations of
women's experiences put forth by radical feminist groups themselves.
When Radicalesbians described the typical lesbian as a woman who
struggled to create herself outside social conventions of the feminine,
they granted her the journey that most heterosexual feminists desired
to undertake. Thus, lesbians were posited as not some outside evil force
that tried to break up the feminist party but rather as women who, like
everyone else, struggled for autonomy from patriarchal definitions of
womanhood. The difference – if there was one – came in the implicit
claim that lesbians were almost automatically compelled to start the
process heterosexual women could begin only after a political or social
awakening. In short, lesbians were rewritten as the pioneers of the feminist community.

The concept of lesbians as the pioneers of the feminist revolution
was quickly adopted by many lesbian feminists in their analyses of gender and society. In the process, lesbian feminists often linked their critique of female socialization to the theory of sexism as the primary contradiction, a combination that had the rhetorical effect of positioning
woman-identification as the crucial step in the eradication of all oppression. Note, for example, the theoretical movements Charlotte
Bunch accomplishes in the following paragraph:

The development of Lesbian-Feminist[6] politics as the basis for the liberation of
women is our top priority. . . . In our society which defines all people and institutions for the benefit of the rich, white male, the Lesbian is in revolt. In revolt
because she defines herself in terms of women and rejects male definitions of
how she should feel, act, look, and live. To be a Lesbian is to love oneself,
woman, in a culture that denigrates and despises women. The Lesbian rejects
the male sexual political domination; she defies his world, his social organiza-

tion, his ideology, and his definition of her as inferior. Lesbianism puts women first while the society declares the male supreme. Lesbianism threatens male supremacy at its core. When politically conscious and organized, it is central to destroying our sexist, racist, capitalist, imperialist system. ('Lesbians in Revolt' 29)

Bunch's rhetorical strategy performs the cultural task of placing lesbianism as a crucial component in the struggle against all oppression. Bunch, of course, utilizes the theoretical structures and arguments of radical feminism in her analysis; but women who were more firmly based in Marxist theoretical frameworks were persuaded by the redefinitions of lesbianism proposed by position papers such as 'Woman Identified Woman' as well. Margaret Small, a contributor to an early lesbian-feminist anthology, *Lesbianism and the Women's Movement,* casts her concept of woman-identification in a materialist mold:

lesbians have a basis for creating new ways of understanding the material conditions. That is because lesbians stand in a different relation to the three material conditions that determine the class position of women – reproduction, production (domestic labor) and sexuality. The lesbian does not have a domestic base that is defined by the production of new labor power and maintenance of her husband's labor power. Her primary relationship to class society is in proletarian terms. That element of slave consciousness which is integral to heterosexual women is missing. Her ability to understand the conditions of proletarian oppression is far greater. She does not have to work through the series of contradictions created by being in the slave position before she can relate to the fact that she's a proletarian in advanced capitalism. (58–59)

Small's analysis attempts to accomplish for Marxist feminism what 'Woman Identified Woman' represented for radical feminism: the placement of lesbianism as outside the conditions that define the lives of heterosexual women and thus as a 'natural' rebellion against the patriarchy (here presented as the elitist segment of capitalist society). And though Small's translation may not have achieved the acceptance within Marxist or socialist feminism that 'Woman Identified Woman' did within radical feminism, it nonetheless points to the influence Radicalesbians' analysis carried outside the realm of radical feminism.

With this new definition of lesbianism in place, Radicalesbians were able to claim lesbianism as central to feminism. Yet while they make this claim early in their essay, they do not fully take up the issue until the final section of the text. Rather, the second section of the essay steps back to critique the concept and use of the term 'lesbian' as it was understood in mainstream society. This section begins strikingly with the assertion that

It should first be understood that lesbianism, like male homosexuality, is a category of behavior possible only in a sexist society characterized by rigid sex roles and dominated by male supremacy. . . . Homosexuality is a by-product of a particular way of setting up roles (or approved patterns of behavior) on the basis of sex; as such it is an inauthentic (not consonant with 'reality') category. In a society in which men do not oppress women, and sexual expression is allowed to follow feelings, the categories of homosexuality and heterosexuality would disappear. (241)

Such a statement may seem odd from those who insist on the primacy of the lesbian 'category' to feminism and its struggle against sexism. But Radicalesbians' rejection of lesbianism as an 'inauthentic' category allowed them both to analyze the separate ways the sexualized category of 'lesbian' as opposed to that of 'gay men' functioned in society and to prepare the way for their accusation of heterosexual feminists' complicity with the oppressive mainstream equation of lesbianism with sexuality.

Radicalesbians approach this implication through the assertion that lesbian baiting historically has been a favorite sociopolitical activity against any woman who dared to be independent. They note that the effectiveness of this tactic reveals the mainstream ideological definitions of a woman as one whose 'essence of being . . . is to get fucked by men' (242). Such a rhetorical structure allows Radicalesbians to assert that if successful, the tactic of lesbian baiting aids patriarchal society in stopping women from becoming the independent, successful people most heterosexual feminists aspired to become. Thus, women who participate in the view of lesbians as only sexual, either through their own fear of being perceived as a lesbian or, alternately, by 'laying a surrogate male role on the lesbian,' succumb to their 'heterosexual conditioning,' which is a result of the 'male classification system of defining all females in sexual relation to some other category of people' (242).

To use the term 'lesbian' as it was understood by mainstream society, then, becomes tantamount to the formation of false divisions among women and works to men's advantage by keeping women 'within the confines of the feminine role.' Radicalesbians' attempts to stretch the category of lesbian beyond (and even, the suggestion seems, exclusive of) sexuality was picked up by lesbian feminists who used it to define the value of female bonding for the feminist movement. Published two years after 'Woman Identified Woman,' Rita Mae Brown's essay 'The Shape of Things to Come' makes an even more careful distinction between the (male) focus on sexuality and (female) concentration on the broader process of female bonding:

Women who love women are Lesbians. Men, because they can only think of women in sexual terms, define Lesbianism as sex between women. However, Lesbians know that it is far more than that, it is a different way of life. It is a life determined by a woman for her own benefit and the benefit of other women. It is a life that draws its strength, support and direction from women. About two years ago this concept was given the name woman-identified woman. That's not a bad name, it is just a fancy way of saying that you love yourself and other women. You refuse to limit yourself by the male definitions of women. You free yourself from male concepts of 'feminine' behavior. (*Plain Brown Rapper* 69)

Brown develops the concept of woman-identification as a sociopolitical issue, but in the process she repositions the term 'lesbian' for the women's movement. By this I mean that she defines the category of lesbian in the way Radicalesbians defined a woman-identified woman; only at the end of her definition, however, does she acknowledge that term as the precedent for her definition. Effectively, Brown participates in the reclamation and revaluation of a socially taboo term, a process Radicalesbians themselves began in the third part of their essay.

The third section of 'Woman Identified Woman' addresses the issue of lesbian baiting in the women's movement. In this section, however, Radicalesbians intensify the pressure on women in the movement to denounce lesbian baiting or to face the charge of collaboration with the enemy if they refused to do so:

As long as the label 'dyke' can be used to frighten a woman into a less militant stand, keep her separate from her sisters, keep her from giving primacy to anything other than men and family – then to that extent she is controlled by the male culture. Until women see in each other the possibility of a primal commitment which includes sexual love, they will be denying themselves the love and value they readily accord to men, thus affirming their second-class status. (243)

In essence, Radicalesbians' analysis functions in such a way as to place the onus of lesbian baiting on those women who succumbed to its pressure (rather than on those who, conversely, engaged in the practice in

30

the first place). Part of the community work of this section of the essay occurs in Radicalesbians' response to feminist leaders like Betty Friedan, Ti-Grace Atkinson, or Shulamith Firestone who insisted that lesbianism was male-identified and, as such, not an appropriate topic for feminism. Radicalesbians' reliance on the assumption of sexism as the primary contradiction gained them a receptive audience among many radical feminists and allowed them to assert that the success of lesbian baiting could be used as a measure of women's desire for male approval.

Other lesbian feminists were quick to pick up Radicalesbians' characterization of the effects of lesbian baiting in the women's movement. Sidney Abbott, for example, used their argument as a definitional element of lesbian feminism itself:

Lesbians have been the ones who listened to what both the women's movement and the gay movement were saying and wove the themes into one coherent theory of sexist oppressions. . . .

To the women's movement, lesbians said, 'Expand your idea of sex role stereotyping to include us, because we are a key proof of female oppression. If any one of you is successful outside the home, what is the first thing you are called – a ballbreaker, a lesbian, that is, a sort of man, no longer a woman or womanly. Expand your concept of woman to include us and your life-styles and you free yourselves; you could free all women.' (139)

Abbott's appropriation reinscribes as fact what had been a theoretical construct within Radicalesbians' conception of woman-identification. Abbott's description of lesbian feminism thus allows her to give credit to the lesbian-feminist movement as the catalyst for an inclusive, liberatory community of women through the actions of those, as Radicalesbians suggested, who had the courage to denounce the tactic of lesbian baiting.

In the last two segments of 'Woman Identified Woman,' Radicalesbians expand their critique of heterosexuality and firmly reposition lesbianism as essential to feminism. They begin this argument indirectly through the characterization of the symptoms of internalization of socially defined femininity and call those symptoms evidence of self-hatred in women:

The consequence of internalizing this role is an enormous reservoir of self-hate. This is not to say the self-hate is recognized or accepted as such; indeed most women would deny it. It may be experienced as discomfort with her role, as feeling empty, as numbness, as restlessness, a paralyzing anxiety at the center. Alternatively, it may be expressed in shrill defensiveness of the glory and destiny of her role. But it does exist, often beneath the edge of her consciousness, poisoning her existence, keeping her alienated from herself, her own needs, and rendering her a stranger to other women. (244)

Radicalesbians' portrayal successfully connects both socially recognized characteristics of femininity and rabid antifeminism to those who would stand in the way of women's liberation. And for women familiar with Betty Friedan's *The Feminine Mystique*, Radicalesbians' description of role discomfiture sounded strikingly familiar, as it paraphrased that work's portrayal of the malaise of white, well-educated, middle-class housewives. With the linkage of Friedan's characterizations to antifeminism, however, Radicalesbians effectively displace those who refused to challenge heterosexism from the center, or norm, of women's liberation.

Radicalesbians' assertion of the misogyny of lesbian baiting allowed them to pose a new solution for women's oppression. That solution came in a self-recreation for each woman beyond the limits of patriarchal femininity: 'As the source of self-hate and the lack of real self are rooted in our male-given identity, we must create a new sense of self. . . . Only women can give each other a new sense of self' (245). Radicalesbians framed their solution within a process of identity construction they had earlier accorded primarily to lesbians. By the end of the essay, then, Radicalesbians can successfully raise the question of the place of heterosexuality in feminism:

As long as women's liberation tries to free women without facing the basic heterosexual structure that binds us in one-to-one relationship with our oppressors, tremendous energies will continue to flow into trying to straighten up each particular relationship with a man, into finding how to get better sex, how to turn his head around – into trying to make the 'new man' out of him, in the delusion that this will allow us to be the 'new woman.' (245)

That this view of lesbianism as a 'natural' critique of heterosexuality strongly compelled many other lesbian feminists is evident both in well-known articles such as Adrienne Rich's 'Compulsory Heterosexuality and Lesbian Existence' and in lesser-known statements such as Charlotte Bunch's 'Lesbian-Feminist Theory.' Bunch writes,

Lesbian feminism as it has developed over the past decade . . . is primarily a critique of heterosexism – the institutional and ideological domination of heterosexuality, as a fundamental part of male supremacy. . . . Its practical application involves an orientation of one's life around women (woman-identification) and a commitment to women as a political force capable of changing society as well as our lifestyle. (180)

This assertion of lesbianism as the primary threat to heterosexism – and thus, for radical feminists, to all oppression – served to strengthen the lesbian-feminist claim to the crucial role lesbianism would play in the feminist revolution.

Radicalesbians' assertions also necessitated the call for the creation of female community. In the final paragraphs of 'Woman Identified Woman,' Radicalesbians state the case for separatism and claim that only through female community – or 'the primacy of women relating to women' – could women create a new sense of self necessary to begin the true revolution. Furthermore, they felt that such affirmation among women would 'melt' the 'divisive barriers' between women and create 'solidarity with our sisters.' For Radicalesbians, then, the creation of a new self – such a creation as lesbians (by Radicalesbians' definition) have been compelled to accomplish – would bring about a community of women capable of achieving the feminist revolution.

In part, Radicalesbians' definition attempted to counter incessant emphasis by many feminists on lesbianism as solely sexual and therefore – like all sexuality – oppressive to women. And in this way lesbian feminism was to take an antagonistic stance to any overtly sexualized portrayals of lesbianism, including those of butch-femme identification prior to the 1960s. But this willingness to mute sexuality in the hopes of appealing to heterosexual feminists also began a line of thought that was to become central to radical feminism: the view of the lesbian as the quintessential feminist.[7] Radicalesbians' statement was thus an effective rhetorical strategy, for it placed the 'well-adjusted' lesbian as one who had successfully completed a journey to a freely chosen womanhood. And intentional or not, the wide acceptance of this definition opened the boundaries between heterosexual and lesbian women: if lesbianism was more than sex; was more, in fact, a method of liberation than it was a sexual orientation, then all women potentially could (and perhaps even should) become lesbians.

By the early 1970s, then, the burden of sexual proof placed on lesbians by works such as Atkinson's 'Lesbianism and Feminism' was clearly turned back from lesbians onto heterosexual feminists themselves. Caught somewhat unprepared, heterosexual feminists found it necessary to defend their sexuality and found themselves vulnerable to the charge of collaboration with the oppressor if they attempted (or refused) to do so. That there was no immediate, organized rebuttal of this redefinition of heterosexuality was perhaps not surprising, even though the lack thereof made lesbian-feminist analyses seem generally correct. And any defense of heterosexual relationships without an effective challenge to lesbian feminists' redefinitions – a challenge that was not forthcoming – could quickly be labeled both antifeminist and homophobic. Thus the overall response by heterosexual feminists usually fell along the lines of Ti-Grace Atkinson's: shortly after Lavender Menace's action and publication of 'Woman Identified Woman,' Atkinson reversed her earlier position on lesbianism and stated that 'lesbianism has been a kind of code word for female resistance' and that women who are 'married to men . . . are collaborators' (Atkinson 131-32).[8]

The community work of the discourse of lesbian feminism as it appeared in essays such as Radicalesbians' 'Woman Identified Woman' thus made several contributions and changes to feminist concepts of separatism and female community. First, it provided an analysis of sexual politics that effectively wrote an entire segment of women – lesbians – into radical feminism's definitions of women's community. In so doing, it strongly challenged the complacency and satisfaction with which heterosexual feminists regarded their own sexuality and, by extension, their commitment to feminism itself. In essence, lesbian feminism added the dimensions of affection and a muted sexuality to feminist ideals of women's relationships with one another, while at the same time it redefined that sexuality to make it carry great sociopolitical significance. Lesbian community, once defined primarily by sexuality, became a community of 'natural' antimisogynist activists. And with their continued call for a separation from men in order to further strengthen women's bonds with one another, lesbian feminists seemed to offer a solution to the brewing divisions, rooted in other differences of social identity, among women.

I have spent what might appear to be a disproportionate amount of time on Radicalesbians' essay, yet the impact of the redefinitions of women, sexuality, lesbianism, and female community offered by 'Woman Identified Woman' is difficult to overstate. Although the essay originated on the East Coast, it was published in books and journals nationwide. In fact, Wolf's study on California lesbian communities of the

1980s cites the importance of the essay (among others) to self-conceptions of those in the communities:

A major influence in reconstructing the thinking of lesbians – as well as women in general – about themselves were feminist writings that described the crippling effects of the oppression of women as a group by men as a group. The oppression and stigmatization of the lesbian because of her sexual and affectional orientation was defined as part of the general oppression of women by men in a patriarchal culture, and especially of women who did not need to relate to men in their personal lives. The following feminist and lesbian-feminist literature has been cited by members of the group as being most influential: Simone de Beauvoir, *The Second Sex* (1949, 1953); Betty Friedan, *The Feminine Mystique* (1963); Kate Millett, *Sexual Politics* (1969); Shulamith Firestone, *The Dialectic of Sex* (1970); Radicalesbians, *The Woman-Identified Woman* (1970); and the anthology edited by Robin Morgan, *Sisterhood Is Powerful* (1970). (18)

Clearly, the contributions of lesbian feminism helped to reshape the conception of female community and the politics of separatism as they were understood in early 1970s feminism. But one last movement that emerged at this time – lesbian separatism – was to have an even greater impact on both the politics and practice of female community as well as on the discourse those communities produced. The next chapter examines the genesis, evolution, and practice of lesbian separatism and the community work of its redefinitions of the sociopolitical functions and value of women's community.

BLOODROOT TWO

During the spring of 1990, when I realized that the research for my dissertation necessitated a visit to New York City's Lesbian Herstory Archives, the choice of a place to stay was once again enjoyably easy. I arranged with Lori for a week's accommodations at the Bloodroot and inquired about commuter trains to the city. The two-day drive from Iowa passed monotonously; I arrived Sunday afternoon in time for dinner at the restaurant.

After supper, I took my book out to the sun porch perched overlooking the shore. While the view did nothing for my desire to read, it inspired a sense of tranquility that would prove exceptionally elusive in the coming week. I had watched the tide for about an hour when Lori came back from the restaurant. She accepted my invitation to stay and talk and asked me what had brought me to the inn. When I told her I was researching my dissertation, she asked about the topic.

'Separatist theory and utopian literature,' I replied.

'Really? You mean like Mary Daly and Sarah Hoagland?'

'In part. More focused on earlier separatist texts, though – and authors like Sally Gearhart and Rochelle Singer.'

'You're kidding!' she said, incredulous. 'You mean they're *letting* you do that?'

'Yes . . .' I said, a bit puzzled. It hadn't occurred to me that 'they' had much say in my choice of a topic. But Lori seemed pleasantly surprised.

'That's great! So, what are you saying about separatism?' she asked.

'I'm not clear on the specifics – I hope this trip will unearth a lot of the missing pieces for me – but I'm interested in the work separatist utopias accomplished in lesbian communities. How they helped shape or change ideas of women's community in general.'

'Sounds interesting,' she replied. 'And what's in New York City?'

'The Lesbian Herstory Archives. The one co-founded by Joan Nestle.'

Her ensuing silence surprised me. I had come to anticipate the exclamations of envy that so often resulted, at least in my midwestern community, from this declaration of my destination. At times, however, I can be hopelessly obtuse to nonverbal cues. I pressed further.

'Do you know Joan Nestle?' I asked, thinking that perhaps simple unfamiliarity with Joan's work or even the archives itself was the cause of her reticence.

Lori nodded. 'We don't . . . agree very much with Joan Nestle,' she said, slowly, in a tone meant to prohibit any further inquiry.

'Oh! Well . . . I suppose it doesn't matter very much . . . Joan's not going to be there, anyway. She said she'd be away for the week . . .' I trailed off, sensing that fact would do little to mitigate her disapproval and feeling suddenly ashamed by its offering. Anxious to change the subject, I asked her about the next morning's train schedule. She gave all the information she had, offered advice on the best unmetered places to park in Fairfield, and wished me goodnight.

Lesbian Separatism and Revolution through Community

Three

Though many lesbians came to separatism as a result of their dissatisfaction in feminist groups, others developed separatist ideologies and practice outside the 1960s feminist context. All-women communities such as the Woman's Commonwealth in Belton, Texas, have existed in the United States since at least the mid-nineteenth century (Andreadis 86–98). Then, too, 1960s and 1970s separatists sometimes came to separatism strictly through a lesbian (rather than a radical-, liberal-, or lesbian-feminist) background. Many separatists conceive of their journey toward separatism as bound to a certain extent by racial or class characteristics; Sidney Spinster's study of the history of separatism, for example, finds that working-class and/or lesbians of color usually became separatists directly through their lesbian identification, whereas white, middle-class lesbians came to separatism more often through the women's liberation movement (99).

Such a varied path to lesbian separatism had consequences for separatist groups, not the least of which is the fact that separatist ideology remains fragmented and often contradictory even today. In fact, separatism can and does encompass more than one method by which a woman understands and lives her life. This chapter seeks to define the major strains of lesbian separatism as it developed in the 1970s in order to analyze lesbian separatism's contributions to feminist visions of female community. Because lesbian-separatist theory quickly became synonymous with and later eclipsed the separatist theories of heterosexual women espoused by groups like the Radical Feminists #28, a clear understanding of lesbian separatism's genesis, theories, and practice is crucial to an analysis of the experiences faced by separatist collectives, whether they were inhabited by heterosexual women, lesbians, or both.

However women came to separatism, separatists who write their histories accord to literature – especially essays and position papers – great importance in the formulation of lesbian-separatist ideology and in the creation of separatist community. Spinster's study, for example, traces separatism's history solely through lesbian and lesbian-separatist journals, newsletters, and books published from 1972 into the early 1980s. But publication was not easy. At a time when even liberal and radical feminists found it difficult to get accurate coverage from the mainstream media, separatists were scarcely heard at all. A few feminist presses (for example, Diana Press) had been established and did publish separatist material; for the most part, however, separatists passed copies of their works among friends or published their own journals. The latter alternative usually was undertaken by separatist collectives, with varied success (Spinster 110). Finally, even when access to mainstream publishers or the media was available, separatists often refused those routes because of their inability to control the makeup of the audience or an unwillingness to provide profits for what were perceived to be male-dominated organizations (Spinster 107).

Even so, several position papers and journals commonly have been cited as highly influential in the formation of both separatist theory and community. One of these, 'Lesbian Separatism: Amazon Analysis,' was written in 1973 by a collective from the Seattle area. Though the essay never was printed (it at one time had been scheduled for publication through Diana Press), it nevertheless was photocopied and passed around the country. Spinster recalls that 'it was never promoted in any way, and yet it was treated as if it was a special Lesbian treasure. It became an underground Lezzie classic' (105). Spinster further cites the c.l.i.t. (Collective Lesbian International Terrorists) Papers, published in *off our backs*, as those which 'gave the largest number of Lesbians their conception of what Separatism is' (Spinster 106–7).

Because of the often-short runs of many separatist newsletters or private distributions like that of 'Amazon Analysis,' to recreate or even find articles that explore separatist consciousness can be difficult. All the materials cited in this chapter can be found in the separatist files at the Lesbian Herstory Archives (LHA) in New York City. Until 1988, the archives had one of the few comprehensive collections in existence. Since then, Sarah Hoagland and Julia Penelope, both separatists themselves, have edited *For Lesbians Only: A Separatist Anthology*. The anthology includes most of what they perceive to be the influential essays on separatism written in the United States (as well as a section on French lesbian separatism), though some of the articles are carried in an abridged form. Because of the availability and scope of Hoagland and Penelope's text, whenever possible I will give citations as they appear in *For Lesbians Only*. Articles critical of separatism – either written from within or outside a separatist perspective – remain uncollected in print though they, too, may be found at the LHA.

Quite early in the radical-feminist movement (during, for example, the mid- to late 1960s), the definition of lesbian separatism would have been fairly simple. For the most part 'separatists,' whether lesbian or heterosexual, chose to segregate themselves from men or male groups. Thus in early lesbian-feminist or lesbian-separatist literature it is not uncommon to find separatists who refer to themselves as 'lesbian feminist,' 'feminist separatist,' or even just 'radical feminist.' The labels often were used interchangeably, as no particular segment of thought had been differentiated. And, in fact, most separatists (lesbian as well as heterosexual) continued to make separation from men their definitive characteristic even after other definitions of separatism gained popularity. Marilyn Frye's influential essay 'Some Reflections on Separatism and Power' uses just such a definition: 'Most feminists, probably all, practice some separation from males and male-dominated institutions. A separatist practices separation consciously, systematically, and probably more generally than the others, and advocates thorough and 'broad-spectrum' separation as part of the conscious strategy of liberation' (64). Note here that Frye retains the notion of separatism as one part of women's liberation. This concept, too, would change for many separatists as they continued to develop the discourse of lesbian-separatist theory.

But while most separatists agreed that separation from men and 'male values' was crucial to their definition of separatism, many quickly pointed out that complete separation was impossible, impractical, and sometimes undesirable. Many early separatists would have agreed with Bev Jo's analysis: 'Separatism is *not* having no contact with the patriarchy. Even the richest lesbians can't afford to do that, and most separatists I know are *not* rich. We have to work, deal with county, state and federal agencies, go to the grocery stores, deal with landlords, etc. We do not relate to males when we don't have to' (74). In part, Jo's emphasis on the class position of many separatists was meant to fend off growing criticism of separatism as a privilege only those who had the material resources could afford. But her suggestion of the need to choose when to separate also became much more developed later in the movement. In a workshop on separatism, for example, Hoagland and Penelope claimed a political value for the careful choice of when and where to evoke one's separatism ('Lesbian Separatism').

By 1970 the term 'lesbian separatist' began to take on different definitions for many women. Deborah Wolf notes that like women in East Coast radical-feminist groups, lesbians in the Bay Area began to feel isolated and oppressed by heterosexual feminists (66). This isolation caused many to feel the need for a specifically lesbian movement. Concurrently, lesbians in the Gay Liberation Front began to perceive that the group's agenda more often met the needs of gay men than it did those of lesbians. Thus by 1973, the *Furies* (a separatist newspaper) published debates on whether separatism meant separating from straight men, gay men, heterosexual women, or all three (Rich, 'Notes for a Magazine' 85). As distinct as each definition might have appeared, the facets of this debate followed arguments that occurred over the value of separatism in the broader context of radical-feminist theory itself. The authors of 'Amazon Analysis' could therefore posit separatism as in keeping with the logical conclusion of feminism:

Lesbian separatism is inherently linked with feminism, the ideology and practice that considers women prime. Feminists are women who get their emotional and physical identity and support from other women; women who are committed to struggling against and defeating male supremacy. . . . Lesbian separatism is feminism carried to its logical conclusion. (Alice, Gordon, Debbie, and Mary, 'Separatism' 31–32)

This ideological move, of course, had an effective precedent: as lesbian feminists had done with the role of lesbianism in feminism, separatists began to cast separatism as the test of one's feminist commitment, especially for other lesbians.

Perhaps due in part to such a rhetorical strategy, yet another type of separatism evolved at this time. As is usually the lot of separatism within the frameworks of other liberation or radical movements, lesbian separatism met more than its share of hostility from both within and outside the feminist movement. Lesbian separatists often found themselves, therefore, under attack even from other lesbian feminists. Separatist reactions to these attacks varied, but one response has been to call for separation from all but like-minded separatists:

BECAUSE WE WANT TO BUILD RELATIONSHIPS ON A MUCH MORE INTERPERSONAL LEVEL AND GROW, WE HAVE FOUND IT NECESSARY TO SEPARATE OURSELVES FROM CERTAIN LESBIANS. . . . [T]here is no desire to develop close, binding ties with those lesbians whom we have major clashes with. For the most part, we want to withdraw ourselves from very oppressive, negative situations into more positive ones. This is the basis of our politics. (Gutter Dyke Collective 29)

Given the differences in definitions posited by separatists themselves, as well as the tenacity of the desire to cling to those definitions (present even in the tone of the above quotation), it is not surprising that the search for a common theory or ideology becomes difficult at best. Yet despite differences in the ways they defined themselves, separatists of the 1970s did share some common theoretical and practical grounds. Again, the following discussion of separatist theory is meant less as a comprehensive definition than it is as an illumination of those ideologies I believe directly affected lesbian-separatist conceptions of the value and function of a women's community.

If one could pinpoint a single theory on which most separatists would agree, that theory would be the radical-feminist analysis of sexism as the primary contradiction. As it was in the development of lesbian-feminist social analysis, this concept was crucial to the political and social critiques offered in the discourse of lesbian separatism. But through the rhetorical strategies of mid-1970s separatism, radical feminism's key theory evolved into an ideology that changed both the practice and politics of female community.

At its inception in the radical-feminist movement, the theory of sexism as the primary contradiction focused most blame for women's oppression on societal institutions of sexism: marriage, motherhood, child rearing, and, through the analysis of lesbian feminism, the institution of compulsory heterosexuality. But the discourse of separatism shifted the emphasis of blame in the theory from a social ill (sexism) to its perceived sole agent (men). This is not to say that such a critique was absent from radical-feminist formulations of the theory; but through separatist discourse, this ideological view of male oppression was far more often articulated than it had been. Take, for example, the position paper issued by the Gutter Dyke Collective, publishers of the journal *Dykes and Gorgons:*

We see sexism as being the basis of all our oppressions – all the other 'isms' that continue to perpetuate themselves (capitalism, nationalistic socialism, imperialism, racism, classism, etc.). Just as sexism is the source of all of our other oppressions, maleness is the source of sexism. In order to rid the world of sexism we must first rid the world of men. But obviously we must also begin to deal with the racial and nationalistic and class divisions that men have created between us. . . . As feminists, we believe that women are inherently collectively oriented. (30)

The Gutter Dyke Collective's statement clearly makes the leap from social institution to biology. The essentialism of this argument was obvious from the beginning and, of course, did not go unremarked by those critical of separatism.[1] In response, many separatists countered that a truly revolutionary feminism required an actual enemy against which to struggle. In fact, separatists often felt that they alone among feminists had the courage to name the oppressor and could therefore avoid the hypocrisy they found in women who refused such a delineation. Mary Daly describes the contradictions she finds in feminists who refused to agree with this lesbian-separatist analysis:

women continue to be intimidated by the label *anti-male*. Some feel a false need to draw distinctions, for example: 'I am anti-patriarchal but not anti-male.' The courage to be logical – the courage to name – would require that we admit to ourselves that males and males only are the originators, planners, controllers, and legitimators of patriarchy. Patriarchy is the homeland of males; it is the Father Land; and men are its agents. . . .

The use of the label [antimale] is an indication of intellectual and moral limitations. Despite all the evidence that women are attached as projections of the enemy, the accusers ask sardonically: 'Do you really think that *men* are the enemy?' This deception/reversal is so deep that women – even feminists – are intimidated into Self-deception, becoming only Self-described oppressed who are unable to name their oppressor, referring instead to vague 'forces,' 'roles,' 'stereotypes,' 'constraints,' 'attitudes,' 'influences.' The list could go on. The point is that no agent is named – only abstractions. (Gyn/Ecology 28–29)

Daly's rhetorical use of sexism as the primary contradiction thus made it difficult for radical feminists not persuaded by lesbian separatism to avoid the charge of maintaining a failed or incomplete feminist vision.

More important, though, separatist redefinitions contained many (often contradictory) implications for the creation and maintenance of a politicized female community. First, if all men were the enemy – and there was a strong sentiment among white separatists that this was the case – then, by extension, all women were at least potential allies. One separatist explains:

All women are oppressed in a patriarchy. The differences among us (race, class, age) need to be confronted and understood, but always with the perspective that no woman is the enemy. Our commonality as women underlies our differences. . . .

All women are oppressed by all men. Men are the enemy, and we make no distinctions among them. Men are not reformable. Men have set up institutions that perpetuate oppression (government, economic systems, religion, etc.) but the institutions in themselves are merely tools of limitability in the hands of men. Female oppression will not be eradicated in the hands of men. Female oppression will not be eradicated by any method of institutional change. (Kane 7)

This emphasis on the sex, rather than the behavior, of one's enemies or allies necessitated (or at least allowed) categorizations of male versus female 'traits,' 'values,' or 'characteristics.' Note, for example, Kane's assignment of social institutions solely to men and, more deeply, to male nature: 'men have set up institutions that perpetuate oppression . . . but the institutions in themselves are merely tools of limitability in the hands of men.' Kane implies that these institutions are not causes of oppression but are simply symptomatic of the nature that gave rise to them.

Such an ideological view of the cause of oppression quickly became applied to nearly every social occurrence or institution identified by separatists as harmful to women, children, animals, the environment, and, on occasion, minority men. Thus for many separatists, men were seen as the inherent cause of every destructive aspect of life on earth. Liza Cowan's compilation of stories and theories written by several separatist groups generated the following analysis:

After I came out and started to spend more time and energy in exclusively female company, I began to realize just how different men and women really are. I realized, too, that seeing everybody as 'human' would help men stay in control and would keep women enslaved. It is in the interest of the patriarchy that women not realize that it is *men* and not 'human nature' that have created pollution, racism, the energy crisis, agribusiness, fast food, and every other symptom of the agony of life in the patriarchy. (224)

Implicit in Cowan's study is a further extrapolation of one's deeds to one's nature: if men were responsible for the creation of oppressive institutions, then they themselves must be the embodiments of the structure and mechanisms of those creations. Thus many lesbian separatists understood men to be naturally competitive, hierarchical, domineering, divisive, parasitic (especially on women), death-oriented, possessive, emotionless, and generally nonsupportive or nurturing of others. The divisions between men and women were so keenly felt that one separatist group wondered if men were not 'from another planet' altogether (Alice, Gordon, Debbie, and Mary, 'Problems of Our Movement' 391).

Such an analysis of men and their characteristics helped to foster a view of women that had great impact on separatist communities: the ideology of the automatic alliance with other women that sexism was thought to produce. Suggested in Kane's statement ('no woman is the enemy'), this ideology of women's natural alliance with other women developed in part from early radical feminist conceptions of the primacy of women's bonds but also as a necessary response to lesbian-separatist theories of male nature. In other words, if men behaved as they did because of their male natures, then women – by virtue of not being men – would act differently from men. Thus women were characterized as nurturing, life-giving, cooperative rather than competitive, passionate, connected with all living beings, nonhierarchical, nonoppressive, and, what was to become quite important, 'inherently collectively oriented' (Gutter Dyke Collective 30).

Lesbian-separatist delineation of behavioral characteristics by biological boundaries was, of course, an extremely fragile system in danger of destruction just as soon as any woman – but more particularly, any lesbian (as women who theoretically had rejected their patriarchal conditioning) – behaved in a manner thought to be oppressive, or 'male.' Yet lesbian separatists were not unaware that lesbians often behaved in oppressive ways. The existence of such behavior, if not reframed, effectively could challenge the ideological structure separatists had built on the theory of sexism as the primary contradiction. And while more than a few separatists accused those women who behaved improperly of not being 'real' women (more often, though, of not being 'real' lesbians), many more offered a theoretical analysis of such behaviors to circumvent the threat they posed to separatist ideology. By the early 1970s, therefore, it was not uncommon to find separatist theoretical discourse that exhorted women to cast out internalized, patriarchal teachings – or, as one author put it, to abolish 'the pig in the head' (Daly, Gyn/Ecology 342). Thus the prevalent separatist view of divisions among women evolved into a theory of such divisions as a false consciousness learned from so many years of patriarchal conditioning.[2] As I will discuss in chapter 5, separatist reframing of women's oppressive behaviors had a highly destructive effect on the practice of female community.

Yet these conceptions of women's nature expanded and maintained by the discourse of lesbian-separatist theory also had, perhaps, a more proactive effect on the politics and practice of separatism. Separatist theories of women as the life-affirming force in civilization compelled many separatists to challenge oppression directly, especially oppressive acts of racism, classism, and heterosexism. It is not uncommon to find actively antiracist, -classist, or -heterosexist analyses and work accomplished through separatist collectives long before these issues became of focus in other feminist communities of the 1960s and 1970s.

The Seattle collective's 'Amazon Analysis' in particular devoted a large part of its space to analyses of oppression in the lesbian community. On the issue of classism, for example, the Seattle collective specified precise methods by which class oppression worked within the lesbian movement:

Lesbians who formed the current lesbian movement were, for the most part, from cross-classed or middle-class families. Because of the type of movement they initiated and perpetuated, poor or working-class lesbians have felt excluded. This movement defined rigid sex roles as lower class (which is not true), instituted middle-class youth-culture chauvinism in many forms, held long meetings at inconvenient times and without providing child care, ignored gut responses in exclusive favor of abstract theorizing, listened condescendingly to women who were not as aggressive or articulate in a university-approved fashion, reacted with giddy excitement to women who got jobs as janitors, bus drivers, or cab drivers because these women had supposedly broken into male fields when working class women have held these jobs for years and don't consider them much fun . . . (Alice, Gordon, Debbie, and Mary, 'Problems' 381)

Similarly, on the issue of racism, the Seattle collective recognized that silence on the part of women of color did not necessarily mean all was well within lesbian separatism:

Many white lesbians have been falsely believing that there was not so much racism among ourselves, not conscious that the reason our community has not been attacked often by third world lesbians for its racism is that for many, if not most, third world lesbians our community is the only place they can be. To attack white lesbians and risk isolation is a privilege third world lesbians often feel they can not afford, though they are constantly oppressed by our behavior. For us to profess to love other lesbians in any more than a sexual way and not put our efforts into reducing the pressures of racism on third world lesbians is hypocrisy. (380–81)

Such an analysis of and call to action against racism and classism is one of the earliest attempts by white women to address these issues in the contemporary feminist movement.

Yet even while they took white lesbians to task for their racism or middle-class lesbians for their classism, the authors of 'Amazon Analysis' never assumed that the lesbian-separatist community might not be the community of choice for lesbians other than those of the white, middle-class majority. In fact, despite separatist efforts to analyze social constructions of difference they felt divided groups of women, the strongest disputes and sharpest critiques aimed at separatists occurred around these very issues. Though nearly every difference that exists among women was at one point or another cause for community dispute, the issues of race and, to a lesser extent, class were represented most heavily in writings on separatism before the early 1980s.

The accusation of racism as inherent in lesbian-separatist ideology and practice was voiced frequently, especially by feminists of color, and today continues to haunt separatist projects. One of the better-known critiques, issued by the Combahee River Collective in 1977, decried separatist refusal to work with men in the struggle against racism:

Although we are feminists and lesbians, we feel solidarity with progressive Black men and do not advocate the fractionalization that white women who are separatists demand. Our situation as Black people necessitates that we have solidarity around the fact of race, which white women of course do not need with white men, unless it is their negative solidarity as racial oppressors. We struggle together with Black men against racism, while we also struggle with Black men about sexism. (16)

The Combahee River Collective implies here that separatism was primarily a white woman's prerogative; other feminists of color stated quite strongly that only white women had enough privilege to become separatists.[3]

Such an analysis, however, ultimately proved inaccurate as many separatist groups numbered women of color among their ranks. But while many women of color aligned themselves with separatism, they often felt ambivalent over the intersections between their separatist and racial identities. Anna Lee, a contributor to *For Lesbians Only,* is quite explicit about her separatist politics but writes of her alienation because of racism in the women's community:

I often feel alienated by the white feminist community which has the privilege to ignore and to minimize racism. White feminists can demand my support, presence and energy without seeing what it is they are asking of me. They can refuse to acknowledge the price I pay: the losing of my protection as limited and limiting as it is. My blackness is visible and the first line of attack on me. I am also a womon and choose to continue my struggle within the wimmin's community. I have stopped struggling with my brothers around their homophobia and sexism. As I have indicated, merging my seemingly separate identities is not easy, but all of them exist within me. It is very important to me to recognize that racism hurts both my brothers and me. While it may manifest itself differently for each of us, it is the blackness that defines the conditions we live under. (87)

Though Lee draws her lines against coalitions with African-American men, she nonetheless indicates the conflicts that the professed separatist commitment to antiracism, combined with the contradictory use of sexism as the primary contradiction, produced within her.

For other feminists of color, the drawbacks of lesbian separatism became apparent over the issue of male children. As I will discuss in the next two chapters, the issue of male children was an especially divisive one for most separatist communities. And for many African-American women, this issue carried racist implications as well. Audre Lorde, for example, described her reaction to the prohibition against male children over the age of ten at a lesbian-feminist conference:

This presented logistic as well as philosophical problems for us, and we sent the following letter:

'Sisters: Ten years as an interracial lesbian couple has taught us both the dangers of an over-simplified approach to the nature and solutions of any oppression, as well as the danger inherent in an incomplete vision.

Our 13-year-old son represents as much hope for our future world as does our 15-year-old daughter, and we are not willing to abandon him to the killing streets of New York City while we journey west to help form a Lesbian-Feminist vision of the future world in which we can all survive and flourish. . . .'

The question of separatism is by no means simple. I am thankful that one of my children is male, since that helps to keep me honest. Every line I write shrieks there are no easy solutions. (34)

Lorde notes further that it is equally important to combat oppression by raising male children who resist and fight their oppressors: 'I wish to raise a black man who will not be destroyed by, nor settle for, those corruptions that are called power by the white fathers who mean his destruction in the same ways that they mean mine' (31).

Ultimately, then, the point of division from separatism for many feminists of color came because, as Elsa Barkley Brown explains in her essay 'Womanist Consciousness,' issues of racism and sexism were often inseparable entities in their lives (610–13). Thus the perceived separatist demand for separation from men and boys of color was for many a highly racist price to pay for a dubious liberation. As lesbians from a group called the Native American Solidarity Committee (NASC) wrote:

We believe that the ideas in Separatist theory are in direct conflict with Native Sovereignty. Although Separatist theory voices a concern with racism, this theory put into practice is unable to directly combat racism. It does not fit racism into its revolutionary theory because of the simplistic view that all men are the enemy – no matter who they are. Separatist theory also dictates an imposed isolation from the majority of people. (13)[4]

In essence, separatism's shortcomings for groups like the NASC appeared in the fact that it could not convince them that racism would or could be eradicated through the elimination of sexism. Further, separatist insistence on the answer that racism was a man-made distinction curable only through the demise of the patriarchy sounded suspiciously like the argument given to women by leftist men on the issue of sexism – an argument that, of course, separatists themselves were quick to denounce.

The issue of class within separatism was no less contentious than that of race, though its discursive representations often assumed different forms. Women who discussed classism within separatism usually did not argue those issues in terms of separatism's distance from working-class men; rather, they based their critiques on oppression they themselves experienced. Issues of class, like those of race, were noted as problematic by separatist and nonseparatist women alike. Redwomon, a strongly proseparatist contributor to Hoagland and Penelope's anthology, recalls some of her experiences with class (as well as race) issues within separatist groups:

Several times I've been kicked out of groups (rap, support, and study) for no good reason – along with other workingclass [*sic*], black or Asian wimin – each time by thin, white, able-bodied, middle-class wimin who always seem to have power and be in charge, even in 'leaderless' groups. I have never heard of a white m-c woman being ejected from anything. The damage done by this elitism is incalculable, both individually and to the movement and community. . . . We must work out our problems in ways that do not attempt to assimilate poor, non-white or disabled wimin into the white middle-class able ideal of manners and appearance. (82)

And for working-class or poor lesbians who did not practice separatism, separatist ideology itself often appeared elitist or arrogantly middle class. In fact, what they learned of separatism through the contemporary publications seemed to demand too much energy needed even for daily survival:

What I get pissed at is the myths and totally off the wall beliefs [separatists] pull out of nowhere to support their attitudes. . . . Some of those lesbians who profess to be together, revolutionary Amazons are the most arrogant, fatuous people around. Besides, I don't know any damn Amazons. We know very little about Amazon culture, and anyway, that stuff went down a long time ago and we're alive *today*. You ain't gonna find me talking trash about how cool and tough and women-identified I am because I don't have time for that shit when I'm still on welfare. ('Separatism . . . Overdose?!' 8)

For many working-class or poor lesbians, then, the perceived demands separatism placed on them were difficult to meet. And if they did decide to practice separatism, lesbians without middle-class privilege often faced a range of class assumptions and practice they found oppressive, whether or not these behaviors were produced by women's 'false consciousness.'

Given my earlier argument that separatists paid at least as much – and indeed probably more – attention to the issue of the social constructions of difference among women than did other feminists, it perhaps seems ironic that they should have faced constant attack for oppressive practice and theory. What was it about separatism that left it more open to criticism than its counterparts in radical-feminist or lesbian-feminist practice? The answers to this question are of course many, several germane to this study.[5] First, and most simply, despite hopes for the opposite, women in separatist groups did and do oppress other women, whether intentionally or indirectly.

But such oppression conceivably might have been lessened or greatly reduced if it were not for tensions within separatist ideology itself. The foundation of sexism as the primary contradiction and more particularly its extension to name all men the enemy, when it did not simply give white, middle-class separatists an easy 'out' from accusations of oppressive behavior, actively stood in the way of any revolutionary connection between women.

Perhaps the most vivid example of this tension in separatist theory comes in the work of the Seattle collective. In its original form, 'Amazon Analysis' quite carefully stated that separatists should respect Third World women's need to work with men, that separatism should not divide women of different races, and that separatists 'should actively oppose the oppression of *all* third world people' (Alice, Gordon, Debbie, and Mary, 'Problems' 381). But shortly after they printed the pamphlet, the collective changed their position and issued an addition to the text, with the preface that although they 'look[ed] forward' to critique, 'one of our errors is so grave . . . that we do not feel we can wait . . . to acknowledge it' (Alice, Gordon, Debbie, and Mary, 'Addition' 307). The crux of this addition was that the collective felt they erred in their original analysis of separatism's place for Third World women.

What the collective issued in place of its earlier analysis was a statement that emphasized the potential alliances among all women and rejected any alliance with men of any culture or with women who continued to insist on such alliances. They now felt that the perceived need to ally with Third World men at the possible expense of other women was a sexist, patriarchal concept. The collective stated that they had in their original stance patronized women of color and concluded: 'We still believe that white lesbians should not impose white culture on third world lesbians. However, we believe that we have accurately analyzed this society. We believe that third world women are as capable as we are of perceiving the patriarchal nature of the society and acting accordingly' ('Addition' 309). 'Acting accordingly,' of course, meant to follow the white separatist program in its refusal to struggle in coalition with men. For those who felt such divisions to be oppressive, separatists quickly took away every step they made toward the creation of revolutionary alliances among women.

Perhaps, however, even these disagreements among lesbian separatists, nonseparatists, and heterosexual women might not have been so deeply felt had it not been for one final consequence of separatist ideological use of sexism as the primary contradiction. Conceptions of the innate, tenacious, and vastly different natures of men and women, and the destructive differences men's natures were perceived to carry, led separatists to conclude that separatism in and of itself was the only effective action in the war against oppression. Whereas radical and even lesbian feminists once viewed separatism as one process by which women could amass enough strength to work for radical change, lesbian separatists now argued that separatism was the only solution for the demise of patriarchy and thus claimed an intrinsic worth for the act of separation itself. In speaking of their ideology of lesbian separatism, for example, the Seattle collective claimed:

Other ideologies may recognize that sexism is bad, and should be eliminated. But unless the root, the cause, is recognized and eliminated, the oppressions and problems that men foisted on us all when they overthrew the matriarchal societies can never be truly eliminated.

No other ideology does this; no other ideology speaks to all of our needs; no other ideology will or *can* destroy patriarchy and male supremacy and build an egalitarian matriarchal society. (Alice, Gordon, Debbie, and Mary, 'Separatism' 32)

The formation of women's community, then, became theoretically in and of itself the revolution, and those who balked at the vision of such a community were at the very least deeply mistrusted. Women who were compelled by radical-feminist analysis as it emerged through separatism understood separatism, especially in its vision of female community, to be an active, revolutionary stance; the only stance, in fact, that could achieve the goals of a feminist revolution.

Thus, the community work of separatist theoretical discourse as it applied to the concept of female community was as complex and contradictory as early separatism itself. First, separatism carried the analysis of female bonding present in Radicalesbians' 'Woman Identified Woman' one step further through the conception of all women as allies in the war against the patriarchy, or, rather, against men. In so doing, lesbian separatists were able to define the ideal characteristics of women in relationship to one another. Further, these characteristics were cast as normal, inherent qualities of womanhood rather than ideals to be attained only after, for example, much hard work. And when women acted in ways that refuted their supposed inherent natures, separatists often criticized them for succumbing to male conditioning or learned male behaviors. Such a tactic, while it may have been meant to create a vision of female bonds that could supersede all difference, worked more often than not to excuse women's oppressive behaviors toward one another. Yet lesbian separatism's strongest priority was to maintain women's bonds with one another: within the framework of separatist theory, female community became tantamount to the revolution.

The renewed emphasis on the value of women's community and sentiments like the Gutter Dyke Collective's proclamation that women are 'inherently collectively oriented' compelled many women – separatist, nonseparatist, lesbian, and heterosexual – to form or join women's collectives during the 1970s. As we might suspect, however, the concepts with which these separatist collectives began provided the basis not only for the most exhilarating visions but also for the most deeply entrenched barriers to their success. The ideology of sexism as the primary contradiction proved to be one of the most substantial barriers of all, especially as its use intersected with issues of race and class.

The next section of this study picks up conceptions of female community as they evolved through the discourse of separatist collective historical narratives. Unlike their counterparts in the discourse of separatist theory, however, the authors of these narratives not only took on the task of describing the hope and enthusiasm with which they embarked on their journeys to put theory into practice, but they also faced the difficult work of the presentation of those experiences for which their theories in no way prepared them. As we shall see, the community work of these narratives thus both parallels and dramatically deviates from that of separatist theory.

LESBIAN HERSTORY ARCHIVES ONE

'You don't need the key,' the doorman said. 'She's up there.'

'But . . .' I hesitated. 'She said she'd be gone all week . . . ?'

The doorman simply shrugged and motioned me in the direction of the elevator.

During the long ride up to the archives, I worried over this new turn of events. I had looked forward to a week of intensive research. A protective archivist hovering in the background – no matter who she was – would only slow me down. Sighing with resignation, I rang the bell.

Joan opened the door. 'Dana Shugar,' I announced myself and extended my hand. She took it, inviting me in. We exchanged the usual amenities and she said:

'I got the list of sources you sent – the journals you wanted are there on the table. After you look through that material, tell me more about your project and I'll try to find other sources.'

'Wonderful – thanks. Do you mind if I take some quotes from the sources as I read through them? I brought pencils . . .' I offered, not quite ready to broach the archivist's nightmare of copying machines.

'Don't worry about it,' she replied, waving away my formalities. 'Pens or pencils are fine – but there's a Xerox machine in the back room if you'd rather. If you use it a lot just leave a donation to help offset the paper costs, okay? Are you a coffee drinker?'

'Diehard,' I smiled, a bit surprised. 'What grad student isn't?'

'Would you like some coffee?' she asked, smiling in return.

'I'd love some . . . thanks!' I couldn't believe it. If this was the archives' usual method of operation, I knew I'd regret not having the means to stay for a month.

I spent the morning reading through the material Joan had pulled. I found a good deal of information I had believed existed but, because of the small or short runs of many radical-feminist journals, could not locate anywhere else. By midafternoon I recognized that the first day's work alone had made the trip worthwhile. I expressed that sentiment to Joan as I prepared to leave for the day.

'Good!' she replied, genuinely pleased. 'But you haven't told me exactly what you're working on.'

'I haven't refined the major premise, but I'm looking at the effects of separatist theory and utopian literature on lesbian communities. That's why I need all these articles on separatism and collectives.'

'Really?' she asked, incredulous. 'And you mean they're *letting* you do that?'

I nodded, grinning at what swiftly was becoming a standard response. 'Yes, and I'm really lucky this trip. I'm staying at a collectively run B&B – sort of a "research immersion"!'

She laughed. 'Where are you staying?'

'The Bloodroot – up in Connecticut.'

Silence. Déjà vu. At times, however, I can be impossibly obtuse to nonverbal cues. I pressed further.

'Do you know the Bloodroot?'

'Yes,' she replied slowly, her voice suddenly flat. 'I am not . . .' she paused, searching for the right word, '*welcome* at the Bloodroot.'

Narratives of Separatist Collectives and Problems of Community

PART TWO

Introduction: Separatist Collective Endeavors

We must move out of our old living patterns and into new ones. Those of us who believe in this concept must begin to build collectives where women are committed to other women on all levels – emotional, physical, economic and political. Monogamy can be cast aside, no one will 'belong' to another. Instead of being shut off from each other in overpriced cubicles we can be together, sharing the shitwork as well as the highs. Together we can go through the pain and liberation of curing the diseases we have all contracted in the world of male dominance, imperialism and death. Women-identified collectives are nothing less than the next step toward a Women's Revolution. – Rita Mae Brown, 'Living with Other Women'

The discourse of separatist theory, especially that of lesbian-separatist theory, in many ways required women to live and/or work in collectives as the full realization of their political analyses. Brown's call (and others like it) encouraged the creation of collectives all over the country: women who lived in urban areas tended to form working collectives (e.g., dedicated to the production of a journal or newspaper, or running a restaurant or bookstore), while women in rural areas bought isolated acreages in order to form residential collectives.[1] Both types of collectives could contain the other, of course; for many women the combination of a working and living collective provided both the social and the economic support they sought.

Feminist literature, especially articles and books on early separatist theory, held a significant place in the formation and life of separatist collectives. One journalist for *Mother Jones*, for example, cast the creation of the Country Women collective in the following way:

Country Women, the soft-spoken, dark-eyed Carmen explains, was born out of a consciousness-raising group started by Carmen's then-lover, Jeanne, who was   57 armed with nothing more than her reading of Shulamith Firestone's powerful book, *The Dialectic of Sex*. (I am appreciative of that fact, because it was and is *the* feminist work that had the most profound influence on my own thinking). . . .

'Jeanne and I were lesbians,' Carmen says, 'but we were not feminists then. We just assumed that a commune meant a mixed commune of men and women. So for two years we had the most sleazy array of men living here. . . .'

After a few short months of their consciousness-raising group, Carmen and Jeanne 'booted the men off the land. . . .' The power of that consciousness-raising group spread to all of its members like a prairie fire. (Koolish 24)

The fact that a publication such as *Mother Jones* found the existence of separatist collectives compelling attests to the visibility and acknowledgment separatist actions achieved in political communities. And the fact that the interviewer herself struggles to find common ground with these women through Firestone's *Dialectic* illustrates both the diverse appeal and catalytic nature such texts had within the feminist community.

But to imply that the relationship between separatist discourse and the creation of separatist communities was one-sided or operated in one direction obscures the complex relationship between separatist collectives, theory, and historical narrative. Separatist collectives, while their creations were inspired by works the members had read, often themselves participated in the formation and evolution of separatist theory. Thus women in the mid-1970s who belonged to rural or urban collectives utilized works such as the Seattle collective's 'Amazon Analysis' or the c.l.i.t. essays in the formation of their collectives, even as they wrote similar essays that would influence in turn other women in the creation of their collectives.

The relationship women in separatist collectives had with literature did not stop at the level of separatist theory, however. Many collectives, especially those that struggled to shape communal living arrangements, wrote and sometimes published narratives of their experiences as a collective. These narratives, now primarily available at the Lesbian Herstory Archives, often recorded the goals or visions with which the collectives began; the everyday experiences, achievements, or failures of collective activities; the goals for the future life of the collective; and, if the collective failed, the process of its dissolution.[2] More compelling to me, however, is the fact that these narratives can be read as a second discursive site wherein theories and ideologies of female community were taken up, examined, and, in many cases, rewritten for separatism.

The second section of this study analyzes two anthologies of separatist narratives in order to illuminate the community work the discourse of separatist historical narratives accomplished in separatism's quest for female community. The first, Michal Brody's *Are We There Yet? A Continuing History of* Lavender Woman: *A Chicago Lesbian Newspaper, 1971–1976,* is a collection of articles, poems, and essays from issues of *Lavender Woman* positioned with interviews Brody conducted during the mid-1980s with past members of the collective. The *Lavender Woman* collective, as the anthology's subtitle implies, was an urban group of women who published a monthly newspaper for Chicago's lesbian community. They did not share a collective living space although they spent much of their free time, as well as their work time, together.

The second anthology, Joyce Cheney's *Lesbian Land,* contains narratives from twenty-five women's land groups, most of them collective in structure, that began as early as the late 1960s. Though several of the narratives have appeared piecemeal in other publications, Cheney's anthology provides one of the largest published collections of separatist land narratives.

I have chosen to work with these two anthologies for several reasons: first, read together they provide examples of residential and business, urban and rural collectives; second, they remain in print today and thus are easily accessible; third, they attempt to provide several different points of view, when possible, from each collective; fourth, they are dedicated to the exploration of both the positive and negative aspects of the collective experience. Each work, too, contains samples of printed materials from the time of the collectives' existence and thus may be examined for the impact they might have had on separatist discourse during the 1970s as well as the mid-1980s. Finally, though perhaps all the selections in these collections were not available in print during the mid- to late 1970s, they nonetheless represent both the tone and content of those narratives that were available during this period. As I examine these works in chapters 3 and 4, I will refer to or quote from other narratives that present similar stories or circumstances.

An analysis of these two texts reveals that the insistence on and enthusiastic struggle for community within the structure of separatist collectives were repeatedly undercut by ideologies of difference and unity that divided women within the collectives themselves. Each chapter begins with an examination of the theories and goals for community held by collective members, especially as those concepts addressed issues of race, class, sexual orientation, and separatism itself, and proceeds to analyze how goals of community were blocked by the operant ideologies within the collectives themselves. Such an examination should illustrate the paradoxical, irresolvable binds in which many collective members found themselves as they tried to practice their politics. These binds, when not confronted, led to a disheartening rate of collective dissolutions during the late 1970s and early 1980s. They also, however, catalyzed the emergence of the final genre discussed in part 3. To begin the analysis of these discursive moments, we turn to Michal Brody's representation of Chicago's *Lavender Woman* collective.

Are We There Yet?: Separatism and Separations in Female Community

Four

Edna: . . . *It's really surprising to me that women have been able to form, I wouldn't say revolutionary, but long-range political goals and work together politically because I don't think that's an easy task. I think that we're much more prone to be individualists and to believe in individual solutions. I'm using the term political in the sense of people getting together to effect social change.*
Michal: *I think that the very fact of our getting together was social change.*
— Michal Brody, *Are We There Yet?*

Michal Brody's *Are We There Yet? A Continuing History of* Lavender Woman: *A Chicago Lesbian Newspaper, 1971–1976* presents the reader with a complex, sometimes contradictory, but nonetheless fascinating narrative structure. Even the subtitle, in its suggestion that a 'continuing history' could end at 1976, exhibits the seemingly paradoxical nature of this narrative. The front cover appears both at one and at odds with the title: it depicts a road on which stand a traffic light (at the moment green) and, directly across the street, a 'No Stopping' sign. Should (as is the wont of traffic lights) the signal turn red, it would immediately contradict the 'No Stopping' sign. The sign, too, appears in contradiction with the definitive boundaries of the title's date, placed just up the road from the sign itself. The combination of the cover's image with its title further complicates our sense of this project: what would be the purpose, we might ask, of traveling on if we are uncertain as to whether we 'are there yet' or not?

The reader's experience of this text as a historical narrative is no less complex. At first glance, the table of contents seems fairly straightforward: an introduction followed by a list of interviews with seven women (who, we later learn, were collective members) and then three chapters that appear to be summary or concluding remarks. At the bottom of the contents page, however, the following note appears: '*Lavender Woman* articles appear throughout the book and are not listed here. They are arranged in very close chronological order' (iii). And upon turning the contents page the reader finds a reproduction of the cover of the first issue of *Lavender Woman* (LW), the first of many such pictorial/textual images interspersed throughout the book.

Brody's book, in fact, presents at least two historical texts or, more accurately, a text and a metatext. By this I mean that while the included articles from LW partially recreate the discourse from its five-year run, the interviews (all presumably done in 1984) create a text that reflects on and repositions those earlier pieces from the distance of at least ten to fifteen years. Further, several of the pieces Brody includes from the pages of LW are 'collective statements': editorial comments or even open letters to their readers issued by the collective itself. These pieces, even more than the 1970s articles written by individual women, might be read as a sort of collective narrative written during the collective's existence.

Any reading strategy that purports to analyze the community work of this narrative thus must grapple with the fact that the text provides more than one historical level. On the other hand, I think an analysis that separates the narrative strands too exclusively would miss the effects each historical period exerts on the other within this text. The interviews, for example, are structured in part as a response to the goals Brody and other members perceived their paper accomplished, just as Brody's choice of which LW articles to include is predicated on the members' memories of the important issues during the collective's existence. Thus my reading of *Are We There Yet?* not only analyzes the community work of Brody's texts as a 1985 narrative in its own right, but it also illuminates the ways members perceived the accomplishments of the journal and the collective during their existence. In addition, both the collective statements and the letters to the editor that appeared in LW can be read as an ongoing dialogue between the *Lavender Woman* collective and noncollective members of Chicago's lesbian community. And while we must always keep in mind that the structure of this text is influenced by Brody's experiences in the mid-1980s, those experiences (as she herself reminds us) were heavily informed by the events of 1971 to 1976.

To coordinate the reading of these textual levels I utilize a two-part approach. I first examine the statements of the collective members Brody interviewed and excerpts from the paper itself that concern the purpose or goals of their collective and its product. Through this analysis three major collective concerns are revealed: the desire to create and write for a specifically lesbian-feminist community, the consternation over charges of racism, and the frustration around the politics of lesbian separatism. I then revisit these concerns as they appeared primarily in the 1970s selections from *LW*, in part to determine what 'work' the representations of race, community, and separatism did during the 1970s in order to elicit reactions in members' recollections ten years later. Of course, my analysis assumes that those experiences recalled in Brody's text in 1985 are those that had the most impact on the collective and on the Chicago community during the 1970s. And while that assumption may be inaccurate, these were the issues that nonetheless became reinscribed and historicized by the construction of this collective's story. I conclude this chapter with an analysis of the discrepancies between collective members' views of the function of *LW* and the view suggested by my interpretation of the final chapters of Brody's text, an analysis that I hope will reveal the community work of all the narrative levels as a whole.

In the introduction to *Are We There Yet?* Brody creates a historical account of both the paper's beginnings and her role in those beginnings. She grounds this account in the social and political upheaval of the 1960s and claims as a direct ancestor the gay pride movement that followed Stonewall. The *Lavender Woman* collective began as a project of the April collective, a group of women who left the Chicago Gay Alliance because they felt that the predominantly male organization did not meet their needs as lesbians. Throughout its five-year existence, the *Lavender Woman* collective claimed approximately fifty members and consisted of white, Jewish, and African-American women (who initially comprised one-third of the group's membership). The paper also claimed a culturally diverse audience (1–10, 130).

Brody tells us very little of her goals or purpose behind *Are We There Yet?* as a historical narrative and even less about her decisions to interview the members she does, compile the clippings she chooses, or publish the book when she did. What she does offer is a statement that is quite careful to disavow any claim to historical objectivity:

The history that follows is not a matter of record in any national publication. It is written the way I remember it, imperfectly, to be sure, and with personal bias. All of history is the same. I've made an honest attempt to be truthful in my accounts, and neutral in my descriptions. But I know, and so should you, that I am writing as a single witness to these events. Other witnesses will no doubt find disagreement between their accounts and mine. That's fine. If a single, concrete Truth were possible, this book wouldn't be interesting or even necessary. Contradiction, and what we do with it, is what we're all about. Are we there yet? (3)

Brody's acknowledgment of editorial bias may seem routine, but the connection between her disclaimer and the book's title signals a greater importance than we might first recognize. To whom does Brody address her statement about the impossibility of a 'concrete Truth'? Why does she feel the need to insist that this history is relative? What group of readers most needs to be convinced that contradiction is 'what we're all about'? And who determines whether or not we're 'there'?

I do not pose these questions facetiously but rather to reveal vital factors in the vision of community held by members of this Chicago collective. For many members of the collective, the experience they gained in the women's movement and in their community brought a welcome change from their experiences in leftist communities, as Brody's interview with Susan Jill Kahn indicates:

When I was in the lefty political sds-type crowds in college, working collectively meant that I handed out the leaflets, did the shitwork, you know, that whole line. My biggest political act was to refuse to fuck a man who had a draft card. On LW I felt like I learned in myself that I was a viable thinker, that I was capable of having political thought. I came up and came out with a very low self-esteem around that. . . . And through LW and some other things I felt like, as much as I had struggles and there were certain places where I was just insecure and scared, on another level I felt like I had found a community and found a place for myself where I was valuable and appreciated and respected, and where I could respect myself. (61)

Kahn's conception of the difference between women's roles in the Left and their roles in the women's liberation movement parallels Robin Morgan's experiences examined in chapter 1. Kahn's sense of a community within women's liberation that provided affirmation for the individual as well as for women as a group also presents her developing awareness of each woman's effect on and contributions to the sociopolitical activism of the collective. This awareness, as we shall see, placed a difficult burden of responsibility both on individual women and on the collective as a whole in a way that was not anticipated by the visions of community posited in separatist theories of collectivity.

Brody's choice to include Kahn's comments on community is a focus she keeps throughout most of the interviews. Her interview with Bonnie Zimmerman, for example, emphasizes that women joined the collective in part because they sought a sense of community from the start:

I had just finished my PhD and moved from Buffalo back to Chicago, which is where I grew up, and I was looking for something to do to get involved with the Lesbian community because I'd been very much involved in it in Buffalo. And Lavender Woman was very visible. Lavender Woman was what I wanted to do because I had done some newspaper stuff in Buffalo. . . . So Lavender Woman very quickly provided a community. I was able to address the issues I'd wanted; there were personal issues and there were political issues. The personal issues, yes, I've never had such a sense of belonging and feeling a part of something as when I worked on the paper. (78)

This passage suggests that Zimmerman's expectations of community were met by her work in the *Lavender Woman* collective. Indeed, the theme of *Lavender Woman* as a community of affirmation appears in these interviews often enough to present either a strong, retrospective consensus on the issue or the desire to create the appearance of such a consensus. The appearance of consensus on issues of community became necessary, I think, if the *Lavender Woman* collective was and is to be perceived as a major force in Chicago's lesbian community. Such a conception is one that Brody herself wishes to encourage.

The vision of community held by collective members extended beyond the boundaries of the collective as well. In nearly every interview Brody asks what each woman understood to be the major accomplishment or contribution of the paper. Zimmerman responded: 'We were a source of news, of information, of entertainment I hope, of infuriation, which is another form of entertainment for the audience; I think that we were something that – when you talked about what was the Chicago community of that time, there were things that defined it – and *LW* was one of those things that helped us feel like a community' (86–87). Similarly, Susan Edwards felt that *LW* had its own identity as a community force: 'I think that it was a forum for people to bounce off of, that people really needed. The isolation of women is so vast. I think that we actually made a dent in that for people. It was an identity, it was something to talk about, it was something to argue about. Yeah, I think that was fantastic' (169). Not only did collective members feel they had formed a community through their work on the paper, they also recall a sense of providing the same sort of community for Chicago women and, as noted in an interview with Betty Sutton, women nationwide (26). Further, the collective envisioned this community as shaped by debate, dissension, and infuriation as well as by news and information. Thus the community of *Lavender Woman* was to be structured by disagreement, even as it governed itself by consensus. The structure of consensus operates to imply failure if consensus is not reached, in other words, if debate continues without resolution. From its origins, then, the collective set itself a nearly impossible task: to create a community predicated on debate and disagreement through a structure of government that, if successful, works to contain or resolve such dissension. The tensions produced within the collective by these expectations, as we will explore later, worked more to augment a sense of failure for collective members than it did to promote a sense of community diversity.

Most of the interviews Brody conducted in the mid-1980s indicate the strong sense of community that collective members felt they had found and conveyed through the pages of *LW*. Other than the suggestion that the paper served to connect women with other women, however, the interviews do not give us many details about the sociopolitical character of the community collective members envisioned when they set out to publish the paper. But Brody's inclusion of the early 'collective statements' printed in *LW* provides at least a partial recreation of those details. An analysis of those statements in comparison with later articles, letters to the editor, or even later collective statements reveals the complex contradictions that perhaps made the emphasis on community seem so necessary to collective members who gathered to recall their experiences.

From its beginning the *Lavender Woman* collective placed its struggle in context with other discourses of resistance. Susan Edwards's article 'Lavender Consciousness' described the collective's battle against oppression in the following way:

We are struggling. To say it again, we are struggling against an oppressor whose primary goal is economic domination. Economic power is secured in this country by the exploitation of the family unit. The family oppresses its children, the husband oppresses his wife, etc. We are struggling against that dehumanization. We are not economic pawns. We want to regain, reclaim and re-establish authority over our bodies, our minds and our hearts. (21)

Edwards combines the rhetoric of the New Left with that of radical feminism in much the same manner as did Shulamith Firestone in her analysis of family oppression (Firestone 142–74). Edwards's use of radical-feminist analyses functions to place the collective within a political framework of revolutionary activism against an oppressive, mainstream society. She concludes that the role of *LW* is to 'chronicle' the defeat of women's oppression and that its radicalism is a result of the acknowledgment of lesbian pride she hoped the collective could present in its pages (Brody 21).

While Edwards repositions the framework of *LW*'s mission within early radical-feminist analyses, other collective and individual statements appropriate specifically lesbian-feminist theories in their descriptions of the paper's vision. The first statement issued by the collective (November 1971), in fact, stated collective views on the value of lesbianism to feminism:

A Lesbian relationship, we are beginning to discover, is not a hazard, or a liability, but a gift and a virtue – a strengthening, redeeming relationship in which we mutually confirm our identities as women, in which we are free to let ourselves be real, rather than meet a male-sexist stereotype which society is always holding up for us to clumsily imitate. . . . Our failure to meet straight standards of behaviour is our ultimate success as real women. In this sense, Lesbianism is a powerful, revolutionary force within the Women's Movement . . . we are the first women who have elected to survive without men. We even find ourselves being exploited by straight sisters in Women's Liberation who see Lesbianism as a kind of revolutionary Bandwagon, [that] they can jump on to get there quicker. (12)

This first statement's incorporation of analyses such as Radicalesbians' 'Woman Identified Woman' effectively places the collective's work on the cutting edge of feminism. A specifically lesbian-feminist theoretical analysis of women's oppression thus became important to the member's conceptions of communal existence and work and informed their choices of publishable material.

As a collective grounded in lesbian feminism, *Lavender Woman* perceived its role as a struggle against homophobia and institutionalized heterosexuality. Through this struggle and, more important, through their work on the paper itself, collective members felt that a politically active lesbian community would be created:

We, of the *Lavender Woman,* feel that this newspaper, written by and for Lesbians, is a powerful weapon against the society that tries, in vain, to keep us closeted and out of sight. More important, the paper will be a tool for growth.

Through it, we can create a positive, viable Lesbian community; increase our political consciousness; communicate our feelings to one another; share with each other our knowledge and gifts and, above all, thank ourselves again and again for each other. (13)

Through its claim that lesbians were the vanguard of feminism, the *Lavender Woman* collective thus celebrated the publication and distribution of its paper as a sociopolitical act.

Yet for the women of *LW* (and collectives like it), the practice of lesbian-feminist politics meant to act in relationship with other women in very specific ways. For example, in a policy that would later prove to be an ironic agent in the collective's demise, *LW* carefully weighed the tone of every article it would print that concerned the actions of women in the community. Betty Peters Sutton recalled:

We knew we did not want women attacking other women. That was the first no-no. That was the biggest no-no of all throughout the movement. Because we felt like we had come out of a background where that was all that had ever happened – women attacking each other over men. That was the first thing. Then we decided that we wanted to be about lesbians in Chicago grouping together to be stronger. We wanted that information to come across in the newspaper. . . .

We were very very careful not to be what we felt was macho oriented. We didn't want headlines that would scream out weird accusations. (31)

This recollection of *LW*'s 'golden rule' is cast in a theoretical discourse we have seen before: women who attack women are 'macho oriented' (or 'male identified'); thus women, particularly women-identified women, should shun this practice. And as it did in the discourse of separatist theory, the dichotomy of a destructive/oppressive male versus a supportive/nurturing female 'orientation' or value system mandated an exclusive unity of women in order that women's liberation might succeed. The collective decided to exclude men both from the pages of *LW* and from the collective itself. More interesting, however, was its decision to exclude heterosexual women as well; Sutton recalls that the collective dedicated itself to a specifically lesbian collective (31).

Yet Sutton also remembers that the collective decided not to print any articles by the Amazon Nation, a lesbian-separatist collective she formed, because the group was 'just too radical or too disruptive. They [*Lavender Woman*] didn't like me after I formed the Amazon Nation' (31). The collective's decision against such specifically lesbian groups as

Amazon Nation threw into contention its golden rule and its commitment to lesbian community. As we will see, the collective's failure to negotiate the distance between its abstract notions of lesbian community and its treatment of lesbian groups such as Amazon Nation became a powerful factor in the collective's eventual dissolution.

Before such tensions arose, however, the collective dedicated a significant amount of column space to its exploration of lesbian-feminist politics[1] and values as well as to its pledge of commitment to those politics. This dedication may in part explain the collective's later views of the paper as a community leader or, as Susan Kahn put it, a 'conscience for the community' (60). And with this role, too, came the commitment to struggle against oppressions other than sexism. Thus it is not uncommon to find articles and collective statements that report events that occurred within the antiwar, civil rights, and student protest movements.

Of the other movements, struggles against racism in particular were of deep concern to the collective. Indeed, Brody's interviews consistently raise issues of racism and race relations among feminists in general and among the collective members themselves. Susan Kahn recalls that even 'in the very beginning we talked about race' (51); Betty Sutton remembers that the early discussions and disagreements often centered on racial issues (30). The pressure for diversity within the collective was strong enough that by March 1973, collective members characterized their community in the following manner:

Some of us have jobs, some don't; some go to school, some are professionals. We are from different economic, social, racial backgrounds from rich to poor from solid middle class to the unimaginable alternatives. We are all 'educated' by the man, but are learning from one another. We invite other groups to submit a report so we can extend our learning family. (45)

This characterization is of interest not only for the value it places on the collective's diversity but also for the fact that the only shared characteristic it presents is the reference to women's social conditioning under patriarchy. The statement effectively works to universalize or homogenize that social conditioning. Perhaps this homogenization allowed a greater sense of identification among the women themselves than did other feminist statements of commonality that seemingly were based more on biology than on social constructions; however, essays such as the Combahee River Collective's 'A Black Feminist Statement' seriously questioned any claim to an easy unity rooted in gender identification. As we will see, the collective's assertion of its harmony quickly became contested by women of color both within the collective and from the paper's audience.

Whether or not the collective's emphasis on women's shared social conditioning worked effectively to unite women in the Chicago community, it certainly provided the necessary factors that allowed many women to make a persuasive case for separatism. Indeed, the collective itself rose from an act of separatism, as an announcement in the second issue of *LW* indicates:

Gay Women's Caucus is now meeting independently [of the Chicago Gay Alliance]. We have thanked the men for their past help and wished them well on their own liberation. Our time is our own. We have transcended our hassles with the men and can now deal with our own needs. We are finally AUTONO-MOUS! We urge all Lesbians to join us in our struggle for ourselves and the Lesbian community at large. There is nothing we can't do with the total support of all our Gay Sisters. WE ARE OUR OWN REWARD! (10)

Several members from the Gay Women's Caucus (who named their new group the April collective) began *LW* during this time of separation from the Chicago Gay Alliance (CGA). In the process of their decision to separate we can chart the course of the convergence of the gay rights and feminist movements for lesbians: women who later founded the April collective were drawn to the CGA during the development of the gay and lesbian pride movement after Stonewall, but they soon became disenchanted with the alliance as their perception of institutionalized sexism grew. Common, too, was the collective's strong sense of euphoria and optimism about the strength of women's unity. Yet the actual fact of the collective's practice of separatism and the decision of whether or not to adopt separatist – specifically lesbian-separatist – politics were two quite different issues debated within the collective itself.

Discussions over separatism within the pages of *LW* initially produced the appearance of an amiable difference of opinion within the collective. By this I mean that when collective members discussed political issues, they noted individual differences but usually stressed areas upon which they all agreed, or at least upon which they agreed to disagree. Collective statements such as the following were not uncommon:

None of us felt the paper should be for straight feminists although Louise wanted us to break down lesbian stereotyping by straights. Susan felt that the paper should cover from an l/f point of view straight women's groups that have lesbians-in-the-closet working for them.

It was evident that we wanted, as Bonnie said, to have a paper by, for, and about lesbians. We all feel that lesbian feminism is the logical conclusion of feminism. We agreed that our lesbian sisters have always been our priority. JR wants the paper to help build and define lesbian culture. . . .

On the issue of men, we want the paper to put women's concerns over gay male concerns. Judy feels that any coalition must be out of our strength. Bonnie feels that man-hating is constructive and positive for women. (95)

In collectives that governed themselves through a consensus decision-making process, as did *Lavender Woman*, to list individual opinions or decisions in a public/community document was rather unusual.[2] And the mild tone through which the collective represents its disagreements gives scarce indication of how much or how little separatist debates might have affected it. In the pages of *LW*, then, the collective presented itself as a viable, diverse, and energetic community of women that was separatist in practice and, at least for a few of its members, in politics.

The early collective statements Brody chose to anthologize thus present the collective as a group that wanted to provide other lesbians with a sense of both regional and national community. Much of their sense of that community came from members' experiences with other women in the collective or in the larger weekly meetings held by the Gay Women's Caucus (later the Chicago Lesbian Liberation). The relative similarity of the members' backgrounds (most were, for example, connected to the University of Chicago or had belonged to the Gay Women's Caucus) influenced the collective vision of the characteristics such a community might have. Because of this shared background and their increasing awareness and acceptance of radical-feminist theory, the members of the *Lavender Woman* collective shaped their vision of community around the values of lesbian feminism, the struggle against all oppression (especially racism and homophobia), and the practice of separatism. Finally, collective members felt that *LW* was not only part of the women's community but was the 'conscience' of the community as well.

To be the conscience, especially the lesbian-feminist conscience, of any community is a job most women today would approach with great trepidation, if they chose to approach it at all. Yet the feeling that such a role was not only possible but desirable during this time arose as much from a sense that women joined together could remake the entire social order (if not the world) as it did from the urgency to create a value system other than that of the patriarchal status quo. However, the assumption of that role not surprisingly created expectations within *LW*'s community of readers, expectations that, whether or not they were met, affected the vision of community held by the collective and by the women who read *LW*. To read the community work of *LW* and Brody's narrative, then, we need to analyze not only what the collective said it wished to do but also the difference between these goals and the responses of those who addressed the progress of the collective's wishes.

The ideal of lesbian unity posited within the theories of lesbian feminism coupled with the encouragement of debate was, as we have seen, crucial to the goals the collective wished to accomplish through *LW*. But the collective's actual practice of several theories within lesbian feminism as it was represented within the pages of *LW* seems to have worked more to divide the community than it did to encourage a community engaged in friendly debate. For example, Susan Kahn recalls the problematic of lesbian sexuality as constructed by the collective:

M[ichal]: We didn't talk about sex, did we?
S[usan]: Oh . . . I don't know. We talked about it, but we didn't talk about our sexual feelings for each other. It didn't fit in with anything else that was happening, like politics. There was no talk about roles. . . . There were no butches. There were no femmes. There were no tops, no bottoms. There were no nothings, you know. (54–55)

Kahn's conception that sexuality did not 'fit in with anything else . . . like politics' is a stark portrayal of the ways lesbian sexuality was written out of the discourse of lesbian-feminist theory, a process that began, as we have seen, in essays such as 'Woman Identified Woman.' From women for whom the 'personal was political' such an acknowledgment seems contradictory; yet it attests to the deeply felt desire among lesbians to be acceptable to the larger feminist community,[3] a desire separatist theory implicitly denies.

The collective's avoidance of sexual issues, while it may have made members more acceptable to heterosexual feminists, served to divide Chicago's lesbian community at a time when unity and visibility seemed most possible. Thus the discourse of community negated the possibility of that community through the very theories that were directed toward the creation of community in the first place. For example, when Kahn remembers collective attempts to forge an intergenerational lesbian community, she recalls the members' unwillingness even to approach those lesbians who had come out before the women's movement:

You know, we talked about wanting to get dykes who had been out for a longer time on the paper and we talked about interviewing some of them for the paper, we tried to stay connected with the community. All the while, I think, being afraid of it. We talked too much about interviewing old dykes and all we needed to do was pop up on a bar stool next to them and talk. So, you know, I think there was a way that we were in the closet and not so proud of our dykey sisters who weren't feminists and weren't young and sweet and political. (54)

Kahn's reconstruction of the collective's perceptions of 'nonfeminist' lesbians and 'feminist' lesbians points to the problematic in the concept of community held by collective members. First, their perception of the bars as the site wherein they would meet older lesbians focuses on a specific segment of the community that, as Kahn previously had said, the collective rendered invisible: identifiably butch or femme women. This may seem oversimplified; yet studies such as those of Joan Nestle or Madeleine Davis and Elizabeth Kennedy have made us aware that the most visible lesbians during the 1950s and 1960s were precisely those who, in the bar culture, proclaimed their identity through fashions of dress and posture. And if we accept Nestle's analysis of the inherent feminism of this visibility (Nestle 105), it becomes apparent that the collective's perception of these women as not feminist or not political drew divisions that refused to validate any activism other than its own and thus placed a large group of lesbians outside this women's community.

Collective members were not unaware of these divisions. In fact, Kahn recalls that 'we tried not to let our differences be apparent because we needed so much to be a community. So we would be just all one thing. Which was lesbians' (54). But the collective's very definition of 'lesbian' was more than 'just one thing' and that difference became more than apparent. By 1974, letters from the 'community' made clear that divisions of difference were quite visible within the pages of *LW*:

Sisters:

It upset me a lot to hear in your collective statement that you think of yourself as lesbian feminists rather than as lesbians. Lesbian/feminists, to my way of thinking, are women who have become lesbians as the ultimate (political) act of rage against men. They have never known the same kind of oppression we, as lesbians, have had to endure. . . . They use the word feminist to dilute that word: Lesbian. If *Lavender Woman* could just go back to the days when you served the lesbians, or try as hard to serve lesbians as you try to serve feminists, you would be serving gay people again. I think the straights have taken over our sexual habits as well as our newspaper under the sheep's clothing of feminism. . . . A long time ago you wrote about women who got thrown out of a bar because they wouldn't buy a drink and about oppression. About the problems lesbians have and how they solve them. I miss that in your paper. I used to feel it was my paper too, but not so much anymore. (116)

However much we would choose a different definition of feminism from that of this author, it is clear that within her definition resides the paradox of lesbian-feminist theory for collective members: their visions of a woman's community created divisions that made the success of those visions difficult indeed.

Even when *LW* confined its goals for community to women who identified specifically with lesbian feminism, however, its analysis of community events seemed to question the possibility of those goals. Joan Nixon, in her article documenting the West Coast Lesbian Conference (1973), uses the dream of community in part to measure the conference's success:

We came to Los Angeles to share the conference organizers' dream – a thousand lesbians finding each other in one place, in one room, would fill the space with a joyous celebration. We would be an army made of lovers and we would build our lesbian culture with our sisters. . . . what we found instead were a series of deadly-serious struggles over issues too complex and deeply-felt to be resolved in three days. The dyke conference became a battleground few had anticipated – a thousand angry women, trapped on the man's territory, fighting each other – lesbian against lesbian, feminist against feminist, woman against woman. Our army of shouting lovers fell into combat with each other.

The oppression we share as lesbian women in a burning patriarchal world was not enough to bind us together, and we did not find an easy joy in each others [sic] company. (63)

Documentation such as Nixon's provided stark contrast not only to the general hope for community of lesbian feminism but also to the specific, stated goals of the *Lavender Woman* collective itself. Here too we begin to see at least a quiet questioning of separatism's ideological use of sexism as the primary contradiction in Nixon's statement that women's oppression was 'not enough to bind us together.' Yet the context of the statement, its tone, and Nixon's image of the participants as 'trapped on the man's territory' continue to reinscribe that ideology as crucial to lesbian community.

Such inscriptions problematized the practice of community not only for those who explored the ideologies of lesbian separatism but also for those who were concerned with issues of racism within the women's community. As I have mentioned, the members of *Lavender Woman* tried hard to be conscious of the dynamics of racism within the collective. For example, Susan Kahn recalls that one of the collective's early acts was to create an African-American section of the paper:

right in the very beginning we were going to have a Black and Lavender section of the paper. . . . It was very clearly a separate part, but an inclusive part of the paper, and I think that the Black women had wanted it that way. And I think it happened pretty easily. I'm not sure, 'cuz I don't remember real well. It wasn't that the women of color only worked on that, but that was their baby. I don't remember whether it created strife or not, whether it created a comfortable separateness or whether the Black women who had that section of the paper felt disenfranchised from the rest of the paper. I know there were talks about it. (51)

Kahn's lack of memory on the issue of African-American women's response to this experiment sits strangely in a narrative that recalls nearly every disagreement and certainly every strongly felt emotion. Perhaps her ambiguity is a testament to an emotion that changed over the course of this attempt: an experiment that first might have been validated from a framework of Black Power quickly could have been seen as more in line with Jim Crow. But I suspect that the vagueness of Kahn's memories had more to do with the fact that African-American women used this section to challenge white lesbians' racism than it did with an actual inability to remember how such a section began. For example, the first issue included an article entitled 'Blacklesbian' that confronted white women on their racism and placed the responsibility for its resolution solely on them. Such a confrontation, of course, implicitly challenged ideologies of community held by the collective and thus might become a difficult memory to sustain for those interested in the continuation of collective history.

The community work of *LW* and Brody's historical narrative on the issue of racism are most evident in the work of and interview with Loretta Mears. Mears was an African-American member of the collective who became involved in Chicago lesbian-separatist politics and practice as well. She left the collective long before its dissolution but continued to write letters to the editor after her departure. Though she states that she left the collective because she functioned solely as a token, she acknowledges that the self-confidence she gained through her participation helped her achieve individual goals later in her life (135–36).

Much of Brody's interview with Mears focuses on the anger, frustration, and pain Mears felt over the racism she encountered in the collective and in Chicago's lesbian community. Mears notes that some of the racism occurred through white women's expectations for the use of language:

Being a standard bearer is a common role for tokens to play, and I was often the token dark woman at those meetings. I mean, there were other dark women there but we just, our presence wasn't powerful enough, we didn't have enough impact. And it ended up being real clear to me that I did really self-destructive and really self-hating stuff in terms of dark women's work on the paper. . . . It's stuff about standards of English, and how something needs to sound in order to be read and understood, and it didn't take me long, as I grew in terms of knowing myself and my own self-hate, to understand that those standards were totally arbitrary, classist and racist. But when I was working on the newspaper I didn't have that consciousness. And it was real easy to get put into the role of telling the white women and the Jewish women on the paper that they were okay, and that everyone ought to meet the dominant culture's standards for language. I was the dark woman whose presence said they were okay. So that kind of pressure takes its toll after a while. (128–29)

Mears felt that racism, with its contradictions for community, functioned even in the medium through which LW hoped to create community. Her analysis provides little hope that the paper could accomplish its goals of diversity or negotiate successfully the mechanisms of racism within collective processes. Finally, for Brody's readers, Mears's narrative serves to indicate that the collective's inability to negotiate the tensions caused by its racist practices stood in the way of its attempts to build a racially diverse, inclusive collective or community.

Given Mears's disheartening portrayal of the work and process of the *Lavender Woman* collective as well as her comparatively short tenure with the group, we might wonder why, if (as Brody claims) the collective truly had a racially diverse membership, Brody chose to include this particular narrative in a project dedicated to the 'continuation' of the collective's history. Brody probably wanted at least one interview with a nonwhite and/or non-Jewish member of the collective, and perhaps Mears's account was the most positive among the women of color; but what compelled the choice Brody made? To answer that question I compared the discursive representations of Mears's experiences in the interview with those in the few articles Brody included that were written by Mears during the existence of *LW*.

Such a comparison begins to explain not only why Loretta Mears became disenchanted with the collective after an initial period of intense participation but also why she (however ironically) remained central to white women's conceptions of their involvement around questions of racism within the community. During a discussion in the interview, for example, Brody and Mears begin to analyze why so much of the anger expressed by women of color was ignored or not heard by white and Jewish women. Brody recalls: 'I remember your writing in the paper always being angry and that you were very strong and articulate about it without being smug or righteous.' Loretta agrees and notes:

It's a role I've played since I was a little kid; it's one I'm good at. I could say the same thing, essentially, as Ruby or Margaret or somebody else would say, in their way, angry and righteous, because they had a right to be angry and of course they were right. They would say it and nobody would hear them. I could say it and people would hear me. Of course, this ended up making all the dark women antagonistic towards me. And it was going to set me up with the white and Jewish women in a way that meant they could use me to say, See, we understand *her*. *She* makes sense. *She* fits in; why don't you? (132)

And while Mears further states that she does not really understand why she is able to mediate among women, she believes she learned the skill because she lived in both black and Jewish neighborhoods as a child.

Although Mears herself may not have been able to pinpoint the process by which she made her anger heard, an analysis of her discursive expression of that anger might provide a clearer understanding of that process. In 1974, after she had left the collective, Mears was contacted by *LW* and asked what she knew about a report of racial discrimination at a well-known Chicago lesbian bar. The dispute was public enough to spark an investigation by the Illinois Liquor Commission and resulted in charges filed against the bar's owners (138). *LW*'s discussion with Mears produced a small announcement in the paper that appeared, six months later, in the April 1975 issue. Mears responded quickly to the inadequate coverage, and her lengthy letter to the editor (here partially reprinted) appeared in the June 1975 issue:

I could not believe the gross misrepresentation of facts that appeared in the April issue of LW under the guise of a news story about the 'alleged discrimination' against minority women at C.K.'s. Not only did it take the only Chicago area lesbian newspaper six months to get around to doing a story on the racism against their black and brown sisters, but when a story finally did appear it was so inaccurate as to boggle the mind.

When I was called by a staff member of LW and asked what I knew about the occurrences at C.K.'s, I said repeatedly that most of what I told her was conjecture and rumors that I had heard, which should be verified with either Renee Hanover, the attorney for the complainants, or one of the complainants themselves. . . . I was assured that this would be done.

This verification was not done because, as I was told, 'there wasn't enuff time before layout. . . .'

I do not see it as my responsibility or that of any of my minority sisters to educate you on the effects of racism. It is not a brown-black problem, it is a white problem and until you take it upon yourselves to see how racism oppresses you and how the man uses it to separate you off from your sisters, how he uses it to oppress us all as women and as lesbians, then that revolution we all claim to want, peaceful or otherwise, ain't gonna happen. (140–41)

I suggest that Mears's anger is heard by white lesbians – even to the extent of reinscription in the collective's narrative ten years later – because as the last paragraph demonstrates, she fashions it through the ideology of sexism as the primary contradiction. Thus she can effectively state all the rage, frustration, and pain felt by women of color over such treatment within a women's community because, in her final analysis, she displaces the blame on 'the man' to whom the tool of racism 'really' belongs.

The refusal to accept all but the mildest criticism certainly was not limited to separatist collectives, but this tendency made the work of community much more difficult, especially as the accepted critique ultimately failed to hold women responsible for their own oppressive behaviors. Yet while experiences with racism strained the bonds of this Chicago community, they were not perceived, as the inclusion of Mears's story might attest, as issues that threatened the entire existence of the community. For the Lavender Woman collective, separatism itself – or, rather, the degree to which women in the collective wished to embrace its politics – became the discursive grounds on which Chicago women drew increasingly irrevocable lines.

As we have seen, the practice of separatism was adopted by the women who formed the *Lavender Woman* collective well before they began to publish the paper. But the fact that collective members practiced separatism before they debated the merits of its politics did not mean they originally took a hasty or unquestioned step. Susan Kahn, for example, recalls the aspects of separatism that initially compelled the collective toward its practice: 'A lot of the function of separatism and lesbian isolation politics was to become stronger identified in yourself and to have the freedom to group with your like kinds and be separate from the people who can oppress you and keep you from yourself. I think separatism is necessary' (59). But new members such as Bonnie Zimmerman brought with them the desire to deepen the collective's separatist politics. Zimmerman describes what she sought from the collective through the politics of separatism:

The strongest position, the most righteous position at that time in lesbian history was the separatist position. So I think that those of us who had a tendency to have very strong opinions and voice them a lot just automatically gravitated towards separatism. I mean I came to Chicago looking for the most political lesbians I could, and the most political lesbians were the separatist lesbians. . . . I wanted to be around somebody who understood that being a lesbian was not just a matter of loving other women. It was also taking a stand against patriarchy. And the separatists were the only ones who were saying it at that time. (89–90)

Zimmerman's sense that only the most 'political' lesbians would gravitate toward separatism may not have been borne out by the expectations or politics of those women who joined the collective before her, but it did provide Zimmerman and others with at least an identifiable community.

The differences in collective members' perceptions of separatism's role for lesbian community went beyond the discussions over process held within the collective, however. In a report on the Midwest Lesbian-Feminist Conference, Karen Vierneisel cast her experiences in a way that would generate a strong response both from members of the *Lavender Woman* collective and from the paper's readers:

For me the significance of each of the workshops I attended was a new perspective on the movement. The questions we have been asking in Chicago are not unique to us. The Columbus women, the Ann Arbor women, the individuals from as far as Oregon and Atlanta, Georgia were all asking the same questions. Our problems are the same. There *is* a lesbian/feminist consciousness, which is not to deny our very real differences. The ritual demonstrates the universal nature of our struggle to define ourselves as lesbian/feminists.

The workshop on separatism and manhating was another example of frustration dialogue. An outspoken woman asked the group assembled if any of us had thought through the separatism issue and declared that those who had were the only women she wanted to talk with. . . . She didn't want to waste her time rehashing the motives or wisdom of separatism. . . . Thirty or so women marched out of the room with her, leaving the rest of us grumbling, hurt, and angry. As much as I understood their desire to talk with each other, the nature of her question exposed the separatist hierarchy in lesbian/feminist politics. Separatists have seen the light. The rest of us are Aunt Bettys. If that isn't divisive, I don't understand what division is all about. (91–92)

The structure of Vierneisel's article functions to illustrate the paradox of female community as it was represented in *LW*: assertions of a lesbian-feminist commonality, consciousness, or 'universal' struggle within the framework of its vision for community continually were undercut by ideological differences that served to divide that community. And Vierneisel's article itself caused further division as strongly separatist women, including Bonnie Zimmerman, wrote in to denounce Vierneisel's analysis (93–94).

Vierneisel's article was but one of several that sparked angry reactions from separatist women who felt under attack in the pages of *LW*. In a July 1974 letter to the editor, a woman who identified herself only as 'Lakey' wrote:

As a former member of the original *LW* staff, as a Lesbian Woman, and as a Lesbian Separatist, I finally feel compelled to write to you. I have become increasingly concerned with the TYPE of unconstructive and subtle war that seems to have been waged in writing against Lesbian Separatism.

In the past several issues of the paper, there have been insidious and unsophisticated nasty remarks about the type of lifestyle and personal/political ideology that some Lesbian Women have grown and learned 'in to.' . . . As Separatists, some of us have been accused of single-handedly dividing the Lesbian community, turning woman against woman, and disrupting the 'sister-love' that might have been. (117)

For women whose visions of community stemmed directly from separatist theories, these splits within that community over the politics of separatism must have diluted, at the very least, the optimism with which they once had embarked on the practice of those visions.

Yet although Lakey's letter clearly indicates the degree to which the issue of separatist politics had begun to jeopardize *LW*'s visions of a women's community, the members of the collective felt that throughout this period they managed to keep internal conflicts over separatism out of the public view. In fact, a full year after Lakey's letter appeared the collective issued a statement that, while it acknowledged members' differences over separatism, claimed that 'during that period of hard times, we never once wrote about our collective's difficulties, never once did an analysis of 'Separatism in Chicago' since we certainly couldn't have agreed on what to say about it' (156). When asked why the collective chose not to address the conflict directly through *LW*, Susan Kahn responded:

I think we were real concerned about putting out a good front. I don't think we wanted the paper to reflect a lot of strife. . . . I think a lot of issues we were afraid to raise for fear we'd raise them in the wrong way and further alienate somebody. . . . I tell you, there's a certain level on which I had no awareness of the effect that I had on my community. (60)

Kahn's perception that a discussion of collective conflicts within the confines of *LW* might have led to community division may have been accurate, but the failure to print just such a discussion (as perhaps Kahn indicates in her comments on the collective's unrecognized community influence) seems to have contributed to the divisions the collective wished to avoid in the first instance. One year after the collective's recognition that the issue of separatism was creating serious conflicts within its community, the collective folded despite efforts that included a revamping of the paper's structure and purpose (157).

Curiously, the structure of Brody's anthology recapitulates the same avoidance on the issue of separatism that initially contributed to so many problems. As I mentioned, Brody does not list in her table of contents the articles, announcements, or letters she includes from the original *LW*. But directly after the last interview appears in the contents, Brody does list a section titled 'Where Some of Us Are Now.' Such a section, of course, usually signals the conclusion of this sort of anthology. Yet two more sections, 'Excerpts from an Unpublished Article' and 'An

Analysis of What Happened,' follow. The titles of these sections, too, obscure their significance: an 'Unpublished Article' might signify something of lesser importance or quality than published articles; 'An Analysis of What Happened' gives us no clue as to what 'What' is or concerns. If we assume that these sections are more afterthoughts than they are significant features of *LW*'s history, we might not bother to read them at all. And if we were to do so, we would miss the most comprehensive discussion on community divisions over separatism present in the book and thereby overlook the problematic that, in Brody's view, contributed most to the collective's dissolution. The structure of Brody's historical narrative suggests that the discussion of separatism was included only partially in her work, as if, somehow, the issue still cannot be contained within the history of *Lavender Woman*'s community. Or, perhaps, it is the contradiction of the community that cannot be contained within the collective's historical narrative.

Brody's title, *Are We There Yet?*, thus correctly forewarns us that this narrative will ask as many questions as it answers. Her goals start us off on a path to trace – and simultaneously continue – the collective's history, but by the end of the journey we must ask whether, given Brody's indirect treatment of the most divisive issue in the collective's past, we have reached our destination or even if we are still on our original trail. Has the destination changed? If not, has Brody's text provided the road map we need? Or are we left to wander aimlessly through the signposts of the past? And who, in any event, are 'we'? Brody recreates the hopes, enthusiasm, and energy she and other collective members recall as part of their history, but does her commentary on the barriers to collectivity just retell the story of *LW*'s past rather than giving us a sense of how those issues might even today be negotiated to 'continue' the history of this collective? Or perhaps we are drawn in not so much to receive answers but to continue this history ourselves. Will we ever get 'there'?

In summary, then, the community work of *Are We There Yet?* operates on at least two different moments in history, although the events of each historical moment influence the accounts of the other. At its onset, the *Lavender Woman* collective wished to become a major factor in the creation and communication of a Chicago (if not a national) women's community. And the articles and interviews Brody includes reinforce this perception of *LW* well into the mid-1980s. The visions for that community included a racially diverse, lesbian-feminist, and (in practice) separatist coalition that would be a political as well as a social force.

However, *Lavender Woman*'s discursive representations of the concepts and theories on which most of its visions were based sparked tensions that eventually factionalized the Chicago community and dissolved the collective itself. Thus what began as an inspired, enthusiastic hope for a change in women's condition through the activism of a separatist community in the end cast doubt on the ability of separatism to unite women at all. Finally, the structure of Brody's anthology itself does little to dispel this perception, as separatism remains the understated tension that continues to affect the narrative of *Lavender Woman*'s history.

BLOODROOT THREE

I was again seated on the sun porch with my unread book when Lori returned from her duties at the restaurant. She accepted my invitation to what would become an evening ritual of conversation. We remarked on the beauty of the sunset against the sea; Lori then asked me how my first day had been.

'Great!' I replied. 'Everything's there I had hoped to find, and I haven't even begun to look at the unpublished materials. It's a wonderful resource. I think almost anything written about separatism or collectives has been preserved. I hope I have enough time to get a look at all of it.' I also hoped to convey my sense of the importance of the archives to the surprisingly reticent women of the Bloodroot.

'Good – it's good you're finding what you need,' she said, noncommittally.

'And the best part is Joan's knowledge of both the materials and historical contexts. She's a walking catalog,' I added, pushing. No one has ever accused me of knowing when enough is enough.

'Joan?' Lori asked. 'I thought you said she was gone for the week.'

'She was supposed to be, but her engagement was canceled. All to my benefit.'

'Hmmm,' Lori said, and nothing more.

'Lori,' I began, somewhat exasperated with what seemed like a lot of unnecessary subterfuge, 'what's the problem between Bloodroot and the archives?'

'It's a long story. . . . We have our differences,' she replied, not unkindly but in a tone clearly meant to preclude further discussion. At the very least it required a change of subject. I obliged.

'The restaurant seems to be doing a steady business. How's the collective doing overall?'

'We have our ups and downs – like anything else, I guess. But the businesses are going well, and we've recently won a battle against a developer who wanted to build more offshore dumps here in Bridgeport. I think our victory surprised the neighborhood a lot. We've earned their respect, at any rate.'

'You deserve it. I can't imagine sitting here and looking at a town dump.'

'You are already,' she said, laughing at my look of surprise. 'See those mounds?' She pointed to several mini-islands that obscured the view of the ocean. 'Those are old, covered dumps. They've leaked toxic wastes into the bay for years. For a long time we didn't see any sign of wildlife here. The ducks and fish have just begun to return.'

'Even more reason to stop the dumping. That's a great accomplishment.'

'Thanks, we thought so too.'

'How's the bookstore doing?' I asked, wanting to return to my earlier question.

'Okay . . . we're a little cramped for space. We don't do a big volume, but the store's only open during dining hours, anyway.'

'So with the obvious demand on the restaurant, why don't you expand into the space occupied by the bookstore?'

'The bookstore's important to us. We can sell the literature we want, and it gives us a way to promote women writers. We even have readings occasionally. It's another way to share our feminism with women in the community – like the cooking is.'

'Bloodroot is very concerned with its place in the community, isn't it? Beyond just surviving as a business, I mean.'

'We're always defining and redefining what we want Bloodroot to stand for, and what our role in the community should be. Have you seen our article in *Lesbian Ethics?*'

I shook my head.

'Wait a minute and I'll get it for you. It describes our position on several community issues today.'

'Thanks, I'd like to read it. Sounds as though it might even be useful for my research.'

'Perhaps so!' She grinned at my fixation and left the sun porch in search of the journal.

Excommunicating the Patriarchy: Oppression, Paradox, and Barriers to Community in Joyce Cheney's *Lesbian Land*

Five

We had thought that we were going to be together forever. We even had a politically correct fantasy of how we'd all die. We'd be old ladies, too tired to organize even one more demonstration. We'd be sitting in our tennis shoes, in our rocking chairs on our porch, and decide it was time. Then we'd all take lessons and learn to fly small planes. Then we'd each rent a plane, fill it with explosives, and simultaneously kamikaze into the eight politically correct targets of our choosing: the pentagon, the chase manhattan bank . . . – Joyce Cheney

Joyce Cheney's anthology, *Lesbian Land*, contains nearly thirty historical narratives of separatist land collectives. These collectives ranged in size from two to many members and existed anywhere from a few months to fifteen years and more. They all were dedicated to the creation of collectives wherein women could live and work with other women. Though they shared the same social, political, and economic goals with business collectives such as *Lavender Woman,* the dynamics within residential collectives often were somewhat different. For example, personal issues such as the sex of one's children, the desire to allow male visitors into one's home, or even the diversity of physical and material resources among individuals carried far more community significance when women lived together.

To read these narratives in terms of the work they did in separatist communities, I will begin with an examination of Cheney's statement of purpose and the structure she chooses for her text. I then explore the goals of community within residential collectives, goals generalized from readings of narratives in Cheney's anthology and others like them. Finally, I discuss the ways these goals were hampered and often thwarted by ideologies of female community and of the patriarchal opposition to that community held by collective members. I hope to show that while the contentious issues in residential collectives may have differed in character from those in business collectives, they nonetheless had similar, destructively irresolvable effects.

As did Brody's text, Cheney's *Lesbian Land* includes narratives that were written both exclusively for this anthology and for publications that appeared up to a decade before. Cheney, however, takes far less editorial control of the stories. She introduces the book with an essay that explains the purpose and scope of her work and then proceeds to include every story as it was submitted. Thus Cheney seems to choose not to try to shape the effects of her work, though the stories themselves are all connected by the shared vision Cheney and her contributors initially had for the anthology.

One editorial gesture does affect the way we read this work as a whole, however. Cheney introduces her book with a lengthy essay she titles 'The Story of the Stories.' The title works to suggest that there might be only one actual story here (however fictional as the connotation of 'story' implies), that all the stories in the book tell the same version of collective experience. And while we might not believe that every story will be the same, Cheney's strategy does indicate her desire to see the stories as an account of a shared experience. As we read, then, we are made aware that whatever the variations among these narratives, for the editor, at least, their commonalities supersede their differences. And Cheney spends a good deal of introductory space sketching out what she believes those commonalities to be.

Cheney divides her introduction into sections that detail her background with collectives (she was a member of Redbird and wrote the story of that collective), her decision to produce this book, the production process, and a discussion of patterns she found in the stories themselves. She also includes an excerpt from her call for papers:

I'm compiling stories of lesbian land, from womyn[1] past and present involved: our visions, goals, realities, and process. WHY? It's exciting and interesting what we're doing and have done on land. We can inspire and amuse each other, and learn from each other. Our spiderweb network of womyn on land includes and excludes womyn of a variety of ethnic backgrounds, classes, and races. With your input, we can make this book reflect all those experiences. (8)

Cheney's excerpt emphasizes the fact that she began her project with a great deal of optimism and enthusiasm. 'Visions,' 'goals,' 'realities,' and 'process' are for Cheney (who makes the equation highly visible with the capitalized 'WHY?') 'exciting' and 'interesting' and should serve to 'inspire,' 'amuse,' and instruct. The one cautionary note occurs in her next sentence, though it is so quickly mentioned and dropped that it might easily be missed. Cheney claims a racial, cultural, and class diversity for these groups yet notes that they also 'exclude' such diversity. But by the next sentence one must wonder how, if women from these cultural groups really were excluded, their 'input' will be gathered to 'reflect' their experience. Cheney's structure thus implies that these women might not have been entirely excluded, at least not to the extent that they are completely outside the realm of lesbian community. In essence, then, Cheney's statement of purpose projects a positive, celebratory tone that only hints at possible conflict.

By the time Cheney writes the introduction, however, she has read all the stories she only envisioned in her call for papers. Consequently, the tone in which she casts the visions she held for her book changes:

I want to pass on a thought on tone that was shared with me by one womon doing a chapter for the book. She said, in general, that she hopes the book is one that encourages womyn's visions of living on the land, that encourages womyn with that vision to pursue it. I also want the book to be a source of strength. That doesn't mean at all over-looking the hard parts. Rather, learning from the hard parts others have gone thru, and keeping things in perspective as parts in a progression: experiments and stages. I hope womyn read of the ups and downs, and get inspiration and realism, not cynicism and paralysis. (8)

Cheney's reproduction of a contributor's comments raises interesting questions for the study of Cheney's work itself. Why did this woman feel it necessary to ask about the tone of the book? Why might she suspect that it would be other than encouraging, especially given the tone of Cheney's original flyer? Perhaps the disclaimer Cheney includes in the next paragraph provides part of the answer; she suggests that it might be too easy to become cynical or paralyzed after reading of the difficulties these collectives had.

Yet the overwhelming weight of Cheney's tone stresses the positive aspects of these stories and pauses on the negative only long enough to admonish us to learn from our past mistakes. Effectively, then, we are to take this work as teaching stories of inspiration for the visions and goals of women's community.[2] And while the goals of these communities often were inspirational, the practice of separatist ideologies codified binary oppositions of oppression within the collectives in such a way as to make the goal of community itself unattainable.

In this chapter, then, I will examine the visions held by residential communities for their actionary existence and the attempts made by many collectives to put those visions into practice. As I will explain, however, binary concepts of opposition (i.e., an 'us versus them' mentality that placed a demonic patriarchy as always 'other') impeded women's abilities to perceive the ways they oppressed other women, especially over issues of class, race, and physical ability differences. As did the *Lavender Woman* collective, many residential collectives argued over the politics of separatism as well. As we shall see by the end of this chapter, women's conceptions of an always-oppressive patriarchy took away any effective method through which they could claim responsibility for their own destructive behaviors and begin the process of conflict resolution.

Of all the types of collectives – music collectives, farming collectives, collectives devoted to spiritual fulfillment, or collectives that existed simply to bring women together – Cheney profiles in her book, she chooses to showcase women's peace camps in her introduction. Further, all but one sentence of the peace-camp excerpts are written by the women in peace camps (such as Greenham Common) themselves. Though Cheney gives no explanation as to why the women's peace camps might merit separate attention (an explanation that seems even more necessary because these camps are represented only in the introduction, not in any of the contributors' selections), the discourse of the camps themselves as it operates within the framework of Cheney's enthusiastic tone offers some clue:

> Like the music festivals, women's peace camps are theory put into practice. The music festivals were the first time many of us saw how powerful and rich an all-woman environment can be. It is more than the absence of fear, intimidation or anger that men can provoke. We see the collective strength of women relying on themselves, working and playing together, building new trust and new structures.
>
> What is male has so demonstratively not worked, that it seems the only thing to do is to start fresh, with the stuff of women's lives for material. We come together to solidify our vision and create alternatives. We know we will not survive if we don't start to build a world as we know it can be, free of violence, suffering, exploitation. (10)

The author's assertion that women's peace camps and music festivals are 'theory put into practice' in part explains why Cheney might have been compelled to include this segment in her introduction. If women's peace camps and music festivals are theory put into practice, then, by association, most women's land collectives can be thought of as activist groups as well. Further, the excerpt utilizes lesbian-separatist theory in its description of women's collectives as viable alternatives to the destructive, violent structures of male institutions. The ideology that women could simply start over again and make things 'right' permeates the above statement as it did most ideologies of female community operant within separatist communities during this time. That this ideology excluded considerations of Freudian notions of subconscious motivation, or even Marxist analyses of the ways social constructions such as class influence behavior, was not an oversight on the part of separatists. Indeed, many women felt that 'starting over' mandated the exclusion of such theorists as Freud and Marx precisely because they were male – and thus corrupt – philosophers.

Finally, the peace-camp authors refer to their collectives as a realization of their vision, a reference that echoes through nearly every story Cheney includes in this collection. Thus the political aspects and activist qualities of women's peace camps work to characterize all the collectives represented in Cheney's text as intentionally politicized or theoretically guided.

What this introductory excerpt does not describe are the specific shapes or characteristics of those collective visions. The majority of the narratives Cheney chooses to include, however, do detail their original visions. Although these visions vary, they tend to follow many ideologies of community found within radical-feminist, lesbian-feminist, and lesbian-separatist theories. For example, Adobe, the founding member of Adobeland, described her vision for that collective:

I want to go the route of a non-profit corporation, and become a charitable organization, with the very real intent of helping poor wimmin, providing a place for wimmin in need to come, a battered womon with her child . . . a place to go. It changes the world if there is a place to go. The vision of this place along those lines is just taking form. For myself, I want a peaceful, serene place, and also the company of other wimmin, so I am going to try to have it satisfy my needs, as well as other wimmin's. (27)

Adobe's vision of a safe retreat for women, evident in her focus on women in need of security (financial, emotional, or otherwise), clearly echoes early radical-feminist conceptions of the benefits separatism held for women. As did radical-feminist theorists of the late 1960s, Adobe implies that women are safe only together, that women cannot or do not harm one another, and that women together bond in ways that they do not within patriarchal systems. Thus, Adobe intends her collective to create a community for herself and for other women; the community's radicalism comes in the changes it theoretically produces in the world of its members.

Other collectives, however, wanted to move beyond the concept of a woman's 'retreat' or space of safety (these concepts were not rejected but kept in addition to others). Gwen Demeter of Silver Circle details that collective's visions for its community: 'Our dream is to create a community of interdependent wimmin, on and off the land, working on changing our patriarchal programming regarding inferiority feelings, competition, compulsivity, tragic life tapes, deprivation mind set, possessiveness, body shame, manipulative behaviors, intolerance, and spiritual beliefs' (129). Silver Circle's goals directly target patriarchal conditioning as a source of women's problems and propose to create a community wherein women would create a new definition of femaleness. The community would actively confront those ideologies that contributed to the need for separatist space in the first place. As such, Silver Circle's goals can be read as a response to Radicalesbians' challenge to create a new sense of what it means to be a woman (Radicalesbians 245).

This adoption of lesbian-feminist theories into the visions of female community was shared by collectives not represented in Cheney's anthology as well. In a 1976 newsletter, for example, members of Ozark Wimmin on the Land clearly envisioned separatist space as a place to challenge and change patriarchal ideologies:

What will it take to end the patriarchal rule, control, and destruction of the earth? Those of us committed to the idea of women development can begin by providing spaces in which we can experiment. We must break all dependent ties to heterosexist thinking in order to create new life forms and processes. We must use our collective women's minds and abilities to end the destruction of the earth and to sustain human and plant life. This movement will take our lifetimes and more. (Ozark Wimmin on the Land n.p.)

The Ozark women envision their collective not only as a challenge to 'patriarchal rule' but also as a way to confront heterosexism. And the impact of lesbian-feminist theories of community is further implied in the Ozark women's call to 'use our collective women's minds and abilities,' a call that, as we have seen, also is implied by Radicalesbians' claim for the value of women's bonds with one another. That the members of Ozark Wimmin on the Land or Silver Circle felt they could remake themselves free from patriarchal conditioning may seem naive or even foolish today, but in a time when the revolution was always 'just around the corner' no change seemed too large or too impossible to accomplish. The enthusiasm with which so many women embarked on these collective endeavors perhaps also helps to explain the uncritical, wholehearted ways they adopted lesbian-feminist and lesbian-separatist theories into their plans for practice.

While the members of Silver Circle and Ozark Wimmin on the Land suggested that their goals could be accomplished through dedicated work within female community, other collectives implied that the act of choosing to live in a collective automatically brought with it changes for each woman. Members from the Web, for example, described their collective's governing philosophy in the following manner:

We believe wimmin are different in wimmin's space; we can give priority to ourselves and one another. For us this land is a space in which we can begin to know and act out of our real selves. This is a beginning for us of taking ourselves seriously, believing in what we dream and what we do. Here we can live with consciousness of the natural world and respect for living things. We live in an interdependent relationship to the earth rather than seeing her as existing for our use. Opening ourselves to the natural world in a safe place opens us to our wommonselves. (141)

The Web's conception of the value of women's land implies that, as Radicalesbians theorized in their essay, women's 'self' exists differently from and somehow independently of behaviors and appearances dictated by social conceptions of womanhood. Unlike members of Silver Circle, however, members of the Web indicated that simply living in women's communities brought out that true self in women. Thus the goal for collectives such as the Web is not necessarily to work on one's social conditioning but rather to create communities wherein those changes would occur spontaneously, initiating a world revolution in which women could live harmoniously with nature and with other women.

The Web's theory of women's land as a space wherein women are 'different' approaches quite closely claims for separatism as revolutionary in and of itself. While the members of the Web did not themselves commit to this claim, many other women in rural collectives did. For example, Senecarol Rising writes of D.O.E. (Daughters of the Earth) Farm's visions for its community:

It is the hope that eventually up to 13 lesbians of diverse age, class and racial backgrounds will live year-round in a close-knit (clan-like) community at D.O.E. Farm. We in no way see living together on collectively operated land as an escape to the country, though we have heard that put down all too often. We view our maintaining lesbian space and protecting these acres from the rape of man and his chemicals as a political act of active resistance. (135)

D.O.E. Farm clearly posits the existence of the rural space for women and of the collective itself as 'revolutionary.' In addition, the collective states its hope for diversity among collective membership, a hope that, like the collective's sense of separatism as the only liberatory act, was primary to lesbian-separatist theory of the early 1970s. That Senecarol Rising frames this vision of diversity as a 'hope' is not coincidental; without experience with the dedication and hard work needed to achieve cultural diversity, women such as those at D.O.E. Farm never felt the need actively to seek ways to attract women who were not white or middle class. Thus the work of female community was perceived to be only in the creation of collectives: one formed a group and waited (or hoped) for the correct mix of women to join. Such a concept implies an ideology of separatism as the supreme radical act; one could do nothing more revolutionary than create women's collective space.

Yet these visions of separatism as the revolutionary act did not preclude visions of other types of activism for many collectives. For example, one of the statements of purpose issued by the Spiral Wimmin's Land Cooperative included the goal to 'help set up a network of wimmin throughout the country that would promote feminism, support Lesbianism, and to challenge sexism, racism, ageism, capitalism, and institutionalized heterosexism in our society' (Spiral Wimmin's Land Cooperative n.p.). Further, Cheney's narrative of the Redbird collective reveals that members opened a lesbian summer camp, won a child custody suit, began an alternative healing center, staffed a rape hotline, ran a women's autoshop, started a shelter for battered women, and began work to build an alternative school for battered children (Cheney 124). The concept of separatism as revolutionary in and of itself did not prevent collectives from commitment to further activism, although it did effectively place separatism as equal with, if not superior to, those other proactive works.

Visions of female community offered by land collectives thus ranged from radical feminism's conception of separatism as a safe space for women to lesbian separatism's analysis of separatism as the ultimate revolutionary act. Residential collective members dreamed of safe communities wherein women of all races, cultures, classes, and abilities could recreate themselves and live in such a way as to undo or challenge the destruction of patriarchal culture. Perhaps Buckwheat Turner summarized these visions best when she wrote of A Woman's Place (AWP) that 'our original dream was a women's utopia. We had a sense of wanting to move actively toward something, rather than simply continuing to react to what society had designed for our consumption' (Cheney 20).

Like the *Lavender Woman* collective represented in Brody's historical narrative, however, many of the groups described in *Lesbian Land* met enough collective conflict to make their experience feel far from utopian. Indeed, Turner herself subtitles AWP's narrative as 'Women's Utopia: Roughing It in Reality.' And despite Cheney's celebratory, optimistic tone, she too notes that these collectives were very often surprised by the variety and tenacity of collective conflicts. In the 'Patterns' section of her introduction, for example, Cheney states that arguments over class issues were most often represented in the discourse of these narratives:

Class, a charged issue in the lesbian community, takes on larger dimensions in a lesbian land environment with the issue of ownership/co-ownership of sizeable investments such as the land itself, dwellings and 'improvements' – wells, roads, electricity, fences, outbuildings. Commitments are made to the land in emotional and physical energy, skills and cash. Always the questions are present, 'Will I be able to stay here? If not, will I have the resources to leave?' (11)

Cheney's description details actions and transactions well within the realm of mainstream legal and economic institutions, institutions that many women professed to leave when they moved 'on the land.' The ability to negotiate these transactions, as well as accessibility to resources with which to do so, left many women open to the charge of class privilege from those who did not have an equal ability. And while these complaints often did not hold up when women pointed out the underpaid, arduous jobs they did to maintain their lands, they nonetheless created divisions among permanent or visiting members of the collectives.

But proof of one's solid working-class status did not mean freedom from classist assumptions, either. Perhaps, in fact, women from working-class backgrounds were more surprised by and resistant to criticism of their classist behaviors than were middle-class women, as one woman of the ARF collective recalls:

We had to work through a lot of assumptions that because we had access to land we were rich women. The fact of the matter is that the majority of women living on this land have always been working class women. . . .

I know for myself, I was not real willing to deal with classism. I felt I've worked all my life, my parents have worked all their lives, so I don't have to deal with classism . . . Some of these women were saying that ARF has got to change. We were brand new. We thought we had gotten the answer, and the answer was anarchy, consensus, and private land! (laughter). (15–16)

The narrative of ARF underscores an unacknowledged hierarchy within the politics and practice of separatism: those with the least privilege in mainstream society often felt they were free of the behaviors that oppressed them. Thus working-class women could accuse middle-class women of class privilege while at the same time feeling certain that they themselves did not carry class bias. The rueful tone of ARF's narrative further reveals the ways in which these women were unable (at the time) to see their own class assumptions: anarchy and consensus were offered as evidence of the collective's antihierarchical, anticlassist behavior, but the concept of private land – even collectively owned – was an oppressive class value from European society that could quickly draw the ire of, for example, Native American women. Thus the theories of class formulated within feminism at this time had a Eurocentric bias that, while it made strides to eradicate recognized class hierarchies from within white American society, did not respond to analyses of class from cultures other than its own.

The tensions caused by these class differences had a variety of destructive effects on the collectives themselves. Ginny Berson recalls that the Furies house (a residential collective for women who published the *Furies* newspaper, some of whom were former members of Radicalesbians) 'didn't work' in part because of conflicts over class (Berson 5). And Concetta Panzarino spoke of the difficulties she had to maintain her rural collective land because of class distrust over issues of ownership:

I never got commitments from any women who wanted to buy the land with me; yet, there have been power problems over my ownership. We worked collectively, but because I own the land, it became my responsibility to pay for repairs, or my fault if this or that went wrong. If a woman didn't pay her share of the phone bill, I paid it. Then women felt I had more control because I paid the bills. Of course that's true, but I also had more of the headaches. (Cheney 43)

The difficulties Panzarino faced came in part because of the differences between separatist ideologies of women's community and expectations of a mainstream government that demanded taxes and bills to be paid on time. When women were unwilling to commit, for whatever reason, to collective financing for their land, someone had to tend to these details or risk forfeiture of the land altogether. Yet because they operated within separatist concepts of class privilege, women such as those Panzarino encountered felt entitled to a consensus government regardless of the material, physical, or emotional strength of their commitment.

These experiences, of course, conflicted directly with the theories that women brought with them to the land. But Cheney's text reveals another, more disturbing phenomenon: collectives that did prosper were often those under ownership or guidance of one or two women. Collectives such as Adobeland or Green Hope Farm began under single ownership by women who had very definite plans for the structure and purpose of their group. And although the character of these collectives may have changed over the years (Green Hope Farm, for example, is now more of a bed-and-breakfast resort than it is a collective teaching farm), the fact of their success in the face of so many disappointments was a direct slap to the Gutter Dyke Collective's ideology of women's 'inherent' collectivity, as well as to separatist dreams of collective ownership.

Though we do not find evidence of it in Cheney's introduction, the issue of class was not the only source of conflict within women's collectives. Tensions over racial difference also became very difficult to negotiate. These tensions problematized relationships between white women and women of color in the collectives and often frustrated white women's attempts to recruit or retain women of color. In a 1976 newsletter, for example, Ozark Wimmin on the Land noted the difficulties they had to convince African-American women to live in the collective:

Eight women are living here now. We try to have a unanimous consensus on everything that we do, which is both necessary and sometimes frustrating. What do we need a total consensus on and what can be individually decided? We are experimenting with collective processes such as how to deal with each other's habits like tobacco, beer, communal sloppiness, not listening, not to mention the other important things like our own sexist, racist, and classist attitudes. . . .

A Black sister came here and said she could not live in Arkansas and she did not think that other Third World women would ever come here to live, but she was glad there was a place to stay. (n.p.)

The Ozark women's representation of race and racism implies a desire for diversity that is simultaneously undercut by the rhetorical strategy they employ. The women describe their lack of diversity in terms of geographic location: Arkansas, by this passage, is too inhospitable a state for women of color to feel comfortable in the collective. Yet, of course, one of the reasons these collectives existed was to create space different from the outside world, space that was to be 'safe,' 'comfortable,' or 'politically active' for all women. Rather, the admission of the collective's 'racist attitudes' might tell us more about women of color's uneasiness in the group than does the physical location of the collective. In other words, while the collective admits to racism, it also continues to choose examples of racial disharmony that avoid responsibility for part of these women's decisions to leave. Arkansas's racial divisions seem to be repeated in, rather than refuted by, this separatist collective.

Tensions over racial issues often affected collectives in ways that divided the groups more deeply than did those over class. As I discussed in chapter 3, many women of color were committed to concepts of female community through separation despite strong opposition from others who felt separatism to be an ineffective solution to racism. Unlike women who experienced classist oppression within these collectives, however, women of color who were victims of racism often did not choose to work with white women on racial issues but began collectives specifically for women of color. The statement of purpose issued by the Sassafras collective asks:

Why do Women of Color want/need separate land spaces? To provide safe and sympathetic environments for women to come where they can be reasonably free of the subtle and overt racism and cultural arrogance frequently displayed in predominantly white, middle-class women's spaces. To provide places where something other than sterile white women's culture can flourish and expand, enriching our entire movement with diversity and balance. To provide a place where Women of Color may discover their personal inner beings and creative selves, where they may bring their children for a taste of 'free-space,' safe from the rampant racism of the larger society. To provide a place where women may gather in numbers and strength, 'sassy' enough to claim their own power in this world, and perhaps establish more places for women of different racial and ethnic cultures to grow without danger of cultural genocide. To provide the land bases from which radical, revolutionary theory and action may originate to help change this world into a better place for all women, children and men. (Average and others 1)

The women of Sassafras represent the creation of their collective as a reaction to the racism they encountered in predominantly white collectives (as opposed to that encountered in mainstream society, for example). Interestingly, however, their discursive representation uses the same separatist ideologies of women's community (e.g., as safe spaces for women wherein they might discover their 'true' natures and use those discoveries as a basis for radical action) that governed predominantly white collectives as well. And in this utilization the women of Sassafras created another paradox for the practice of feminist separatism: their explanation for their separation from other women contradicted separatist ideology of female community while it simultaneously reinscribed that ideology in order to give meaning to the act of their separation and to the existence of their community. Effectively, then, Sassafras was the creation of a separatist community of women of color from the ideologies that its members found ineffective for women of color in other separatist communities.

Given the tensions such a paradox can produce, it is of little surprise that the practice of separatist ideologies in women-of-color communities fared little better than they did in predominantly white collectives. Juana Maria Paz, author of *La Luz Journal* and contributor to Cheney's anthology, writes of her experience in a women-of-color land collective, La Luz:

Being here was one of the cruelest experiences of my life. Many times I felt raped or deliberately ostracized. Not that that's any different from what I knew in the outside world. The devastating thing for me was that I expected it to be different here. . . .

For all our rhetoric, some of us, including myself, have been racist, classist, and oppressive to womyn with less privilege than ourselves. (Paz 9, 11)[3]

Like working-class women who (despite the strength they gained from naming and resisting class oppression) were surprised to find themselves perpetrating that same oppression on others, members of women-of-color collectives awakened rudely to evidence of their own racist or classist behaviors. Thus even though policy statements issued by collectives such as Sassafras convincingly utilized the rhetoric of radical feminism for the formation of their community, representations of experience such as those of Juana Maria Paz contradicted the dreams for separatist communities of women bound together more closely through experiences of racism or classism as well as those of sexism.

Though conflicts over racism and classism reverberated quite deeply through these rural land collectives, they were at least echoed in other types of separatist collectives (such as that of *Lavender Woman*) and in the larger feminist community as a whole. As such, women in residential collectives could discuss or explore their conflicts within a sympathetic yet indirectly attached group of others, perhaps with the hope of at least temporarily resolving some of the conflicts within their own collectives.[4] But other conflicts were more unique to the experience of rural land collectives and thus held special significance for the groups represented in Cheney's anthology.

Rural living, especially on a small budget, requires grueling physical labor to maintain self-sufficiency, even more so to make money beyond that needed for survival. And while such work remains difficult for those born and raised to it, it was much more dreadful for city women whose only experience with road building, for example, was a flash of annoyance as their evening bus was delayed by road-repair crews. Many collectives found it necessary to expect a good deal of physical labor from all their members to sustain the group as a whole, especially if the individual women could not or would not contract such work out to professionals. Yet lesbian-feminist and separatist ideology simultaneously requires that any woman-only space (ideally) must be accessible to any disability a woman might have, as is evident, for example, by the efforts of the Michigan Womyn's Music Festival to provide wheelchair ramps and paths; interpreters for the hearing impaired; accessible toilet, shower, workshop, camping, and concession facilities; and Braille programs and maps for its annual gathering in the midst of the Michigan woods (Cheney 97). Thus disabled women who felt initially encouraged by the policy of open women's space often were surprised to encounter covert (or overt) hostilities generated from assumptions of each member's need to contribute physically to collective life.

While assumptions of physical contributions were difficult enough to confront and resolve for women with visible disabilities, they became unbearable for many whose physical limits were not as apparent. A woman from the Golden collective remembers the hierarchy of physical ability that operated in that group: 'There was one woman who was persecuted not so much because she couldn't do the hard physical things, but because she chose to take a lot of time to heal her body and her soul in meditative ways. It did get painful to see person after person pressured off the land because the 'workers' would criticize them and make life hard for them' (Cheney 51). Practices that valued diversity in women's community were put aside quickly in many collectives when that diversity seemed to threaten the community's survival. And like women of color in predominantly white collectives, disabled women sometimes found it necessary to create a separate disabled-women's collective to have their needs recognized and met, as the narrative of Concetta Panzarino's Beechtree attests (41–45).

Perhaps even more divisive for land collectives than the issue of physical ability, however, was the issue of children. 'Children' signified a variety of experiences for women in living collectives, and problems mentioned in their narratives ranged from differences over how children should be raised to which children could be allowed on the land altogether. Buckwheat Turner notes that concepts of child raising produced one of the strongest conflicts at AWP:

Seven women with eight children originally formed the caretaker collective. Some of the initial monthly income that helped pull the place through the first winter was child support from ex-husbands. There are no children living at AWP now, although some visit, especially during the summer. One of the most intense conflicts the first year was on how to raise children. With everyone living under the same roof, many adjustments were necessary. (21–22)

Because the debate over whether social conditioning as opposed to biological inheritance as the prime motivator of human behavior was such a charged issue for separatists, child raising – more particularly, how (or even if) women should raise children – became a large area of contention for many separatist collectives such as AWP. And perhaps more than one woman at AWP (or among this narrative's audience) felt it ironic to argue how best to raise a child free from patriarchal influence while doing so on money earned through the patriarchal support of that child.

Separatist ideologies of patriarchal conditioning had an even deeper effect on debates over children in the collectives, however. Recall that while separatists admonished women to free themselves from their conditioning, many made no such allowances for men: men were irresolvably destructive; women did not have to be passive or weak. And if men were inherently oppressive, boys – at any age – must also carry the ability to oppress those marked as inferior to themselves. Similarly, separatists who felt that both men and women were culturally conditioned argued that this conditioning took place at such an early age as to be almost congenital.[5] Thus one finds in separatist theory of this period claims that while they may seem innocent, boys were as oppressive as their fathers and certainly did, for example, oppress little girls.[6]

Separatist conceptions of the character of boys led to many arguments as to whether or not boys should be allowed in women's residential collectives, and if so, at what age they should be required to leave. The arguments were not as destructive for those collectives in which no children (or, at least, no male children) were present, yet even these collectives had to confront the issue when male children came to visit. D.O.E. Farm, for example, suffered a large split over its policies on boys: 'Changes have been somewhat easier to deal with since the first big split. Many wimmin considered that first change, from welcoming boys to limiting them, as too fundamental a breach of the original intention to be able to continue their involvement. Those conflicts have left me with no illusions that living and working cooperatively is easy' (134). And while more than one separatist mentioned the irony of further divisions among women (this time self-inflicted, created by debates over males),[7] such realizations did little to encourage acceptable resolutions of this issue among most of the collectives.

When we examine the historical narratives of these groups, then, it becomes apparent that many more issues than those of class created tensions and conflicts within separatist collectives. Conflict resolution thus became an important (if not crucial) aspect of collective life, and women spent long hours working through the various problems as they arose. Yet few groups were able to create a process by which disagreements consistently could be resolved, as Turner's discussion of AWP indicates:

Through the years, various means have been used to negotiate conflicts: consensus decision making, charismatic leadership, covert leadership, and majority vote. . . . The constant choice seems to be whether to place the most value on the process of getting something done, or on the accomplishment of it. In general, AWP honors the process only to the point of endangering its own continued survival. When that point is reached, process has been abandoned. (22)

Again, issues of survival severely taxed the practice of politics when experience began to conflict with ideology. And though consensus decision making was the preferred method of government for most collectives, many found, as had AWP, that this process was at best arduous and, more often than not, ineffective.

What happened, then, when process failed? Many collectives suffered a great deal of attrition, though in several cases new women replaced the lost members. Some signed over their collective ownership to single- or couple-owned land. In the majority of cases, however, collectives simply ceased to exist as collectives. Of the American land groups mentioned in Cheney's book, for example, one-third had completely dissolved by the time the book was published. Of the remainder, another two-thirds either began as or converted to private ownership or had disintegrated to the point that only one or two women were left on the land. Thus approximately 22 percent of the groups (six total) represented in Cheney's text survived as collectives beyond the publication of the book. And the dissolutions were often less than collectively decided as well. Recall, for example, the Redbird collective's dreams for its final action with which this chapter began. In the paragraph following those dreams Cheney narrates the process of Redbird's actual dissolution: 'Redbird died a less glamorous death. The collective broke up in the spring of 1979. A year later, the school was sold to pay off school debts. As for the house and land, some womyn signed away their ownership, one womon was forced to sign off, and the rest own it together. The house has been rented to dykes and heterosexuals' (123). Cheney's discursive representations of the visions Redbird had for its end, juxtaposed to the story she is able to tell, provide a stark contrast that works to dim hopes of a 'utopian' existence in any point of the collective process.

Cheney herself, however, does prepare us for the 'deaths' of these collectives in her introductory essay and suggests a framework within which we might read these endings. For Cheney, many women left their groups because of the hardships of country living:

Why did we form lesbian lands? To pursue vision. And why did many leave? We found out country life is hard. Where are the jobs, the hot baths, the harmonious song circles, the peaceful retreats, the sunny afternoons? In addition, we found land payments due, cars stuck in the mud, bugs, cold, endless group meetings, loneliness and isolation, especially if we were not youngish, white and able-bodied. As we experienced what the realistic picture of country life is, we saw that it is a package deal, with pros and cons like any other. (12)

Although Cheney alludes to the conflicts over race, physical ability, age, and even group process, she casts them in such a light as to indicate that these difficulties rose from the physical difficulties of country living. Such a formulation, of course, became quite fragile with the realization that similar conflicts were also the downfall of nonrural, nonresidential separatist collectives such as the *Lavender Woman*. Perhaps because rural women had access to news from their city counterparts, then, explanations such as those Cheney offers were not often repeated in the narratives of land collectives.

Women from the collectives themselves often cast their failures or reflected on changes they should have made in ways that differ from Cheney's explanations. For example, Buckwheat Turner's characterization of the attrition from AWP as 'burn-out' describes strongly internal, rather than environmental, influences as destructive factors:

Reasons for leaving, in general, come under the heading 'burn-out.' Unresolved personal issues, lack of personal money, group scapegoating, and the pressures to succeed in the ways of the outside world (more education, professional development, travel, etc.) all contributed in varying degrees to each woman's eventual exhaustion. . . . The unfortunate thing is that many women have left with a sense of failure, a feeling that they were unable to fuse their lives completely with the ideal vision of A Woman's Place. (22)

Turner's characterization carries none of the disillusion with country living that Cheney described; rather, it is evident that interpersonal tensions and 'group scapegoating' – a code, I think, for the pressure to conform often produced by the process of consensus decision making – were more problematic for members of AWP.

The perception of these tensions as a major factor in the dissolution of many collectives led some women to challenge portions of lesbian-separatist ideology altogether. When they began to think about what they might have done differently in their collective, for example, the members of Golden questioned the value of diversity itself:

I'm realizing it isn't enough just to live with other lesbian feminists who want to live on the land. We need more affinities. . . .

One thing I'd want in another community is to be around more wimin who are more like me. And that's hard for me to say, because at Golden I really encouraged a diversity, and thought diversity was something that would help us grow. Now I feel that, in a lot of ways, the diversity made it really hard. We were coming from so many different places, and had so many different goals, and were all so scarred as lesbians living in the patriarchy, that we were bound to take some of that out on each other. (51, 53–54)

Reflections such as that of the Golden collective seemed to suggest that collective experience could not match the ideals of community posited in separatist ideology. But more ironically, such statements also implied that these ideologies might in and of themselves threaten the survival of the very collective they helped to create.

One further suggestion in the narrative of Golden, however, became a far more common explanation for collective failures than any we have examined thus far. Note the ways in which 'the patriarchy,' present above as the cause for lesbians' oppressive behavior toward one another, is also written into the narrative of the Heraseed collective: 'The gulf between our patriarchal origins and our utopian vision made it hard. We carry around so much old stuff inside us, old behavior patterns. We are letting go of them as best we can, but the process is a slow one' (60); of Cheney's Redbird: 'I learned to be wary of led groups or group pressure to conform. We are different. We thought we were doing something so radically different. In some ways we were. In other ways, we brought the patriarchy with us. Us/them. Better than/worse than. Fault/blame. The *right* way' (124); or of Juana Maria Paz's La Luz: 'What we didn't see (I thought I did) was that we were the same people we had been before we came here, and we brought that past, meaning the patriarchy, with us. It will be a long and continuing process to purge ourselves of the culture we grew up in. Perhaps we cannot even do it in our lifetime. Perhaps only our daughters, who will not learn the ways of men, will be truly free' (Paz 12).

Not only does this focus on the effects of the patriarchy refute such theories as that of the Web's members, who believed that 'wimmin are different in wimmin's space' (Cheney 141), it also blames the failure of these collectives on the very institution cited as the raison d'être of the collectives in the first place. In these historical narratives women's rhetorical use of the patriarchy seems to bind them in an intolerable paradox: perceived as vulnerable only to the community strength and separatist actions of women, the patriarchy nonetheless makes the success of that community and those actions ultimately impossible.

But 'the patriarchy' makes another, far more insidious appearance in the discourse of these histories. As we have seen, any state apparatus – the legal system, city or state governments, business organizations, the military, the police, and so on – was cast in separatist theory as a major mechanism of the patriarchy through which women were oppressed.[8] Thus any contact with such institutions was to be avoided, if not shunned altogether. Yet some collectives, as the story of the Pagoda attests, found security in legal procedures and structures they might otherwise have dismissed:

The association is our community legal agreement. . . . I'm an anarchist . . . Still, I am glad for the association. A major conflict that happened soon after the formation of the association . . . could have split this whole place up if we had not had some structure. Some would have sued us. They threatened to, but we had a pretty strong base. Even now, when some women who've been involved decide to move on, some close sisters' actions in selling their cottages have been surprising. If it hadn't been for the agreement, they would have sold for a profit, taken anything they could get, from whoever had offered it. (112–13)

And Cheney herself recalls that the Redbird collective resorted to lawyers when mediation attempts during the collective's dissolution failed: 'The actual breakup was like any divorce, just as we were like any marriage, where we thought we were going to be together happily ever after. We fought and fought. Some of our final negotiations took place in our lawyer's office. Our friends agreed to mediate, and one by one they burned out' (123). This – grudging – reliance on mainstream institutional help can be dismissed as hypocritical, of course, but I think it is far more interesting in its indication of the difficulties even determined women encountered as they confronted their socializations. While I am not willing to claim that the route these collectives took worked because it was the 'right' one, I do feel that it was effective in part because women expected it to work and because they were familiar with the ways in which it could (or could not) help in the resolution of collective arguments.

Although narratives such as that of Redbird and the Pagoda thus indicate the collectives' reliance on mainstream institutions, they represent these choices in a way that does not indicate the internal struggles that must have occurred over these decisions. Other collectives, however, were far more direct in their narration, as the account of the breakup of AWP indicates:

The worst conflict in our seven-year herstory, the one we took to the patriarchal legal structure, happened in the fall of 1977. Several unresolved issues were building up. . . . We were unable to resolve this conflict among ourselves, and painfully settled it by bringing in patriarchal lawyers and law enforcers. Many women left AWP, never to return, several of whom had put years of their lives and thousands of dollars into the place. (22)

Turner's language operates on at least two distinct levels in the cultural register of separatism. First, it once again displaces the responsibility of women's behaviors and choices onto an externalized, evil force – the patriarchy – in such a way as to deny women's agency during times when those choices were complicitous with forces seen as inherently oppressive to women. In so doing, Turner's rhetoric places women in a powerless position: unable to resolve their own conflicts, women's only choice seems to be to turn to those who will behave in an even more oppressive manner. Second, Turner's narration of the collective's choice to utilize 'patriarchal' institutions reveals the complex and contradictory signification the patriarchy carried for the practice and politics of female community: the always-evil oppressor could become a sometime-savior at the (obscured) behest of women themselves.

The significance of the patriarchy as a complex sign for separatism comes, I think, at the expense of the practice of women's collective endeavors. Because patriarchal institutions could be counted on to resolve insurmountable differences among collective members while at the same time they remained an ideological evil, the discursive representation of women's actions allowed no real recognition of the ways women were implicated in the continuation, maintenance, or even flourishing of that system nor of the ways women benefited from it. Thus no truly effective methods by which to confront, much less overcome, internalized social constructions of difference could be developed, as the blame always lay outside women's 'real' natures. Yet when women acted from their 'inauthentic' (patriarchal) conditioning, they did so in ways that, in the retelling, seemingly had permanent, irreversibly destructive effects on the women's communities to which they belonged.

As a historical narrative, then, Joyce Cheney's *Lesbian Land* works within its community to characterize the visions, experiences, and disappointments of the collective endeavors of that community. Cheney's purpose is to inspire others and provide the opportunity for women to learn from our collective mistakes. And indeed, many of the dreams and visions with which these collectives began, and through which some succeeded, could conceivably work to inspire further creations of women's communities.

Yet the consistent representations of conflict and differences among women present in the narratives themselves work in ways that more often than not contradicted these visions. Expectations of an easy sisterhood gave way to destructive arguments over issues of race, class, physical ability, and child care that were enacted repeatedly throughout many collectives' stories. And though the collectives offered several explanations for the failure of their dreams, the most common one – too much patriarchal energy among women themselves – operated as a paradoxical sign that blocked effective conflict resolution and thus continued to contribute to the collectives' dissolutions. That these seemingly irresolvable conflicts reverberated deeply both in and outside the collectives became quite apparent in the late 1970s and early 1980s, as I will discuss in the following summary.

'Morning!' I greeted Joan as she answered the bell.

'You're early,' she replied, a touch of testiness in her voice.

'Sorry. You shouldn't have told me about the express subway, I guess. It made the trip much faster. I'll leave later tomorrow.'

'Never mind,' she said, waving away her bad mood and my chastisement. 'What are you going to work on today?'

'I think I'll tackle all the back issues of the journals. I'm anxious to see how these arguments over separatism played out in the literature.'

'You'll need a dust rag,' she warned, grinning.

'I hate dusting.'

'Somebody's got to do it,' she countered, laughing at my expression.

I bit back my rejoinder about dykes and dusting. 'I guess it's a small enough price,' I grumbled. 'Where are the journals stored?'

I spent another morning in an ecstasy of discovery that usually occurs too rarely in research. I was so thoroughly engaged with the material that I checked my watch in disbelief when Joan touched my shoulder and asked, 'Don't you want to break for lunch?'

Wired by the unending supply of coffee and excitement, I shook my head. 'No, I think I'd rather keep reading. There's a lot here, and I've only got a few days left. Thanks anyway.'

'Okay,' she shrugged, leaving me once more to my studies.

Later that afternoon, however, she approached me again. 'Look, you really should take a break. You can't do this all day long. Want to take a walk?'

I was ready to agree with her. 'Thanks. Actually, I could use a break.'

We left the apartment and turned toward Riverside Park. 'So,' she asked, 'how's the work coming?'

'Fantastic! And it looks like the unpublished papers will be just as fruitful as the published material. My only worry now is that I won't have enough time to read it all.'

'Hmmm,' she nodded, apparently familiar with the dilemma. 'If you need to, you're welcome to spend a night over. That should give you some extra time.'

I thought I had grown accustomed to her generosity. This offer, however, left me more than a little speechless. 'Thanks, Joan . . . that means a lot to me. You're very kind.'

'You're very welcome,' she replied, and then looked at me for a few moments. 'Dana – can I ask you a question?'

I nodded, though such a preface always makes me apprehensive.

'Why are you doing your dissertation on separatism?'

I laughed, perhaps relieved. 'A couple of reasons, I suppose. The first one horrifies everyone but me. I spent four years working on another, very safe dissertation, including a month-long research trip to four archives, only to find the exact study completed a few years earlier by a British graduate student. The whole thing was a fluke, and she never published it. But it was too close for me to try to work around it with any believable claim of originality. So I decided that if I was going to finish the degree, I would do a study on what I wanted to do, whether or not anyone else thought it would get me a job.'

'Sounds like every grad student's nightmare,' she sympathized. 'But why separatism?'

'Separatism as a personal and political stance has always fascinated me – but then, I'm usually intrigued by things most people rush to dismiss or denounce out of hand. Often I find they carry far more social significance and influence than anyone wants to acknowledge – the dismissal signals fear more than anything else. The dismissal of us that comes from homophobia works the same way, you know?'

Joan nodded. 'But you're in English, aren't you? How did separatism even become a possible topic for you to pursue?'

'I didn't start with separatism as my topic. I started with what I thought were lesbian utopian novels. Only through thinking about these utopias as social documents did I realize that my project had a lot more to do with separatism and women's communities than it did with something most scholars dismiss as lesbian escapist fantasy. It's become a way for me to explore my fascination and to understand the value of and problems with separatism for women.'

'One thing's certain – it's a very different topic!'

'I'm pretty lucky, really. I get to have fun writing my dissertation. It's a topic that has remained exciting for me; I'd lost that with my first one. And with what other topic could I use the excuse that I needed to go to the archives, much less stay at the Bloodroot, as part of my research?'

My comment was meant to elicit a laugh, but the mood shifted suddenly and I was faced with that maddeningly flat affect once again. Enough was enough.

'Joan, my turn for a question. What the hell is it with you and Bloodroot?'

She hesitated, surprised. 'It's a long story . . .'

Where had I heard that before? 'I'm listening,' I said, sensing that she wasn't unwilling to tell me. 'So?'

'A lot of things, I guess. Mostly they don't like the work I do on sexuality. They – and many others – weren't very happy about my presentation on butch-femme relationships I did at the Barnard conference on women's sexuality, much less the conference itself. Nor do they like the fact that I've posed for *On Our Backs*. And *Restricted Country* really made them angry.'

'Why? Weren't you primarily looking at your own experiences in new terms? I found the contextualization of butch-femme sexuality alone invaluable. The book has been one of the most honest and enjoyable works I've read in a very long time.'

'Thank you. But it's not just the approach, it's the subject altogether. I think butch-femme, lesbian pornography or prostitution, and s&m are almost interchangeable sexual practices for them; they all receive the label of woman-hating or male-identified.'

'Okay, fine, so you don't agree on sex. But why should that make you treat each other like you each surprised the last remaining cockroach on earth? Isn't the community a little small for that vehemence?'

She smiled, probably at my apparent naiveté. 'You'd think so, wouldn't you? But don't you have the same problems in Iowa City?'

'Over sexuality? Not really. Perhaps it's just not the topic of fashion right now . . . I don't know. I haven't given it much thought. But I have a feeling that it has more to do with our history than anything else.'

'In what way?'

'About ten years ago the community split seriously over the issue of boys at the women's coffee house. Women with young boys didn't want to – or couldn't – find child care every time they worked at or visited the coffee house. But many separatists wanted at least some space to be with other women, free from male presence. They couldn't reach a compromise; the coffee house shut down instead. It sobered up a lot of women. I don't know if we've found less destructive ways to argue, if we're avoiding argument altogether, or if our most contentious members simply pack up and move on. It is a university town, after all. Whatever the cause, this one's not ripping us up.'

'Sounds wonderful,' Joan replied, a little wistfully.

'Maybe, but it's got drawbacks. I feel like the proverbial country cousin: I have to come to New York just to realize the intensity of the argument, and I still can't say I'm convinced the fight is worth the leverage it's giving the right wing against us. Then there's *Common Lives* . . . we were floored by the intensity of the negative response to the pieces we published on s&m. Perhaps we would have been better prepared had we dealt with it at home first.'

'Perhaps. But I don't know if that would have made a major difference, unless you chose not to publish the works at all. But look at my experiences with the Bloodroot! Even after several years of this argument, I'm certainly not welcome at the restaurant, nor will they carry any of my works at the bookstore.'

'So how are you handling it?' I asked, hoping for some insight.

'I'm not giving in to that type of pressure. You can't rewrite history, women's lives, or even sexual desire to make them fit a political agenda – no matter how ideal. You'd think lesbians of all people would know that, or at least listen long enough to learn it. Aren't we the ones who keep insisting, "You've got to listen to what women have to say"?' she demanded.

I nodded, smiling slightly. I was beginning to recognize where the flash and intensity of *A Restricted Country* originated and understand the love that stood behind it.

Summary: The Community Work of Separatist Historical Narratives

Both Michal Brody and Joyce Cheney embarked on their projects with the goal of continuing the dreams with which their collectives began. Collectives such as *Lavender Woman* and those represented in Cheney's text created a space wherein women could practice their visions of change for themselves and for a women's community, change that included social as well as personal activism. Brody's title, especially in its focus on a 'continuing history,' indicates her desire to maintain those visions; Cheney directly tells us that her intent is to inspire further collective action. Cheney also guides her audience to just that reading of the narratives themselves:

One writer questioned whether a book about lands, several of which no longer exist, will encourage or discourage dyke readers. The book is full of opportunities for encouragement! Wild womyn! Wild visions! Wild times! We learn from our sisters. Sometimes we learn to do it the same; sometimes, to do it differently. We learn to go gayly forward. (12)

Cheney hopes that her readers are encouraged by this anthology; yet her exclamatory structure suggests an overemphasis on the positive, and not unnecessarily so: many of these narratives dwell on descriptions of their difficulties and dissolutions.

In whatever ways these collectives represented their failures, however, it became clear to many separatist theorists that their visions of female community through the practice of separatist collectives were seriously called into question, if these visions survived the collective experience at all. Sarah Hoagland, professor of philosophy at Northeastern Illinois University, has commented on collective failures in her recent book, *Lesbian Ethics*. Her commentary indicates the extent to which conflicts over social constructions of difference had become an issue outside collective structures themselves:

I observed many [lesbian] organizations grow and then fall apart. This collapse occurred for a number of reasons. In direct response to our efforts to challenge the oppressive values we lived under and to create alternatives, we faced outright violence, severe economic limits, legal threats, f.b.i. penetration and disruption, and all manner of other male sabotage, such as feminist men filing discrimination suits so they could enter our events or transsexual men claiming a right to lesbian space. In addition, we carried deep within us the values of the fathers, including classism, racism, ageism, antisemitism, sizeism, able bodyism, and imperialism, as well as sexism and heterosexism – all of which informed our perceptions and none of which we immediately, nor have we yet, divested ourselves of. And of course we made significant mistakes as we traveled this new path, such as believing that because we were all women or all lesbians we could automatically trust each other. (1–2)

Hoagland cites all the conflicts (and more) apparent in the narratives we have examined. Again, too, she reinscribes the explanation of patriarchal influence on women as part of the cause. And the other causes she lists – 'legal threats . . . economic limitations . . . f.b.i. penetration . . . male sabotage' – effectively displace the problematic outside the control of women themselves as well. Only in the last sentence, structured nearly as an aside with the use of 'of course,' do women carry any of the responsibility. Even that responsibility, however, is cast as the positive mistake of trusting one another too much.

These discursive representations of the failure of collectives in terms that made their success almost beyond the control of women led other separatists to question the value of female community through residential collectivity itself. For example, even as early as the mid-1970s, the Seattle collective doubted the effectiveness of rural groups as a strategy to build the 'lesbian nation':

Several things do seem clear to us as far as long-range strategy. . . . There is no way that lesbians are going to be permitted to simply withdraw quietly to some area and to begin to take control over our lives and our community. Even those lesbians with enough privilege to talk of buying land have no way to make sure that the government will not come in and destroy all they've built. . . .

This is not to say that we're opposed to setting up rural lesbian communes or farms. . . . But a lesbian farm is NOT the lesbian nation, because the lesbians on that farm have no real power to control their community in terms of the outside society. (Alice, Gordon, Debbie, and Mary, 'Directions' 40, 44n)

The Seattle collective's doubt about the efficacy of (here rural) separatist collectives as the ultimate radical stance reveals the re-visions of female community created by discursive representations of those collective histories: if, because of the overwhelming influence of the patriarchy, women cannot control even the environments within their own communities, then those communities cannot be a possible solution to the destruction of that patriarchal system. One of the strongest arguments for female community through collective action thus proved to be its worst undoing.

Yet, however many times concepts of female community were battered by the failure of separatist collectives, the yearning for community persisted. Cheney's call for renewed emphasis on community was echoed even by women such as Juana Maria Paz, who had felt so deeply betrayed by her past experiences in rural collectives (Paz 91). But it also became apparent to many feminists that the visions for these communities had to change if they were to negotiate the problems presented by collective experiments. I contend that the discursive moment wherein the ideal of female community was taken up and revised came in the sudden interest and participation in the genre of separatist utopian literature. To read the genre in this context, however, requires an analysis of the utopian gesture that has only recently been articulated. That analysis and a reading of two separatist utopian novels are the subjects of the final section.

BLOODROOT FOUR

Questions such as 'Are you for censorship or freedom of speech?' have no mean-ing. What kind of boredom is there in lesbian lives to produce a market for On Our Backs, *or the violent, racist emanations from Lace Publications?*

Those of us who call ourselves feminist make our Selves and other women a priority. We are angry and political; we make judgments for our Selves. Lesbians discuss substance abuse, work towards 'survival' of alcoholism, incest, patri-archal religion; yet some don't seem to recognize that sadomasochism is our own internalization of men's womanhating. – Bloodroot Collective, 'Bloodroot: Brewing Visions'

Wednesday is 'women's night' at the Bloodroot; the restaurant often of-fers some form of entertainment after the dinner hour. That particular Wednesday Linda, a singer/songwriter from New York, promised to enchant our evening. Before she was scheduled to begin, however, I took the opportunity to browse through the bookstore. I could not find any of Joan's work available for sale, even though *A Restricted Country* had undoubtedly proved profitable for other women's bookstores. I did find Susanna Sturgis's *Memories and Visions,* an anthology of femi-nist fantasy literature, and bought it in the hopes of gleaning informa-tion useful for my study.

During dinner Dot, a member new to the collective, joined me to dis-cuss graduate schools. She hoped to return to school soon, she said, and wanted to know what I thought about the different strengths of several schools. She was excited that I was working on women's communities and asked me how my research was coming.

'Wonderfully,' I replied. 'I'm finding more at the archives than I ever thought possible. But I'm finding that has its disadvantages, too.'

'What do you mean?'

'I thought the excitement would wear off after a day or two. It hasn't, and with all the coffee I'm drinking, I'm not sleeping.'

'At all?'

'Maybe one or two hours each night.'

'That's not good. Ever try homeopathy?'

'No . . . I've worked mostly with herbal remedies – teas, infusions, that sort of thing. Why?' I asked. 'I'm not sick, just exhausted.'

'Homeopathy works sort of like a vaccine. You take a very concentrated dosage of a remedy that in normal situations would cause the symptoms – in your case, caffeine. It produces the opposite effects of its usual results.'

'Like giving coffee to a hyperactive child?'

'Partly, yes. I've got doses of caffeine at the house. If you want, I'll give you some to take just before you go to bed.'

'Great, thanks! I'll stop by after the concert.'

We continued our discussion until Linda began to tune up; Dot and I settled in for an evening of 'women's music.' Women: 'adult female persons.' Music: 'vocal, instrumental, or mechanical sounds having rhythm, melody, or harmony.' Women's music, then, should be harmonious(?) sounds by, about, or for that social group we call women. An accurate description, as dictionaries are wont to provide, but nonetheless untrue in its contemporary usage. Music by, about, or for lesbians, then. More accurate in actual demographics, perhaps, but still untrue in its failure to capture this genre's essence. I sat and listened to the music – music still created primarily in separate spaces such as the Bloodroot or the Michigan Womyn's Music Festival, unless its message is neutralized enough to slip past the guardians of the top-forties gates. Music that, at its most powerful, catalyzes and supports women dedicated to social and community change. And when Linda sang a humorous song decrying the pain accompanying sadomasochism, I laughed and applauded along with everyone else.

On my way back to the inn, I happened upon Linda as she relaxed after her set. 'Thanks,' I offered after I introduced myself, 'I really enjoyed your music tonight. Have you ever done any shows in the Midwest?'

'No,' she replied. 'Why do you ask?'

'I live in Iowa City – we have a fairly large women's community. There's an active organization that brings musicians from all over: Holly Near, Castleberry and Dupree, Odetta, Lucy Blue, Ferron – and a lot of local women, too. If I tell them about you, would you be interested in coming?'

'Sure!' she said and gave me her address. 'But if you're from Iowa City, what are you doing here?'

I explained the reason for my trip; she asked me where in New York City I was doing my research. 'The Lesbian Herstory Archives,' I replied warily, by now uncertain of the response.

'Oh!' she brightened visibly. 'Say hello to Joan for me, will you? We go back a long way.'

'Of course,' I smiled broadly. We said goodbye and went our separate ways: she to the train station, I to my dose of caffeine and the best night's sleep I'd had all week.

Separatist Utopian Literature and the Re-vision of Community

PART THREE

Introduction: Fantasy and the Revolution

The relationship between the 'utopian' and the 'revolutionary' . . . is a question which is not only central to any discussion of radical cultural practice, but essential in a critical analysis of feminist texts, literary and theoretical. For it is the vital, necessary, and intensely ambivalent relationship between what is and what might be that creates the structural tensions and ideological ambiguity in feminist writing and thinking. We might recognize, in theory, that to choose between (utopian) thought and (revolutionary) practice is not only absurd but ultimately impossible. – Angelika Bammer, 'Visions and Revisions: The Utopian Impulse in Feminist Fictions'

The experiences and stories of women who attempted to practice separatist politics through collective experimentation made it extremely difficult for women still nourished by dreams of female community to move toward their visions. At this juncture in separatist history (during the mid- to late 1970s), the contrast between separatist desire for an ideal community and the problems or failures of collective practice opened an opportunity for separatist authors to work once again within the community. But the needs of the separatist community had changed: separatists now shared a body of theoretical discourse, and enough written and oral history had circulated among women both within and outside collectives to inform them of the difficulties faced by separatist groups throughout the country. Consequently, the genre women turned to in their quest for community also changed. I suggest that at this point, the creation of and interest in separatist utopian literature was at least in part a response to the opportunities presented by the changing needs of separatist community: fantastical enough not to be limited by the disheartening experiences of collective endeavors, the genre of separatist utopias functioned, as Bammer implies, to reestablish the importance of revolutionary practice within the framework of radical thought.

To be more specific, separatist utopian writings during the 1970s and early 1980s worked within their communities as cultural documents that sought to intervene in and neutralize destructive, binary oppositions constructed within the theories and narratives of the communities themselves. This process of neutralization in turn functioned to define and encourage new methods by which women could continue their struggle for female community. The cultural history I (re)construct here implies a reading of separatist utopias that, while it is developed from theories by Marxist and feminist scholars of utopian literature, nonetheless diverges from them in at least one important way.

Because both Marxist and feminist critics are concerned with the ways cultural ideologies and material realities shape individual and social behavior, their analyses of utopian literature are crucial to my understanding of separatist utopias. However they view utopian literature, most critics continue to recognize the debt owed to Thomas More's pun for their understanding of the genre: the 'good place' (*eutopia*) that is also 'no place' (*outopia*). Yet Marxist theorists in particular traditionally viewed utopian literature as an escapist, antirevolutionary genre, as Jean Pfaelzer explains:

Marxist theorists traditionally argued that utopia represents a tempting but flawed proposition about history – a facile and thus dangerous guarantee of a serene future. Friedrich Engels found that when such early utopians as Saint-Simon, Fourier, and Robert Owen defined their task 'as to manufacture a system of society as perfect as possible,' they disregarded the working class as the necessary determinant of social change. By promising the good place prematurely, indeed magically, utopia became a potentially dangerous diversion from the difficult task of forging a new society. . . . Engels believed that by failing to generalize from the particularities and peculiarities of immediate reality, utopians divorced the future from the present; essentially idealists, they saw no preconditions of the future except right thinking. (4)

Like their formulation of the religious impulse within Marxist theory, Marxist theorists considered utopia as more harmful than helpful to plans for revolutionary activism.

From the 1940s through the 1970s, however, Marxist critics began to shift their definition of the important features of the genre from utopia as a static, dangerously easy society to the processes or mechanisms of social change envisioned in the texts.[1] Darko Suvin, for example, carefully defines utopia as strictly a 'verbal construction' that

> as a definitional element by-passes, I hope, the old theologizing quarrel whether a utopia can be realized, whether in fact (according to one school) only that which is realizable or on the contrary (according to another but equally dogmatic school) only that which is unrealizable can be called utopian. . . . If utopia is, then, philosophically a method rather than a state, it cannot be realized or not realized – it can only be applied. ('Defining the Literary Genre of Utopia' 135–36)

Suvin's argument refigures utopia as a 'method' or a process to be applied within society toward the realization of sociopolitical goals – not as a realistic prescription in and of itself. Further, Suvin emphasizes that utopia need not be perfect, only 'organized according to a more perfect principle than in the author's community' ('Defining the Literary Genre of Utopia' 132). Suvin thus shifts the critical focus on utopia from a genre that prematurely promises the good life to an understanding of the active role the genre might play in the process of change within the author's community.

While Suvin concentrates on the reconceptualization of the sociopolitical function of utopian literature, Fredric Jameson implicitly expands the boundaries of Suvin's theories through an exploration of the specific ways that utopian literature acts in society. For Jameson, the utopian impulse functions in society through the (literary) creation of processes by which socially operant, destructive binary oppositions or conflicts are neutralized (as opposed to, for example, resolved). In other words, a utopian text posits a world where current, socially constructed binary oppositions no longer carry meaning. Jameson (reading Louis Marin) argues that utopian literature thus can be considered a type of praxis:

> To understand utopian discourse in terms of neutralization is indeed precisely to propose to grasp it as a process, as *energeia*, enunciation, productivity and implicitly or explicitly to repudiate that more traditional and conventional view of Utopia as sheer representation, as the 'realized' vision of this or that ideal society or social ideal. . . . [I]t is possible to understand the Utopian text as a determinate type of *praxis*, rather than a specific code of representation, a praxis which has less to do with the construction and perfection of someone's 'idea' of a 'perfect society' than it does with a concrete set of mental operations to be performed on a determinate type of raw material given in advance which is con-

temporary society itself, or rather, what amounts to the same thing, to those collective representations of contemporary society which inform our ideologies just as they order our experiences of daily life. ('Of Islands and Trenches' 6)

Jameson's construction of the function of utopian discourse confers upon the genre a revolutionary status; if utopia has the potential to act in its society in the way Jameson suggests, then indeed utopia as process can be seen as a potentially radical act. Thus Angelika Bammer's sense that '(utopian) thought and (revolutionary) practice' are ultimately inseparable is derived in part from Marxist scholars' analyses of utopia as a process, made all the more important to feminism in its function as an agent of social change.

Of course, not every feminist scholar examines utopias within the Marxian framework of process or change. Though critics such as Frances Bartkowski, Angelika Bammer, and Jean Pfaelzer in part read utopias as sites of cultural meanings, others examine the genre for its incorporation of feminist 'themes' or 'values,' for representations of traditional literary tropes, for visions of alternative institutional structures (i.e., government, child care, education, economics, and so on), or even as representative of the difference an author's gender makes in the creation of literary utopias.[2]

Whether or not feminist critics choose to work within the structures of Marxist analysis, however, their examinations of separatist utopias fail to analyze the ways these texts envision processes designed to catalyze change in the communities from which they come. For example, Bartkowski dismisses separatist utopias such as Sally Miller Gearhart's *The Wanderground* as essentialist and thus implicitly not feminist; she analyzes Suzy McKee Charnas's *Motherlines* only as it relates to *Walk to the End of the World*, Charnas's dystopian, male-dominated fantasy (167, 81–108). Critics such as Jennice Gail Thomas who search these texts for feminist themes are interested in the commonalities separatist utopias have with other feminist utopias (e.g., Marge Piercy's *Woman on the Edge of Time* or Ursula K. Le Guin's *The Dispossessed*); the issue of separatism is seen as either coincidental or, more inaccurately, as that which makes the work utopian (25, 189–91).[3] Natalie Rosinsky's examination of the literary tropes in feminist utopias analyzes separatist texts and literary conventions of the hero under the moniker of 'The Battle of the Sexes'; that separatist strategy relied on withdrawal from rather than battle with men seems to elude her completely (65–104). And Lee Cullen Khanna's analysis of the difference between utopias written by men and those written by women does not distinguish separatist from non-separatist feminist utopias and thus cannot provide a way to read the work these texts do within their specific communities.[4]

I do not mean to imply that the above analyses and others like them are unimportant. They have allowed us to read these works as part of the larger genre of feminist utopias and to aid our definitions of what a 'feminist' canon in general might look like or include. But they do not interest me as much as does an analysis that provides an understanding of the ways these texts functioned within the specific communities from which they came or for which they were written.

Like Jameson and Suvin, then, I feel that separatist utopias worked within their communities as potential agents of social change. Moreover, I agree that their community work is most visible in their attempts, through discourse, to intervene in and neutralize destructive, seemingly irresolvable oppositions constructed within the discourse of separatism and separatist communities. However, I argue that the function of these texts was not to change a few aspects of separatist community but to reenvision that community entirely so that the derailed process of community building might be reconceptualized and begun anew.

To illustrate these contentions, the last section of this study examines Sally Miller Gearhart's *The Wanderground* and Suzy McKee Charnas's *Motherlines* as representative yet unique examples of separatist utopian literature. In reading them in this manner, I hope both to explore one final discursive moment wherein separatist concepts of female community were utilized and recast as well as to suggest a new reading of separatist utopias that analyzes the work such texts did within their communities.

'We May Not Be Together Always': The Community Work of Sally Miller Gearhart's *The Wanderground*

Six

First published in 1978 by Persephone Press, Sally Miller Gearhart's *The Wanderground* went through two more editions and today is in print through Alyson Press. *The Wanderground*, as its subtitle *Stories of the Hill Women* suggests, is a work composed of short stories that weave a community tale. The community of women exists outside a large, destructively patriarchal city in which the women, disguised as men, maintain a physical presence to learn of any potential threat to their community. The novel's time frame spans from the past-imperfect of antifeminist backlashes, restrictive regulations (dress codes, curfews, work limitations) for women, and witch hunts that led to the community's creation, to the future-perfect of an (almost) safe space where women are free to develop new psychic, spiritual, reproductive, and physical powers.

Like the separatist collectives it reflects, *The Wanderground*'s community governs itself by consensus, tries to live in accordance with ecofeminist principles, and attempts to affirm 'women's experience' in an otherwise-patriarchal world. Also like the women in those groups, the women in the novel face a variety of both individual and community conflicts. But the definitive difference between the utopian gesture and historical experience comes in the novel's presentation of these conflicts: whereas the existence of many separatist collectives was seriously threatened by discord among group members, the conflicts in *The Wanderground* are approached in such a way as to neutralize these operant, irresolvable oppositions.

This chapter discusses the sections of the novel that best illustrate what I define as its utopian gesture. In so doing, I demonstrate how the novel as a utopia 'worked' within the communities for which it was written and from which it came. My analysis therefore is not meant to be a comprehensive examination of the novel even in its relation to lesbian feminism or lesbian separatism. It should, however, offer a reading that explains the novel's appeal to and impact on its community of readers more clearly than have most previous analyses.[1] To begin the examination of *The Wanderground*, I provide biographical information about Gearhart and explore her political philosophies so that we might place her thoughts and experiences within the context of the separatist debates and community conflicts of the 1970s.

Like many lesbian-feminist activists in the Bay Area, Sally Miller Gearhart came to her politics through the theories of radical feminism (Wolf 60). Gearhart has subscribed to radical feminism's basic theory of sexism as the primary contradiction, though as is evident in an article she co-authored for the *Lesbian Tide*, Gearhart makes a distinction not commonly found in most separatist appropriations of this concept:

> I believe that the primary contradiction is man over woman. My socialist sisters get very upset and say, 'No, indeed, it has to be capital over labor.' Or, they say, 'We simply can't make a choice.' But I believe that all other power relationships did grow from male dominance over female submission whenever back in that dark corner of history the first exercise of power in human relationships took place.
>
> Now the prime contradiction is different from what I call the immediate contradiction. It's absolutely plain to me that the immediate contradiction is that of capital over labor, imperialism. It is people who are starving and in pain. (Gearhart et al., 'A Kiss Does Not a Revolution Make' 25)

Gearhart's distinction between a 'prime' and an 'immediate' contradiction allows her to remain within the radical-feminist/lesbian-separatist theoretical framework and to challenge indirectly the monolithic place of the theory of sexism as the primary contradiction within separatist ideology itself. Though the distinction reveals an ambivalence on the issue of separatist ideology, it does give her room to distance herself from separatist conceptions of oppression that, as we have seen, alienated so many women in separatist business and residential collectives. As I will explain, Gearhart's seeming ambivalence over her adherence to essentialist conceptions of gender and her gesture toward theories of social constructionism play a crucial role in the community work of *The Wanderground*.[2]

Though Gearhart may not entirely endorse the basic ideologies of lesbian separatism, she has acknowledged the value of separatist goals in her life. In 1974, for example, Gearhart explained why she felt separatism was important:

I need and want to say something about dyke separatism and about why I believe in my heart that I am a dyke separatist, but cannot act on it now. It falls under that category of getting my head together, or functioning with alternative organizations. There may be a time in the future when I'll be able to act on it again. I know I believe in it. I know that it's the logical and psychological and historical extension of what I believe cultural feminism to be. I don't see much difference between a heterosexual cultural feminist who wants to build a female culture free of men and a lesbian separatist who wants to do the same thing and in fact is doing it. (Gearhart et al., 'A Kiss Does Not a Revolution Make' 29)

The connections Gearhart makes between cultural feminism and lesbian separatism contradict other separatist authors such as the women of the Seattle collective, who, as we have seen, strove to define lesbian separatism as a distinct theoretical and practical stand. Note that Gearhart clearly desires to erase that difference through her declaration that she would not distinguish between a heterosexual cultural feminist and a lesbian-separatist engaged in collective practice. Such an erasure avoids those facets of lesbian separatist theory and practice (detailed in chapter 3) that sought to distance lesbian separatists from heterosexual women who, by continuing to define themselves as heterosexual, at least theoretically refused to sever all ties with men. For Gearhart, then, the importance of lesbian separatism rests not in its identification with an erotic politics but in its goals to create and expand women's communities.

Gearhart's identification with lesbian separatism runs deeper than a philosophical commitment to some aspects of its ideology, however. In an interview with Leila Klasse, Gearhart described her practice of separatism:

First of all I have to say that though I would love in my heart to live only with women, that I cannot do that in my life right now because I feel myself too active in the city, in the women's studies program at San Francisco State where we work with men. . . . I will spend probably the usual ten months in the city and then hopefully be able to collapse for two months of the year on some of the land which six of us have bought. So I'm not a separatist even though I would love to be, and even though I think ideally that's the way women live best, with other women. . . .

There's a sense in which we can't really separate at all, ever, even women buying land in Wisconsin or Minnesota have to deal somehow with the system, and that system is still the male system that is out there, so even though we're very pure in being away from men, we're still often playing with men's toys. . . .

But then there's another sense in which any woman who's coming to any kind of lesbian consciousness is beginning to become a separatist. (Klasse 13)

Gearhart's sense of the value of separatism in her life compelled her to form a land collective with five other women. Note, however, the uncertainty that surrounds her definition of separatism: Gearhart claims that she is 'not a separatist' because she is not completely separate from men, yet she recognizes that no one can be entirely free from the dominant social order. This ambivalence easily might be criticized as merely an attempt to avoid taking a stand. Yet her hesitancy to do so reflects a contradiction within the practice of separatism itself: separatist theory claims that the degree to which one practices separatism measures one's commitment to feminism; however, complete separation was impossible, a fact separatist theorists such as Marilyn Frye or Bev Jo openly acknowledged. Here again, then, separatism seems to draw Gearhart more for its visions of female community than its theoretical debates over the degree to which one must maintain a separate space.

Whether or not Gearhart chose to define herself as fully separatist, she certainly had direct experience with the politics, practice, and conflicts that characterized separatist collectives during the 1970s. And as Gearhart suggested in a 1979 interview, the genre of fantasy allows her the unique opportunity to promote that collectivity: 'I think that fantasy's a capacity that men certainly have too. But I feel, because we have a political purpose before us in the women's movement . . . that maybe we have more of a handle on how that fantasy can be used to gather up our collectivity' (Sturgis, 'Transcript of an Interview with Sally Miller Gearhart' 5). Gearhart's nod to a 'male' and 'female' capacity for fantasy suggests, of course, that she believes there are abilities or ways of thinking that women and men do not (cannot?) share. The implied essentialism of this belief compels us to ally Gearhart more firmly with the essentialist foundations of lesbian separatism, though Gearhart often prefers to distance herself from those tenets.

More important, however, is Gearhart's belief that fantasy can be used to promote women's collectivity. Gearhart's conception gives the genre a social significance in much the same way Suvin's theory does: for both, fantasy is a process that can work within its culture to encourage social change. For Gearhart, such a process is conceived as a response to the difficulties of collectivity she witnessed in both the theories and practice of lesbian separatism. *The Wanderground*, then, offers an opportunity to understand how the genre might have worked in separatist circles to revitalize the concept of female community.

As I mentioned, *The Wanderground* is structured through short stories rather than a more conventional, unified plot. There is no single protagonist in this work; each story involves women who may or may not appear in other stories. The novel's structure and lack of a central character work to enhance the sense of collective living as it was represented in separatist theories of community explored in chapter 3: no person is more important than any other, no leader's existence characterizes or provides a foundation for the community's existence, and commonality – rather than individuality – is prized.

Other innovations, too, work to define this text as both fantasy and ideologically separatist. The community of *The Wanderground* develops its own language, a language that functions as a sign for a specifically 'female' experience.[3] More significantly, Gearhart creates a spiritual system for her community that parallels much of the focus on spirituality in the women's community during the 1970s. For the women of *The Wanderground*, spirituality is a way to connect all living things, a way to reclaim the female principle in spirituality theoretically lost during the rise of ancient Greek civilization, and a way to deepen their connections with other women. Spirituality thus becomes political in its use as a weapon against women's oppression: recall that for separatists, anything that affirmed women or women's experience was a revolutionary act. Gearhart herself claims that 'the spiritual is political,' by which she means it can be used to oppose the destructive patriarchal forces within the world ('The Spiritual Dimension' 187).[4]

Though I do not intend to provide a detailed analysis of the novel's innovations, I think they deserve notice because they represent the characteristics of communities that women such as those in Brody's and Cheney's anthologies sought. I do intend to focus on five issues or debates raised by the novel that reflect sites of contention within those nonfictional collectives: (1) Is external or internal opposition the greatest threat to women's collectives? How are these forms of opposition related? (2) How should conflict between individuals be negotiated? And how can individual bias or confrontational behavior be accounted for: in short, what is the place of the individual in the community? (3) Is gender a result of biological predetermination or is it socially constructed? (4) How do collective beliefs on the question of gender formation affect the members' relations with men and other women? (5) How should communitywide conflict – the failure to achieve consensus – be negotiated?

The issue of external and internal oppositions to collective security is developed in the beginning chapter of the novel, 'Opening.' 'Opening' presents two problematic events through the perception of Jacqua, a young collective member who 'hears' these events with extended psychic powers characteristic of the hill women. The first event, an argument between two long-term lovers, is represented as 'anger . . . from two older sisters who had overvisited with each other' (1).[5] Such a characterization challenges the valuation of closely knit, monogamous relationships among women through the implication that these relationships create more friction than harmony. But that challenge, as we shall see, is undercut by the representation in this chapter of an even greater threat to the women's community.

Jacqua's attention to the argument is quickly diverted by a sound she only slowly recognizes: someone, perhaps clad in armor, clanks through the outskirts of the Wanderground. Scarcely knowing what to make of such an anachronism, Jacqua 'listens' harder. But the person has stopped short and Jacqua can no longer trace the sounds. As she ponders the implications of this event, Jacqua suddenly wonders whether or not the intruder could be a man: 'Could it be that it wasn't a woman at all but a man? One from the City, standing stock still there within their Wanderground?' (2). Jacqua's question opens the opportunity for Gearhart to present the community's theories on and ideologies of men.

As a young woman, Jacqua is of a generation that has been born (through ovular merging)[6] into the community of the Wanderground rather than having had to leave the City to create (or find) the community. Thus she has never had extensive experience with men and knows of them only that which her elders teach. When, for example, she wonders whether the armored figure is a man and thus a threat to their community, she is compelled to recite the community's creed: 'It is too simple . . . to condemn them all or to praise all of us. But for the sake of earth and all she holds, that simplicity must be our creed' (2). The creed simultaneously challenges the essentialism of separatist theory and inscribes that essentialism as the basis for separatist action (if not theory). Such a negotiation of the essentialist problematic may simply reflect Gearhart's own ambiguities, but it also stands in contrast to the rigid stance of separatist theorists such as the Gutter Dyke Collective on the issue of men. While the women in the Wanderground seem willing to adopt essentialist constructions, they are less willing than many of their nonfictional counterparts to apply these constructs without reservation.[7]

Jacqua's question causes her to ponder the problem of men beyond her recitation of the community's creed. She knows from her studies that women once lived with and loved men. But the idea of loving men is alien to her conceptual framework and she wonders how, even historically, it could have been possible: 'It was uncomfortable and backwards in her mind. She tried it on from every angle but it would not adjust; some of its bulk stuck out over the sides while other parts of it were too short to approach the edges. Yet somehow once it had been so. 'Maybe it was a different kind of love,' she mused. 'Or maybe they were gentles' (2). Jacqua's reference to the 'gentles' is the reader's introduction to a group of men whose existence, while not negating essentialist constructions of maleness within the novel, complicates a simplistic dismissal of the work on the grounds of that essentialism. The gentles are gay men who recognize that the only hope for the earth's survival is the destruction of the patriarchy and concurrent ascension of 'women's' values and ways of living. Consequently, the gentles aid the women in their City surveillance and pass along information important both to their community's survival and their presence in the City. This is not to say that the women exist in easy alliance with the gentles, however: there is little contact among them and that contact occurs only in the City, only individually, and only when necessary. Yet alliance with the gentles clearly exists in contrast to the call by separatists, such as we have seen in the conflict between the *Lavender Woman* collective and the Chicago Gay Alliance, to sever all ties with gay as well as straight men.

As Jacqua recalls past images of men and the problematic of 'maleness,' her attention is rediverted by the sounds of the now more quiet argument between the two older women. Again Gearhart characterizes their disagreement by the statement that the women 'had spent too many days together without speaking their hearts to the rest,' a pattern that Jacqua is said to know well because 'it was one of the first lessons' for young members of the community (3). The women who argue are City-born women who were lovers before their arrival to the community and thus are said to hold 'too hard to each other and to the old ways of trying to love' (3–4).

Gearhart's characterization of this internal conflict effectively in-scribes some of the tensions within the nonfictional collectives that sep-aratists ascribed to their patriarchal conditioning. Recall, for example, that collective narratives such as Joyce Cheney's on Redbird blamed in-ternal discord on 'patriarchal' influences that women brought with them to the community. The remaining events in Gearhart's first chap-ter, however, place this paradigm in a context designed to defuse its paralyzing, destructive force.

Even as she listens to the waning argument between the city women, Jacqua's attention is once again disturbed by the clank of armor. The ar-mor-clad figure now has been joined by Seja, one of the hill women. Seja attempts to talk to the stranger, who nonetheless remains poised to beat Seja with a cudgel. Finally, Seja points to the knife that the stranger carries, kneels on the ground, and exposes her own throat in a position of vulnerability meant to reassure the stranger of Seja's friendly inten-tions. To Jacqua's amazement the posture works: the stranger finally al-lows Seja to remove the oversized armor that binds her body. Free of the armor, the woman turns to walk with Seja into the heart of the Wan-derground (4–6).

The potential conflict between Seja and the newcomer has been averted by Seja's invocation of an ethic of trust. As such its resolution seems to stand in contrast to the inability of the two City women's com-munication skills to achieve such a result. Yet as we learn portions of the history of the armored woman, Margaret, in later chapters, we are compelled to restructure the dynamics of the apparent comparison Gearhart creates in this first chapter. Margaret's appearance in the Wanderground is a result of a gang rape by two men who clad her in the armor and chased her off by throwing stones at her (21). At her arrival, Margaret suffers from the psychological and physical shock that pre-vents her even from speaking about the attack. Seja's actions begin a long process of healing for Margaret that takes the span of the book (and more) to complete.

The structure of 'Opening' thus sets up an apparent conflict that is destabilized by dynamics later revealed. Whereas Jacqua's assignment of the argument's source to women's social conditioning suggests that community discord lies within the group of women themselves, Marga-ret's history serves to remind the readers of the 'agents' of that condi-tioning. While 'Opening' stresses the importance of learning new methods to communicate and resolve conflict, its deeper contexts reinscribe the ideology that no woman is as great a threat to women as men can be. Yet Jacqua's thoughts on the gentles also cast doubts on any absolutist conclusion: men certainly are named the enemy, yet some exceptions are, at least theoretically, allowed. It seems that 'Opening' thus works best to inscribe the maxim that despite women's very real anger and potential to harm one another, the possibility of and need for alliances against a greater threat must serve to overcome those inner conflicts.

This maxim is scarcely unique to Gearhart's novel. But its commonalities with the writings of separatist theorists such as Eileen Kane end with the processes Gearhart envisions to recognize and diffuse the damage that unacknowledged oppositions among women caused in separatist collectives. These processes are envisioned in a chapter Gearhart entitles 'Sisterblood.' 'Sisterblood' tells the story of two women of extremely contradictory personalities, Ono and Egathese, who must unite to heal a badly wounded dog. Ono finds the dog, Cassandra, with both paws caught in a steel trap. Knowing she needs help to administer first aid to Cassandra, Ono tries to 'summon' Egathese (through mental telepathy) in order to ask her advice (33–34).

To reach Egathese, however, is not as easy as it is to reach many of the other women. Afraid to be discovered so close to the edges of their land, Ono quietly persists in her call until Egathese responds. But her response is less sympathetic than perfunctory, an event that causes Ono to recall Egathese's bias against dogs:

Ono remembered Egathese's carjer, one of those personal bands of prejudice where hard things had to be worked out or at least understood. One of Egathese's carjers was her antipathy to dogs. Ono slipped into a mantle of tolerance, though underneath she wondered if Egathese were not all carjery, so many people and things did she dislike, so grumpy was she always. 'And I guess all that is my own carjery,' Ono thought to herself. (34–35)

That Gearhart creates the word 'carjer' to mean women's personally held prejudices indicates the need for a new conception of character within separatist collective living. In other words, if such a concept were operable within the lexicon of separatist ideology, the adoption of a new term would be unnecessary or at least superfluous. Indeed, Gearhart usually reserves her created language for the superhuman, psychic, or physical powers these future women have developed.

Through the invocation of the concept of carjery, Gearhart creates a space wherein individual quirks or dislikes are accepted and understood. Women within the Wanderground therefore do not spend large amounts of time 'working' on each other's 'patriarchal behaviors' but instead acknowledge that personal bias exists in everyone. Their lives depend much less on the tensions and intrigue that plagued nonfictional collectives caused in part by the constant surveillance of every member's verbal and nonverbal behaviors.

Yet such an acknowledgment within the novel did not mean that prejudice strong enough to cause repeated friction among women went unchallenged, as the continued interchange between Ono and Egathese demonstrates. As soon as Ono completes her thought on Egathese's carjerous nature and admits her own bias against Egathese, Egathese herself interrupts Ono:

'Right.' Egathese had over-received her. 'Better deflect next time when you're open if you don't want me to know all your niggardly thoughts.'

Ono was suddenly flushed with anger. Without even knowing she did it, she told Egathese that she was a crotchety old woman, a bitch – apologies to Cassandra – and that it was a wonder anyone had ever loved her; that, as a matter of fact, she seriously doubted if anyone ever had. (35)

The tensions raised by the conflict between Ono's and Egathese's personality differences escalate to the point that they jeopardize Cassandra's healing. Ono's rage against Egathese causes Egathese to break contact; Ono cannot care for the dog alone.

Once Ono calms down, she concentrates again on reaching Egathese. Egathese fails to respond. Ono finally resorts to a call that she knows will goad Egathese into a response and produces the desired effect:

'Stop it,' [Egathese] flooded back to her. 'You're making me sick with that sticky mollycoddling. I don't want it, Ono. Can you understand that? Talk with me straight and clear. You are a hard woman yourself and not so young either. You do not need those sweet smellings any more than I do. . . .'

Ono was not surprised. She had gotten this response before, and had even sat with Egathese once in sister-search. It was true. The old woman didn't respond to anything but stiff straightness. For her, meanings lay always in the line or maybe in the mass, but never in their interplay. Even her mindstretches seemed sometimes to probe rather than to enfold. Ono answered with seriousness.

'I ask then for sister-search, Egathese, when we go back to the ensconcement. You are carjerous for me.'

'Done.' The extensions were clear now, direct and efficient. 'How is the dog?' (36–37)

Allowances for carjery are made only until disruptive conflicts arise, an event that necessitates a direct confrontation through the 'sister-search.' Again, Gearhart's creation of new words for this old phenomenon suggests at least the need for a different approach to the problem, if not the need for an entire reconceptualization of the problematic itself. Within the community of the Wanderground, both time and geographic place are set aside in order for women to work through their individual conflicts. Such a spatial relocation emotionally and physically removes the tensions that need not endanger the immediate tasks at hand, while it simultaneously keeps the responsibility for the resolution of those tensions firmly on the women themselves. Ono and Egathese thus are able to complete Cassandra's healing process together.

This focus on the individual or individual problems in any collective generally questioned separatist ideologies, operant in groups such as the Furies,[8] that strove to deemphasize individual difference in favor of building collective characteristics and behaviors. As I have mentioned, the structure of and characterization in Gearhart's novel does deflect some attention away from a 'cult of individuality' within the fictional community: there is no protagonist, no single point of view, and characters seldom stand out as memorable individuals in the book. But the sanctity of the individual is in some ways at the heart of the novel and informs many of the processes that work to define Gearhart's text as a utopia. One such process occurs in 'A Time to Sing,' a chapter that both addresses the question of the individual in community and explores the issue of gender construction.

'A Time to Sing' tells the story of the impatience of a young woman, Troja, in her unsuccessful attempts to contact her lover, Rula-ji, through a 'mindstretch' channeled by other women. The chapter opens as Troja once again fails to make contact:

'She cannot be reached.'

'Try again!'

'I tell you, Troja, she cannot be reached. She's clearly elected not to receive any enfoldment. We've been trying for hours.' Blase's impatience punctuated the response.

'Then invade, Blase, invade! We can't wait any . . .' Troja's message trailed off

into thin nothingness. There was a long stretchsilence. An incomplete gram-
matical structure hung over the miles between them, meaning without movement. Troja sent first. 'Blase?'

'Here.'

'I didn't mean . . .'

'I know.' . . . Troja's violence had shaken her. She needed all her energy to
address it.

'I will sing the Kore story,' Troja was sending now.

'Will you wait until ministrations?'

'No. You may not be available tonight and it was with you that I tore the cloth.
I'll sing it now if you'll hear.'

'I'll hear.' (69–70)

Troja's recitation of the Kore story is intended to atone for what the
others call a 'man's crime,' the unwelcomed use of force against another
woman (70). Gearhart's invocation of this essentialist construction – a
'man's crime' even though attempted by a woman – in part reinscribes
separatist conceptions of women's false consciousness as a result of
their patriarchal conditioning. But Troja's atonement, the retelling of
the Kore myth, complicates that construction and helps to neutralize
the problematic of essentialism while it simultaneously places the inviolability of the individual at the heart of *The Wanderground*'s ideology
of community.

The Kore myth (as Troja sings it) begins with a description of the
daughter-mother/lover relationship between Kore and Demeter. Hek,
nephew of the god of the underworld, Dis, falls in love with Kore and
asks to marry her. Kore is happy in her love for Demeter and refuses
Hek. Saddened, Hek turns away only to be confronted by Dis, who demands that Hek prove his manhood and take Kore by force. Hek refuses and says, 'Oft will I ask her, but never can I take her if she does not
choose to go' (74–75). Hek's response immediately compels us to see
him apart from essentialist constructs of men as always willing to violate
women, a shift in perception that complicates the construction of essentialism itself within the novel.

Dis's response, on the other hand, complicates nothing: he is furious
with his nephew. In his rage he curses Hek and turns him into a
woman:

> Smote he his nephew
> With worst of his curses,
> 'Make now the outer form

Fit the truth within:
Be forever woman, impotent she-man!
Hek no more your true name
Be now Hecate!'
Thus the shroud of manhood
Fell from Hek that day. (75)

To increase the punishment Dis takes Kore for himself and forces Hecate to watch as he rapes Kore.

But Dis's actions have an unintended effect. Hecate becomes Kore's maid and, as such, is accepted as a lover by both Kore and Demeter. Though Hek loses his manhood, his respect for Kore's wishes earns Hecate the love Hek could not win. The myth closes with a chorus that is meant to summarize its lesson:

'For though we be entered where the way was not opened, never will they bring us if we do not choose to come. And never may we enter where the way is not opened, never may I bring her if she does not choose to come. Never may she enter where the way is not opened, never may she bring me if I do not choose to come.' (76)

For the community of the Wanderground, the Kore myth serves to teach that love and friendship are gained only through the recognition and respect of every individual's inviolability as a human being. This inviolability becomes a right and a requirement among those in the community; responsibility for its violation rests with both those who commit and those who witness the wrong.

For *The Wanderground*'s community of readers, Gearhart's utopian use of the Kore myth serves a second purpose. Troja sings the myth to atone for a crime ascribed to the character of men. Her song, however, tells of a man who, because he refused to act in a way supposedly natural to his male essence, was turned into a woman. And as a woman, this once-man earns the very thing he sought and seemingly lost in the first place. Gearhart thus disconnects the theoretically clear cause-and-effect relationship between essence and action: if one's actions determine one's gender, as is suggested by the fate of Hek/Hecate, then one's gender cannot entirely (or simultaneously) be said to determine one's actions.

Yet, of course, Troja is said to have intended a 'man's' crime, which at least appears to rely on essentialist theories of identity. I suggest there-

fore that in 'A Time to Sing,' Gearhart does not destroy the binary opposition of 'man' versus 'woman' and its relationship to individual actions created through essentialist constructions but instead confuses
the cause and effect of gendered behavior enough so that no theoretical base for its ideological use can be determined. Rather than a direct
challenge to or negation of separatist ideologies of identity, Gearhart's
utopia provides her community of readers with a process that destabi-
lizes the ideology of identity enough to neutralize its potentially destructive effects. Thus a woman might be chastised for 'acting like a
man,' but through the recitation of the Kore myth the boundaries of a
'male' or 'female' identity are made so unclear as to no longer carry a
meaningful referent within the realm of experience.

The break (or at least softening) of the link between gender and behavior in 'A Time to Sing' not only allows Gearhart to envision a process
that neutralizes the impact that essentialist definitions of identity had
on separatist collectives, it also makes room for an acknowledgment of
strong cultural differences among women themselves. In 'Ijeme's
Story,' for example, a hill woman marvels at the differences between
herself and a woman who lives in the City:

She was a thing out of history to the hill woman: a thickly painted face, lac-
querstiffened [*sic*] hair, her body encased in a low-cut tight-fitting dress that ter-
minated at midthigh; on her legs the thinnest of stockings, and the shoes – were
they shoes? – Ijeme could not believe they fit the same part of the anatomy that
her own boots covered. How could she walk in these spindly things? And with
the flimsy straps that fastened them to her ankles and feet? The dangles that
hung from the woman's ears jangled in tune with her bracelets. She clutched a
cloth-covered purse to her side.

Amazed as she was, Ijeme knew that she was in the presence of a woman –
but not a woman as she knew women. (63)

Ijeme's narrative continues to describe the woman in terms of her geo-
graphical location (the City) and her appeal to men. The City woman's
existence and her difference from the women of the Wanderground
offer no new paradigms for the book's readers, but Ijeme's response to
this woman and the continued existence of their distinct cultures does
create a relationship that offers new conceptual processes for separatist
ideologies of women's community. The overdetermined nature of female community within separatist theory made it crucial for separatists
such as Charoula to insist that all women had to participate in separatist

practice to achieve the goals of a feminist revolution (Charoula 3). Gearhart's novel, however, posits a community that can coexist with very different communities of women without the necessity of its own destruction. Further, though Ijeme is tempted conceptually to separate herself entirely from this other woman, she is compelled to remember that 'what we are not, we each could be, and every woman is myself' (63). Through the vision of the possibility of differences that, while they may erect boundaries among women, do not necessarily threaten the existence of either group, Gearhart negotiates the tautological bind that the concept of the necessary universality of female community created for many separatist collectives.

Differences among women, however, are less problematic for the fictional community than are the conflicts that arise because of the perceived differences between men and women. We have seen the effect that the 'Opening' chapter had in the novel's inscription of the problematic of men: men are, the story suggests, far more dangerous to the community than women ever will be. Indeed, subsequent chapters such as 'The Remember Rooms' continue to reinforce that paradigm. The remember rooms are places wherein women recreate audiovisual images of the history of each hill woman. Their historical repertoire includes rape, mutilation, assault, and countless other acts of violence against women by men and is imparted to younger community members so that they will never forget the history of women's subjugation. The rooms also document the increased restrictions imposed on women spurred by antifeminist backlashes, the pursuit and torture of women who dared to try to escape from the cities, and finally the 'Revolt of the Mother,' a phrase Gearhart creates to describe a rebellion of 'nature' that rendered men and male technology impotent outside the boundaries of the cities. This revolt has ensured the tenuous safety of the hill women: unable to rape, kill, torture, or even work outside the City, most men feign a disdain for any rural pursuit (138–66).

The story of 'The Remember Rooms,' however, excludes the origins of the gentles' community and the history of their relationship with the hill women. As we have seen, the presence of the gentles helps to unsettle fixed notions of male behavior. In fact, one hill woman, because of her working relationship with a gentle during a City rotation, is compelled to reflect on her ideologies of male behavior. Her reflection occurs as a result of the thanks he gives her for a mind 'enfoldment' she did not realize he could consciously feel:

'You're welcome,' Betha said, astonished and pleased to realize that he could respond to an enfolding of care. . . . He was not a woman, after all, and there seemed only the thinnest possibility of mindstretch between them. Somehow men – even gentles – found it difficult or impossible really to share power. . . .

Yet Aaron did respond to enfoldings. 'What makes him a man?' she pondered. She had asked that question in one form or another all her life, but particularly since she began training for her rotation and particularly since she had been living in the City. About most men here she could give a quick easy answer. About the gentles she could not; her absolutes began to get fuzzy around the edges when she tried to make them apply to a man like Aaron. (115)

Betha's questioning of accepted ideologies of male nature from her position within the separatist community itself allows Gearhart to take another step away from the maintenance of a strict separation within the practice of her fictional collective. While the ideological use of sexism as the primary contradiction remains within Betha's theoretical framework (she does, for example, firmly believe that men and women 'are no longer of the same species' [115]), her willingness to maintain a distinction between theoretical purity and practical necessity diffuses the conflicts that a rigid adherence to the theoretical position caused. The apparent paradox embraced by Betha and other hill women in the City works to displace the destructive effects of the entrenched oppositions in which separatist women in nonfictional collectives, such as A Woman's Place or D.O.E. Farm, often found themselves.

But while 'The Remember Rooms' chapter does not contain the history of the hill women's relationship with the gentles, it is flanked by chapters that depict the greatest conflict, sparked by the gentles themselves, that the hill women face. Because this conflict creates the strongest argument among the women in the novel, I suggest that it is the site for the clearest illustration of what I have termed the book's community work. Throughout the novel the reader is increasingly aware of a growing concern among the hill women that the effect of the 'Revolt of the Mother' is not holding. City men have made increasingly successful raids into the country, killing animals and raping women, as the story of Margaret (with which the book opens) attests. And the gentles indicate that they may have information about the raids, information they will divulge if the women consent to meet them as a group in a remote country location.

The gentles' request becomes the focus of the most vehement debate in the book as it is told in 'The Gatherstretch.' Given the histories of the women who first came to the Wanderground, not a few in the group feel that they should have nothing at all to do with the gentles. Their strongly held beliefs reposition into the fictional community the divisive debates over the practice of separatism that, as we have seen in Brody's narrative, were cast as destructive to the survival of separatist collectives. Every woman in the Wanderground joins together to discuss the request, and, as is completely expected by the women themselves, opposing stands are quickly reached:

As Li laid open to the presencing of them all the considerations of the Twelve [the community's representative council], the sense of curiosity and concern was gradually disturbed by an irritation. . . . It was an opposition, a mixing of fire and water. Even before the discomfort was offered up in any formal fashion Zephyr knew its nature: to some of the women it did not matter that the gentles were men sworn to isolate themselves from women; if they were men then there was no reason for concourse with them. Zephyr was impatient. Such an old story. Such ignorance, she felt. The hill women needed the gentles. Women from rotation could say how much. Why always these purists, why always the moralists? She called herself up short. She relaxed her impatience. Far more than she herself wanted to hear, she wanted the dissenting women to be heard. She sighed, then she moved her own presence toward the center of the gatherstretch.

'I name an opposition that lies with us,' she sent. 'It's the belief that we must have nothing to do with men. Will you own it now, you who believe it?'

'I own it.' 'And I.' 'And I.' 'I own it.' 'It is mine.' Immediate responses came from individual women in all quarters. They came with varying degrees of intensity. As Zephyr and the others waited in silence more women joined the owning until altogether more than fifty women declared their opposition to any negotiation with men. (126)

The process Zephyr invokes to hear the women's opposition not only makes room for debate but encourages it. If opposition is fully encouraged rather than avoided, the fact of disagreement among community members no longer carries the threat of disruption or dissolution that it did in nonfictional collectives such as Golden or A Woman's Place. Debate, opposition and difference thus are integrated into the community and the women have little to fear from the fact of opposition itself.

The women's recognition that conflict is one facet of community life, however, is not equivalent to the creation of a process by which to counter the difficulties that a failure of consensus can produce, as the women of the Wanderground seem to have discovered. During the ensuing debate over the gentles' request, women from both sides continue to present their views: reasons for and against meeting with the gentles. The gatherstretch grows more and more hostile until women begin to shout one another down, refusing to listen to or speak with each other. But whereas such an experience within nonfictional collectives often created serious divisions among group members or even began the group's dissolution (recall that the dissolution of A Woman's Place began with repeated failures to achieve consensus), the utopian community creates a process whereby this irresolvable opposition no longer threatens the concept of women's unity. Just as the consensual process in the novel appears to be utterly destroyed, one woman invokes a ritual that effectively neutralizes the unspoken tensions that threaten to lock out any useful solution:

'I ask for the Regard of Tui!' her opening said.

Silence. Miraculous silence. The remembering of who they were. Tui. A moment for the hope of agreement. A moment for the readiness to struggle, a moment for re-commitment to care, whatever the eventual outcome would be. Gradually the presencing grew strong again. Some unity, some bonding on a fundamental level struck an ultimate sense in every gatherstretching woman. . . .

Earlyna asked for the First Acknowledgement: 'Can we, on both sides of the matter, yield?' 'The hardest question of all,' Zephyr thought. She looked hard at her conviction. Would she be willing to refuse the gentles? Yes. If it came to that. And that was all that was required of her – not that she yield, but that she be willing to yield. Every woman in the gatherstretch was examining herself for that willingness. It took a long time. It took particularly long for Wal-kara and others who dissented to find their willingness to go along with a meeting with the gentles. Finally the acknowledgement came: every woman open, every woman willing.

It was Li who asked for the Second Acknowledgement. 'I am called to remind us that at any moment we can cease to be one body. No woman has to follow the will of any other. Always we must know that we can separate, even splinter or disperse one-by-one, for a little while or forever. We rest our unity on that possibility. Do we acknowledge this?' 'No,' thought Zephyr, 'I was wrong. This one's the hardest question of all.' Breaking away, separation, the lack of clear wish in the gatherstretch: it was all threatening, even sickening to her. Yet she knew it was vital. So did all the others. (129–30)

Through this creation of a process for the examination of discord among group members and the provision of a mechanism for the dissolution of the group if conflicts cannot satisfactorily be resolved, Gearhart makes the oppositions among women no longer carry destructive meanings – no longer threaten the group process.

Such a conception, of course, differs from a mechanism that avoids dissolution altogether. What *The Wanderground* does, then, is not to work as a process to avoid opposition or its effects but rather to reframe opposition (or dissolution) in such a way that it is no longer perceived as a failure of group process. If a collective's unity rests on the possibility of its dissolution, then dissolution itself is only one more step in the process of that community's continued existence. Indeed, the gatherstretch closes with a communal ritual that accepts the possibility of irresolvable differences:

> I embrace the possibility: I may yield.
> I may not. Yet I may.
> I embrace the possibility: We may not be together always.
> We may not. Yet we may.
>
> I may not. Yet I may.
> We may not. Yet we may. (130)

Through the imagination of a space wherein this community as a group might exist differently, the experience of difference no longer has the power to threaten the concept of that community.

'But does it work?' Such a question might well be asked of the processes Gearhart envisions in *The Wanderground*. Yet, as Jameson and Suvin remind us, the question of the 'reality' of a utopian society as it compares to nonfictional communities misses the mark of the community work these texts do. The point of *The Wanderground* as I have constructed it is not that it supplies exact blueprints by which separatist collectives might build their own communities but rather that it creates a neutralized, conceptual space wherein women can rethink their ideologies about women, men, separatism, consensus, and community. And the ability to think oneself 'beyond the box' creates the possibility for a renewed growth and continuation of those (albeit changed) communities.

This construction of *The Wanderground*'s literary functions, as I have mentioned, is not shared by every reviewer or scholar who discusses the text. But the reviews of the book did in some ways predict the variety of responses to the work in the academic analyses that followed. For example, in reviews written by authors or for audiences unfamiliar with the existence of separatist collectives, the analysis of the work's utopian gesture often rests in its vision of a separate world for women. Such a response is best exemplified by Bonnie Zimmerman's review for the primarily liberal-feminist audience of *Ms.* magazine, in which she used the text to introduce the concept of separatism and separatist collectives.[9] As a former member of the *Lavender Woman* collective, Zimmerman of course knew that these collectives existed, but she could not be as certain about her audience's knowledge. Similarly, scholars such as Jennice Thomas or Nan Bowman, who seem unaware of the existence of separatist collectives, describe the text as utopian because of its separatism.

However, reviewers who, through lesbian-feminist journals such as *Conditions* or *Sinister Wisdom,* reached audiences more familiar with the politics and practice of lesbian separatism, tended to focus their analyses on the particulars of the life of the fictional community. For Julia Penelope (co-editor of *For Lesbians Only*), the most important purpose of the book is its ability to teach her how to live: 'The Wanderground is unique in that . . . the tensions that hold the stories together are drawn from the world of struggle that we all know too well, and it was from these tensions, and the confrontation of them, that I learned new things about myself and what I want to live for and how I want to live' ('Imagining Our Future' 71). And for Catherine Madsen, who reviewed the book in *Conditions, The Wanderground's* strength rests in the story of the gatherstretch: 'I think the strongest point . . . is Gearhart's presentation of the moral dilemma which the hill women face, and in these sections she becomes a thoughtful chronicler of lesbian-feminist political opinion. 'The Gatherstretch' presents a dispute over separatism with such care that no woman's position is disparaged' (138–39). Though Penelope does not specify what tensions and confrontations she means, it is clear that both she and Madsen interpret the important work of *The Wanderground* as centered more in its visions of community process than in its creation of that community per se.

The impact of *The Wanderground* became apparent in feminist literature other than that of the book's reviews as well. Sidney Spinster, for example, cites *The Wanderground* as an example of what separatists should look toward in their quest for community:

The idea of eventually taking over territory is a popular one. When parting with Separatists I am close to, so that they or I can search for a better place to live, we often express the belief to each other that we'll all live in the same place some day. How we will do that without putting us all in danger is unclear. Visionary works like *The Wanderground* are vitally important for Separatists to write, so that we can figure these things out. (119)

Spinster clearly sees *The Wanderground* as a text that works to build community in its ability to negotiate the 'danger' separatist collectives face. As such, she promotes the novel in her own work on the 'Evolution of Lesbian Separatist Consciousness' and thereby places *The Wanderground* as central to her visions of the continued growth of separatism itself.

Women within residential collectives themselves also incorporated *The Wanderground*'s visionary presence into their ideologies of community. In 1986, members of a second-generation separatist collective,[10] HOWL, called their collective 'a wanderground' and wrote:

We hope to see HOWL become one of those few places where we can continue to train, to revision, to recreate home, family, community. We know from our community women's herstory the difficulties and struggles in group projects of this scope; too much structure, not enough money, the multitude of 'isms.' Let us, in a leap of the imagination, invite our questions and fears to become our allies, our teachers, our guideposts in keeping this project moving and growing. (HOWL n.p.)

Through their juxtaposition of HOWL as 'a wanderground' with their visions for this new collective, the members of HOWL invoke the fictional community as their guide; they privilege a community that 'works' rather than adopting a variety of separatist ideologies as markers for their collective path. Such a historical shift is further indicated by the group's emphasis on its own 'questions and fears': whereas collectives of the 1970s often created their communities in part to distance themselves from their fears, the women of HOWL now place those concerns as their 'allies,' 'teachers,' and 'guideposts.' The process of neutralization posited by Gearhart's utopia thus is inscribed by the members of HOWL as central to their community's actionary existence.

Finally, Gearhart's novel has been used as a symbol by which nonseparatist women also identify their creation of female community. Gearhart herself relates this story about the 'lonth,' her Wanderground term for a subconscious portion of an individual that has the ability to control both voluntary and involuntary bodily functions:

The best story I ever heard about the lonth is that . . . there was a group of women who really wanted this other woman to be a part of them, and she tried and she couldn't because she had these kids to take care of at home and a husband who wouldn't take care of them, who just would not. And she couldn't ever get away, and her guilt was so great, and she'd always have to bring the kids so that . . . she couldn't even come to the meetings. And one night they were all meeting and lo and behold, the door opened and in she walked! And she said, 'I just put myself on lonth and walked out of the house! And he's still back there taking care of the kids.' (Sturgis, 'Transcript of an Interview with Sally Miller Gearhart' 22)

For many lesbian, heterosexual, separatist, and nonseparatist women, Gearhart's *The Wanderground* was important to their lives in its inscription of the processes by which the barriers to female community might be neutralized or negotiated.

But *The Wanderground* did not appeal to every woman's – or every separatist's – concepts of the changes separatism should undertake. In fact, at least one separatist has used Gearhart's text to represent all that she feels is wrong within separatism:

Although I define myself as a Lesbian separatist, and have for over four years, it is often frustrating for me to read articles or letters in womyn's publications by other dykes defining themselves as separatists. More often than not it ends up being something written by some privileged, white, middle-class, able-bodied, thin womon whose analysis of oppression is that 'sexism' is its primary (if not sole) form, and that all other issues – such as racism and classism – are either false 'divisions,' or else will magically disappear at some point (probably after all womyn move to the country à la *Wanderground*), when we all blend together into one homogenized Lesbian culture/lifestyle. (Dykestein 279–80)

Dykestein uses *The Wanderground* as symbolic of separatist refusal seriously or adequately to address oppressions of race and class – in other words, culturally determined, biologically, and socially marked differences among women – within its practice. For Dykestein, while *The Wanderground* may indeed work to create a 'homogenized' lesbian community, that homogenization is accomplished only through the exclusion of women previously marginalized within feminist and separatist ideology.

Such a critique of *The Wanderground* is, in fact, at least partially shared by Gearhart herself. Six years after the novel first appeared, Gearhart wrote that the book made 'no successful attempt to paint ethnic differences among women or to identify conflicts that might arise because of such differences' ('Future Visions' 307). Thus despite *The Wanderground*'s success in its creation of a conceptual space wherein the conflicts over the politics of separatism might be negotiated, Gearhart and others felt the novel fell short in its relation to separatist oppositions over issues of cultural oppressions among women.

Other separatist utopias, however, appear to more fully address the difficult issues of racism and classism within separatism. Gearhart writes of Suzy McKee Charnas's *Motherlines* that 'Charnas deliberately and carefully distinguishes between the Motherlines, delineating particularly Nenisi and the (Black) Conors. Her painting of a whole nomadic culture that barely forces out survival from a bleak landscape sets a tone of hardship, and the resulting behavior is far from the familiar patterns of middle-class life' ('Future Visions' 307). Yet while Gearhart lauds Charnas for her portrayal of racial and class differences among the Riding women, she faults the book for the failure of its author to 'convince the reader of any awareness on her part of the injuries committed on the basis of race' ('Future Visions' 307). I suggest, however, that Charnas's focus on racial or class conflicts among the women appears both at the level of plot that Gearhart notes and on (at least one) level of metaphor as well. In so doing, I contend that Charnas's utopia works within separatist community to envision mechanisms whereby tensions created by the ideological position of race, class, or other social constructions of identity differences in separatist theory might be rendered powerless to destroy the communities within which they operate. That reading and an analysis of the impact Charnas's work has had in separatist communities are the subjects of the final chapter.

LESBIAN HERSTORY ARCHIVES THREE

In 1981, I wrote an article called 'Butch-Femme Relationships: Sexual Courage in the 1950s'. . . and published a short story called 'Esther's Story.' . . . That year marked for me the second McCarthy period in my life. Only this time, many of the holders of truth were women.

They called the organizers of conferences where I was speaking and told them I was a 'sexual deviant,' labeling me as a dangerous person who betrays the feminist cause. The place where I earn my living, Queens College, was visited . . . to warn a group of students and professors about me. 'Don't you know she is a Lesbian? Don't you know she practices s&m? Don't you know she engages in unequal patriarchal power sex?' (Butch and femme is what is meant here, I think.) I was told this when I was called to the Women's Center on campus and asked . . . whether the accusations were correct. Only those of you who remember the cadence of those McCarthy words – 'Are you now or have you ever been . . .' – can know the rage that grew in me at this moment. . . . 'I cannot answer you,' I said, 'because to do so would bring back a world I have worked my whole life to see never come again.' – Joan Nestle, 'My History with Censorship,' in *A Restricted Country*

I arrived Thursday morning prepared to make a final, twenty-four-hour push to read through the remainder of the archives' files. The Bloodroot generously agreed to watch my car overnight although they were to lose one night's profit by my stay in the city. Thursday evening is also the night the archives' collective gathers to conduct business; I looked forward to meeting the rest of the women who do the work crucial to the archives' existence.

Before the collective was to arrive, however, I hoped to finish studying the unpublished documents on separatism. I spent the morning reading theoretical and historical essays, some obviously written for 149 college courses, and finally turned my attention to documents written by members of 'second-generation' (mid- to late 1980s) collectives. Though relatively few in number, these writings were immensely interesting in part because their authors wrote with a decade's worth of collective dissent, failure, and occasional success behind them. One document in particular generated enough excitement that I unthinkingly exclaimed:

'Damn! Would you look at *this!*'

'What?' asked Joan, coming up behind me.

I jumped. Like most people who think out loud, I am astonished every time someone responds. 'Oh, hi . . . I didn't realize you were in the room,' I hedged, slightly embarrassed.

'What's so fascinating?'

'I'm just reading about a 1986 collective . . . HOWL. They talk about all the problems of collective life and then call their collective a 'wanderground.' Do you know how great that is?' I demanded, my excitement quickly returning.

'No,' she said, chuckling. 'But I'm sure it's enormously important.'

'Absolutely! It means that . . .' We were interrupted by a buzz signaling the doorman's need of Joan's presence.

'Would you excuse me for a minute? I really should find out what he wants.'

'Sure,' I said, not a little grateful that the bell put an end to my babbling. Several moments later Joan returned, bearing a small box.

'My book is here!' she exclaimed.

'What book?'

'The anthology of short stories I edited with Naomi Holoch. *Women on Women,* it's called. It's got a story you'd like – Joanna Russ's 'When It Changed' – about a lesbian utopia.'

'Sounds interesting. Allow me to be the first to buy a copy.'

'My pleasure – I'll even autograph it for you.'

'You're on. And speaking of books, I have one for the archives, too, if you don't already have it.'

'Oh? What's that?'

'Susanna Sturgis's *Memories and Visions.* I bought it for the introductory material on utopias and science fiction. I've gotten what I need from it, and I'd be happy to donate it. I found it at Bloodroot's bookstore,' I added, watching her reaction.

She took the book. 'I don't think we have it. Thank you.' If the book's origin upset her, she didn't show it. Instead she opened the box, pulled out a book, inscribed it, and gave it to me.

'Thanks, Joan. I'm going to enjoy reading this,' I said as I glanced over the table of contents.

Shortly before seven that night the rest of the collective began to arrive. I met women whose names were both familiar and unfamiliar to me. We had only a slight chance to talk, however, as most of the evening became occupied with sorting and labeling the week's mail. I watched as everything from diaries, biographies, letters, essays on separatism, softball, and s&m and journals as diverse as *off our backs, Lesbian Contradiction, On Our Backs,* and *Lesbian Connection* were scrutinized, cataloged, and filed. Speaking engagements, participation at future rallies, and requests for donations were discussed and decided upon. By ten o'clock the last member of the group got up to leave, but not without giving me some good advice about places to stay on Fire Island. I worked several more hours and, when I couldn't see well enough to read any further, went in to bed.

'Morning,' Joan yawned as she came into the kitchen. 'Up so early?'

'Just finishing up some loose ends I left last night,' I replied. 'I'm happy to announce, however, that I am com-plete-ly finished. Done.'

'Great! That must feel good.'

'Sure does, and I've got you to thank for most of it. Coffee?' I asked, gesturing to the pot.

She shook her head. 'Don't drink it. Just let me stumble to the fridge instead.'

'No, not this morning. I want to take you to breakfast, okay? Is there a place nearby you like?'

'You don't have to do that,' she replied, surprised.

'It's my pleasure,' I said simply. 'Shall we go as soon as you're dressed?' She nodded; we left for the restaurant a short time later.

'So,' Joan began after our food arrived, 'do you think you've got enough material for your dissertation?'

'Enough material!' I exclaimed. 'That's an understatement. Enough for both the argument and most of the proof. And I'm beginning to think that even the experience of this trip may eventually find its way into the book.'

'What do you mean?'

'My committee keeps pushing me to put myself in the book – to quit posturing on some vague notion of objectivity. And this week has convinced me that there's very little distance between the twenty-year-old arguments over difference I'm studying and the ones on sexuality I hear today. We've changed our objects of disagreement, but we haven't changed the ways we argue them. So who knows? It may be my point of entry. Now, however, I need to focus on getting the academic part of it written.'

'Oh, you will – I've no doubt about that!' she said, laughing. 'But if you're ever low on encouragement or you need someone to read parts of it, call me. I'd be happy to look at it for you.'

How is it that she consistently manages to leave me speechless? I thanked her in my thoroughly inadequate way and paid the bill, and we rose to leave.

'You're leaving for home today?' she asked as we neared the apartment.

'Yes, I'm stopping to see my folks in Chicago, but I should be home in three days or so.'

'Do you have a bit of time before you go? There's something I'd like you to see . . .'

'The trains leave every hour or so. There's several I can catch,' I replied as we reached the door. The doorman opened it for us, and we walked toward the elevator.

Femmish or Womanist? Conflicts between Communities in Suzy McKee Charnas's *Motherlines*

Seven

Suzy McKee Charnas's *Motherlines* is the second novel of a trilogy. The first, *Walk to the End of the World,* is a dystopian tale of sexism carried to its 'logical conclusion.' Charnas prepares us for the third novel, *The Furies,* in the final pages of *Motherlines.* As a separatist utopia, *Motherlines* both parallels and diverges from the concerns of separatist collectives represented in Gearhart's *The Wanderground.* Like *The Wanderground, Motherlines* presents groups of women who must negotiate conflicts that threaten to disrupt or destroy their communities. Unlike Gearhart's text, however, Charnas's fantasy envisions processes whereby social constructions of seemingly biological differences among women – differences that parallel the constructions of race or ethnicity in American society – might be negotiated in such a way as to neutralize their destructive effects. But before I begin to discuss the ways *Motherlines* worked within feminist communities, I will offer some biographical information about Charnas to contextualize her position(s) within the debates that characterized separatist collectives. As we will see, such a contextualization both illustrates the pervasiveness of separatist ideology within feminist communities during the 1970s and challenges some of our more limited conceptions of separatism today.

During the turmoil of the civil rights era and the growth of the radical-feminist movement on the East Coast, Charnas lived in New York City and taught in its public school system. In 1968, just as radical-feminist groups began to form in large numbers, Charnas married and moved to New Mexico, where she has remained with her husband and children through the development of her writing career.[1] As became apparent in the creative process of her novels, however, Charnas's marriage and subsequent move did not mean that she removed herself

153

from the radical-feminist concerns and activism that so enlivened the East Coast.

Charnas originally conceived of her first fantasy novel, *Walk to the End of the World,* as a tale of a world dominated by a rigid religious hierarchy. But through the book's various drafts, Charnas recalls that *Walk* retained only one common element: 'I could not help recognizing that the thread holding it all together was one basic value . . . and that was misogynistic sexism' (Wilgus 22). *Walk* emerged as a dystopian novel of a decaying, patriarchal world wherein women, called 'fems,' are enslaved for the purposes of hard labor, domestic service, and childbearing. The plot focuses on three men, each a social outcast, who travel through the 'Holdfast' in search of one of the men's father. The Holdfast's fems remain primarily in the background until one, Alldera, is required to join the men as their message-carrier because of her running ability.

At this point the world of the fems becomes more clearly defined. As in most slave cultures, the fems are seen by their masters as stupid, lazy, conniving, and complicitous with all the evil or unfortunate occurrences in the society. Holdfast men think the fems capable of only the most limited speech; the fems convey their history, often through song, in a language unintelligible to the men. Further, the fems' hopes are kept alive through stories of 'free fems,' women rumored to have escaped to a growing group of fems living in the wastelands beyond the borders of the Holdfast. Many fems dream of and plan their own escape with the hope of reaching these legendary women before they die.

Such dreams, however, create problems for other fems in Holdfast society. The men have imposed a rigid hierarchy wherein 'boss' fems are severely punished for any infraction, however minor, committed by fems in their charge. This system creates harsh conditions for the fems from birth: rebellious 'cubs,' as femmish children are called, are killed by older fems; adult fems who might create problems for their seniors are often maneuvered by those in charge into low-status, hard-labor work details. Dreams and talk of escape thus threaten the positions of both more privileged fems and those who choose to pursue their dreams.

To curb such rebellious actions among the fems, Alldera has been chosen by an older fem, Matris, to escape into the wilderness and later return with a story of impending rescue by the free fems. Matris hopes that such a story will replace plans for present action with dreams for the future among the discontent and thus ensure the survival of them all. The novel ends with Alldera's escape from the Holdfast, an escape that prepares the reader for *Motherlines*.

Interestingly, Charnas admits that she included Alldera in *Walk* as an afterthought. Alldera was born, Charnas relates, out of a need to balance the overwhelmingly male presence in the novel:

This fem, Alldera, was filling the place taken in so many stories, SF [science fiction] and mainstream, by 'the girl' – she who stands for (and invariably lies down for) that half of humanity that is otherwise absent from the foreground. I know that's what Alldera was doing in the story because I remember saying to myself, there has got to be a woman in here someplace or things are going to look awfully lopsided. Readers, friends as well as strangers, will think you are very odd. ('A Woman Appeared' 103)

Alldera's role, however, quickly changed as Charnas moved through the plot of *Walk*. Because of Alldera's comparatively unique function in this genre (there were, as far as Charnas knew, few literary models for any of her female characters in fantasy ['Dear Frontiers' 67]), Charnas was at a loss to create a stock character in the figure of Alldera. Thus Alldera grew from Charnas's own experiences and those of her friends: 'So I had to make Alldera up, and I composed her using aspects of a friend from my school days and aspects of myself' ('A Woman Appeared' 104).

Alldera's character became so distinct that Charnas felt it 'reshaped the novel entirely' ('A Woman Appeared' 104). More important, Alldera grew to a point that she required her own story, finally told in *Motherlines*. *Motherlines* picks up Alldera's tale as she wanders the desert wasteland beyond the borders of the Holdfast. Charnas describes what she originally had planned for this utopia:

A second book, a sequel to *Walk*, hove onto my mental horizon with Alldera at the helm. Her setting was to be a plains tribe of free, nomadic women, Amazons of the future. I was interested in the potentialities of an Amazon-like society unconstrained by our distorted and fragmentary notions of real, historic Amazons. This time, at least, I had some idea of what the book was about before I began. ('A Woman Appeared' 104–5)

As we will see, however, *Motherlines* deviated from its original conception almost as much as did *Walk to the End of the World*.

Charnas's transition in focus from men and religion to a woman who struggled against the Holdfast's extreme form of sexism may seem to us today to be a familiar shift, followed in content by works such as Margaret Atwood's *The Handmaid's Tale*. Charnas herself initially felt bewildered by the change, though in hindsight she recalled:

Looking back, I now recognize the obvious. During that same winter of 1972–3, I was doing what so many other women were doing and are still doing: reading books like Shulamith Firestone's *The Dialectic of Sex* (Bantam, 1971) and *Sisterhood Is Powerful* edited by Robin Morgan (Vintage, 1970) and participating in consciousness-raising sessions with other women. As my awareness matured – and my anger at finding myself trapped in a powerless class of women – Alldera pushed her way more and more to the heart of the story as I was writing, changing everything around her as my own perspective on her fictional world changed. ('A Woman Appeared' 104)

The structure, plot, and characterization of *Walk* thus changed as Charnas's sociopolitical awareness emerged through her encounters with radical-feminist theory.

More interesting, perhaps, is the fact that Charnas had some direct experience with feminist/separatist collectives, though her experience was not with a rural, residential collective as was Gearhart's. Charnas describes her collective experience as an outgrowth of a consciousness-raising group: 'Let me note in passing that during this time [while writing *Walk*] I was part of a local consciousness-raising group that turned its collective hands and heads to the production of a series of local TV programs by and about women' (Wilgus 22). Charnas's experience with the politics and practice of separatist collectives in New Mexico thus both parallels and diverges from Sally Miller Gearhart's participation. While each woman took part in collective practice within the framework of the modern feminist movement, the differences in their personal lives shaped the ways each received and perceived the politics of separatism within feminism.

For Charnas, separatism is but one method by which to combat sexism. During a discussion of *Motherlines*, Charnas explored her perception of the novel's separatist politics:

[*Motherlines*] also turned out to be about separatism as a solution to sexism – the heart of the book is the all-woman culture of the 'Riding Women.' Some readers will call the Riding Women monsters, since many people find monstrous the idea of women living good, full lives without men. I do not, though separatism is not my blueprint for Paradise and not the only answer to sexism that I hope to explore in fiction. ('A Woman Appeared' 106)

As in *The Wanderground*, then, the issue of separatism is present not as an ideal in itself but rather as part of an analysis that suggests how women might better live their lives in relationship with one another. Yet while Gearhart embraces separatism as the framework in which she would ideally live, Charnas rejects separatism as a personal choice and as the sole solution to sexism, though she acknowledges a place for it in feminism.

Finally, Charnas believes that the genre of fantasy is written from distinctly communal experiences:

I think that fantasy comes not from saga/myth/fairy tale prototypes nor from personal dream-codes, but from a kind of shared reservoir of ideas that women are party to these days, if they care to be and dare to be. . . .

Fantasy is a fine tool for feminist writers and readers, and a lot of women are using it to extend our sense of ourselves and our potentialities, or even just to entertain women without insulting us. ('Dear Frontiers' 66, 67–68)

For Charnas and Gearhart, then, feminist utopias result from socio-political theories (Charnas here implies, I think, radical feminism) and can be used to change the ideas or practice within those social movements.

I include this biographical information and delineate each author's views on separatism not to imply some direct connection between the choice of separatism and other factors such as sexual orientation but rather to suggest how much cultural currency the politics and practice of separatism carried within feminism during the mid- to late 1970s. In other words, while we today might expect someone with Gearhart's philosophical commitment to separatism to have participated within separatist collectives or write within that collective framework, our contemporary view of separatism often obscures the participation of women like Charnas whose political philosophies were less radical. Indeed, women such as Charnas had a unique view of the controversies that surrounded separatism: persuaded by though not committed solely to its practice, these feminists had the opportunity to witness the conflicts surrounding separatism that occurred both within separatist collectives and among groups of feminists who disagreed on the value of separatism to feminism.

It is especially from these tensions among groups of feminists, I think, that Charnas created the different worlds of women in *Motherlines*. *Motherlines* tells the story of both the free fems Alldera escapes to find and the Riding Women whose existence is unknown in the Holdfast.[2] These two groups coexist in the desert, but their relationship is less than amiable: though they trade goods annually, each group expresses a deep hatred, rooted in ideological and seeming biological differences, of the other. I suggest that the community work accomplished by *Motherlines* rests partly in the novel's negotiation of the irresolvable oppositions among the distinctly different groups of women it portrays. The ways the novel anticipates, frames, and neutralizes these oppositions speaks to problems feminists experienced in their relationship with other women whose experiences or philosophies differed from their own, problems often predicated on social constructions of race, sexuality, or class. I proceed with a chronologically based description of the novel constructed to explain the depth of animosity felt by the two groups of women and suggest the connections such animosity had to conflicts among groups of feminists during the 1970s. This chapter concludes with an analysis of the processes by which the text neutralizes the oppositions present in the novel in ways that offer similar processes for separatists engaged in the work of community building.

Motherlines opens as Alldera wanders through the desert after her escape from the Holdfast. She soon comes to the bitter realization that she is pregnant as a result of a rape perpetrated by one of two men in the Holdfast. She walks aimlessly for months in the wasteland and grows increasingly weaker as she finds fewer and fewer things to eat. Several times Alldera attempts to induce an abortion, but

the cub seemed as tough as she was herself and would not die. She felt its heartbeat and its growing, living weight dragging at her body as she traveled. There were moments of intense pleasure at the thought that this cub, at least, the men would never have. Most often she thought, this cub will kill me, it is a weapon of the men planted in me to ruin my escape. (5)[3]

Alldera's 'cub,' as we will see, becomes a key part of the novel's community work.

As Alldera grows certain that she will die, she discovers 'monster' tracks in the muddy bank of a river. Alldera reasons that whatever made the tracks will either feed or eat her and follows the trail until she reaches a cloth bag wedged in a tree. She opens the bag to discover a food cache that ensures her survival for at least another month. Alldera decides that the creatures will return to the food cache and settles down to wait for them (3–7).

The 'monsters' do indeed return. When Alldera finally sees them in the distance, it is through a haze of feverish delirium. She is repelled by their appearance: four legs protrude from a massive body out of which also grows the torso of a 'man.' Alldera watches with horror as the monster comes apart and nearly faints when the 'man' approaches her. As she slides toward unconsciousness, Alldera realizes that the man is actually a woman who has somehow tamed the beast on which she rides. Our introduction to the Riding Women is thus cast in a milieu of fear, mystery, and revulsion. Though the women are Alldera's only hope for survival, their obvious difference from all that she has known nearly causes her to flee from them back into the desert. Only her loss of consciousness and the women's swift response prevent Alldera from successfully completing her escape (7–14).

The women carry Alldera back to their camp, where they keep her in a healing sleep until she is ready to give birth to her child. Through her semiconscious state, the women later tell her, Alldera absorbs some of their culture, dialect, and ideology. She regains full consciousness just before she gives birth to her daughter, an event celebrated by the entire camp (25–30).

Alldera's awakening affords us our first opportunity to experience the intricate lives of the Riding Women. Alldera learns that she will raise her child with four other 'sharemothers,' a practice that will ensure family ties within the camp for Alldera and the baby. Just why the women are interested in creating a family for Alldera is unclear to her: 'Family, kindred; suddenly Alldera was afraid. Perhaps they took her for something other than what she was, to give her such unreserved welcome, warmth in which her bones and sinews seemed to be dissolving. When the mistake was discovered they might turn on her' (30). But before Alldera can discover why she is important to the women, she is interrupted by the arrival of a hard-featured, unsmiling woman called Sheel. Sheel speaks sharply to Alldera, deriding both her appearance and her history as a slave (30–31). Though Alldera is a bit relieved by this more-familiar display of animosity, Sheel's anger reads as characteristically out of place in this utopian society that appears to embody the separatist ideal of cooperative community among all women.

Sheel's animosity stems both from a deep-seated hatred of fems in general and from a specific event of which Alldera is unaware. Alldera was found on a routine check of the food caches maintained by the women for escaping fems such as Alldera, a check that Sheel tried to persuade the patrol to omit on their way home. Had they done so, Alldera almost certainly would have died. This possibility horrifies many women in the tribe; the judgment against Sheel includes half the horses of her band to be forfeited to Alldera's child, for whom Sheel must also share comothering duties. Sheel's hatred for fems makes her even more angry over the ruling than she otherwise might have been; the tensions between Alldera and Sheel, as we will see, come to represent much of the tension between the women and the fems as a whole.

As Alldera spends time in the tribe to recover from her ordeal, she learns a great deal about the ways their society functions. Kinship and family ties are indeed important to the Riding Women: each woman is a genetically similar descendant from an original group of women who were altered by male scientists to reproduce parthenogenetically with the aid of a catalytic 'fluid.' These experiments occurred before the 'Wasting,' an environmental disaster that destroyed much of the earth's life forms and gave rise to the society of the Holdfast as well as that of the Riding Women. (Though the Wasting reads as far more negative than Gearhart's 'Revolt of the Mother,' its results – the maintenance of a separatist community – are the same.) Because the women's reproductive method produces scarce genetic variation, distinct traits develop and remain little changed in each of the 'Motherlines.' If one generation of a line fails to produce children who live to reproduce, a line may be eradicated altogether. Further, the distinct gene pool means that no new lines can be produced (60–62).

For the Riding Women, then, the birth of Alldera's child signifies the potential of a new Motherline, as Nenisi Conor, a member of a black 'race' in the tribe, explains to Alldera: 'New seed, new traits, the beginning of the first new Motherline since our ancestors came out of the lab. That's how important your child is to us. My ancestor, a woman almost exactly like me, stepped out of the lab and lived, and now though she's generations dead there are many of us Conors. So it will be for your child's blood descendants' (62). When Alldera protests that her child will never reproduce parthenogenetically and suggests that the women are 'raising a free fem among you, that's all,' Nenisi replies:

'No, we don't think so. When you came to us, that child was still forming inside you. We made you sleep to rest and strengthen you both. We fed you the milk of our breasts and the food chewed in our mouths, the food of Motherlines that we feed our babies. We fed your child, through your blood while she was still in your womb. We think she's become like our own children. We still feed her – that's why we do all her nursing. You see how healthily she grows, how fast, just like other babies here. We don't have our forbears' [*sic*] wisdom or the wonders of the lab to change her to be like us, but we've tried to do it with what we have.' (62)

Although this utopia would not win awards for biological theory or methodology, the genre's ability to suspend disbelief enables us to realize that Alldera's child represents new potentials for both the women and the fems to whom the child was born. Just what that potential includes is unclear to us and Alldera alike; however, its ramifications become far clearer as the story progresses.

As Alldera's stay in the camp lengthens, she begins to distinguish between the Motherlines and, finally, between the members in each line. To her relief life in the camp seems far more tolerant of difference than was her existence in the Holdfast: cooperation rather than competition forms the basis for the women's culture. In fact, the women seem almost to ritualize the place of difference in their tribe, as an exchange between Sheel, an older woman (Jesselee), and an adolescent girl who rails against several tribal members exemplifies:

'Let's talk about the Stayners for a minute,' Sheel said. 'Myself, I don't like that line. The Stayners pick their noses. . . .

'And I don't like the Ohayars because they're sneaky. The Fowersaths are quick-tempered, the Mellers borrow things and don't return them, the Churrs have ice cold hands, the Hayscalls mumble till you think you're going deaf.'

Jesselee joined in zestfully, 'The Clarishes are vain, the Perikens exaggerate everything, the Farls are lazy and their fingers turn back in a sickening way and make a horrible wet cracking noise doing it besides. As for the Morrowtrows' – she was one herself, of course, gappy-toothed and wide in the jaw – 'they like to stick their noses into everything that happens, especially to children of their own families. . . .

'. . . you'll be related to women all your life whom you don't love or even like – raid mates, pack mates, relatives of your mothers, captives – you may even find that you don't care for your own bloodchildren. Liking women has nothing to do with being related to them, and you might as well work that out and get used to it right here in your own family.' (230–231)

Sheel and Jesselee's advice reflects the ways difference is negotiated in the culture of the Riding Women: each line has its specific traits and, to that extent, both positive and negative characteristics are acknowledged as simply part of a woman's inheritance. Because the traits change little from one generation to the next, even less-attractive characteristics are oddly reassuring, as they place that woman firmly within the history of her family and of the tribe.

For Alldera, such an acceptance of difference is at first a welcome relief in its contrast to life in the Holdfast. But as we watch her become more familiar with the women's culture, we begin to understand that their tolerance has distinct limitations. For example, though Alldera herself is as 'different' from the others as anyone within the camp could be, the women pointedly refuse to speak with her about her past, though they inscribe it into the tribal history by naming her Motherline the 'Holdfasters.' When she finally confronts Nenisi about their behavior, Nenisi responds,

> 'Why think about that? It's over.'
> '. . . It is part of my past, part of my life.'
> 'No. This is all of your life. . . . I hate to see you unhappy. I think that maybe I treat you a little like a child sometimes, and you don't like it. That's good, that you don't like it. Only to me you are still something of a child. . . . And you are not done learning to be a woman. . . .'
> 'I wasn't wakened from a nightmare, you know,' Alldera said. 'The first life was real too. It's as you say – like being born twice.'
> Nenisi looked at Alldera sideways from her eyes with the warm-stained whites, the centers like wet dark stones. 'I'll try to remember that you're growing out of your childhood.' (71)

Nenisi's answer adds to our growing awareness of an unpleasant characteristic of the entire tribe of women: a seemingly immovable resistance to change. Here represented by Nenisi's refusal to acknowledge a past other than that of the tribe, her response to Alldera is mirrored in the behavior of the rest of the women as it concerns Alldera's femmish history.

Implicitly a result of their unchanging genetic makeup, the women's resistance to change precludes improvements in their daily lives, traditions, or outlooks. For example, when Alldera suggests to Nenisi a change in the structure of the granaries so less grain would be lost to scavenging animals, thus improving the chances for the women's horses to survive the dry seasons, 'Nenisi threw out her hands in a gesture of incomprehension. "More for what? We gather enough seed heads for the horses and for our flour. If we had more – well, there'd soon be too many horses to feed and care for and milk. Women aren't slaves to tend the earth. We just live here as best we can"' (72). Yet each year, the women undergo what is to Alldera a painful process of culling the herd because there is too little grass for all the animals. Alldera grows increasingly frustrated with the women's lack of desire to improve their lives (a desire that often meant the difference between life and death for the Holdfast fems); the women cannot understand her restless quest for change that to them seems 'unnatural.' This confrontation between Nenisi and Alldera parallels a larger ideological conflict between the women and the free fems.

The women's reliance on their genetic stability as the basis for their value system produces one further problematic characteristic: a seemingly inbred hatred of the free fems. Sheel, of course, does nothing to hide her feelings from Alldera and maintains her sarcastic demeanor throughout most of the novel. Alldera initially mistakes Sheel's distrust for personal enmity but begins to realize that a certain suspicion is shared by nearly all the women. We are never entirely certain why such animosity exists, though Nenisi's explanation to Alldera of the separation maintained between the women and the fems provides a good indication:

> [Alldera] said: 'You took me in among you; why not the free fems too?'
> 'You have a child here; kindred. The free fems aren't related to anyone. . . .'
> 'How can they be so different that you can't take them in among you?'
> 'Their beginnings and ours differ,' Nenisi said. (59)

Nenisi's answer differentiates the lab-produced, parthenogenic beginnings of the women from the heterosexual origins of the fems as the root of the irresolvable split between the women and the fems. For the women, the fems' method of reproduction codifies the fact that they are an inherent slave race, inherent because their creation relies on male participation in what the women perceive to be a singularly female function (as far as its human component is concerned). And in the experience of the women, the relationship between men and fems has never been anything but that of master and slave. Since for the women one's means of reproduction determines one's personal characteristics, the fems can be nothing but slaves regardless of whether they are actually 'free.' The women pride themselves on their independence and are fiercely protective of their freedom; the fems' slavish 'nature' repels the women as everything they despise and fear. The women therefore prefer to keep their distance from the fems, though they do help them during their escapes and conduct annual trading events with them. That Charnas's construction of the women's suspicion parallels tensions created by social constructions of race among 1970s feminists becomes increasingly clear as the story progresses.

Alldera soon discovers that the animosity between the women and the free fems is far from one-sided. During a trading session two fems spot Alldera and try to persuade, then force, her to escape to their camp. When she refuses and protests that she is not held prisoner, the fems become verbally abusive and attempt to kidnap her. Failing that, one fem taunts her: '"Have they gone and mated you to one of their stallions, then?" she cried. "You got fucked by a horse and you like it, is that what's happened?"' (58). Though Alldera quickly escapes the free fems, their words linger in her mind. Her first response is to attribute the remark to slander born of jealousy, but subsequent events finally reveal to her a far more disturbing base to the fems' accusations than she had imagined.

Alldera learns that the women do indeed 'mate' with their stallions (85). Though Nenisi has told her that the women use a fluid to induce oocyte division, Alldera neglects to inquire about the origin of this fluid. When she finally asks Nenisi what she means by 'matings,' Nenisi tells her that the stallions' sperm have been developed as a catalyst for the division, though they cannot fertilize the eggs themselves. Nenisi attempts to explain the elaborate ritual the women have developed around the annual matings, but Alldera is far too overwhelmed to listen and does not want to understand. Nenisi's revelation culminates a string of shocking events Alldera witnesses in the camp; Alldera decides to leave to join her own 'kind' in the tribe of the free fems (88). Her departure does not resolve any of the conflicts between the two camps; the animosity is, in fact, far too raw at this point to suggest that such a resolution might be possible.

As readers, we have been introduced to the intrigues that characterize the free fems' camp long before Alldera joins it. We witness the fems' life through the eyes of Daya, a former 'pet' fem raised to the comparatively luxurious life of a kept whore. Terribly scarred by her master's male lover for some minor infraction, Daya now holds a precarious role among the free fems, who jealously despise her past role but revere her storytelling abilities. In the camp of the free fems, Daya manipulates people and events to garner the favor of the fem boss, Elnoa, an endeavor in which she is only partially successful. The fems' life thickly contrasts that of the women: giving their obeisance to a single leader, the fems are bound to one another through a shifting mixture of loyalty, disfavor, intrigue, suspicion, and the 'plan,' an endlessly revised plot to return one day to the Holdfast in order to rescue the remaining fems. Finally, their hatred for the Riding Women (or the 'Mares,' as the fems prefer to call them) provides a common value that is in part based on the Riding Women's vow to stop the fems should they ever try to enact their 'plan.'

After her stay with the women, Alldera is less than tolerant of the fems' behaviors that result from so many years in captivity. She quickly earns the enmity of many of the free fems, who distrust her both for the length of time she spent with the women and for the fact that she left her daughter with them. As she did for the women they so despise, Alldera's child represents to the free fems a new, though slight, hope for survival as a race or culture. Because they cannot reproduce without men, the free fems are not increased as a group unless more escape from the Holdfast to join them. Yet since Alldera's escape no others have joined them, an event that helps to confirm increasing fears that everyone – male and female – in the Holdfast might have died from that society's shortage of food and basic necessities. Alldera's child thus represents at least an immediate continuation of their society, if not the hope of reproduction itself. In this one hope, at least, the fems and the women are united.

The lack of any viable means of reproduction for the fems does not keep them from trying to conceive, however. Each year the fems hold a fertility rite during which they attempt to induce conception through an herbal douche prepared by Fedeka, the femmish healer. The liturgy that accompanies the rite begins with a statement of the ways the fems perceive their difference from the women: '"We gather tonight, fems," [Kobba] said, "to try once more to find a starter that will make new life in us. The Mares conceive without men, and so will we – but we won't turn to beasts to do it"' (123). That the fems' revulsion for the women stems from their means of conception – or origins – is further reflected in the fems' names for them: 'mares' and 'horsefuckers' are two frequent examples.

Charnas thus frames the oppositions between these two groups as based in the fundamentally different means of conception each practices. The animosity, of course, has more to do with the ways these origins are socially constructed than it does with the biological procedures they follow. For example, the horse matings are perceived by the fems as penetration (always a degrading act) perpetrated by an animal that in Western ideology claims a 'supermale' status especially in relation to the size of its genitalia. For the fems, then, the horse matings are the ultimate act of degradation and symbolic of the slavery they pride themselves on having escaped.[4]

Further, the means of reproduction and its social constructions within both camps also shape the cultures of the camps. For the women, the horses carry both a material and an ideological significance. The horses provide them with food, clothing, shelter, transportation, species survival, and, in the camp's system of barter, one means of economic exchange. But the horses also symbolize the women's own place in their universe, as Sheel tersely explains to a fem who derides her for her refusal to believe in an all-powerful goddess:

'I would know if there were some single great moon-being controlling all movement in the world – the tides, the growth of plants and creatures, the weather. That's the sort of thing the Ancient men believed in. We women know better. We celebrate the pattern of movement and growth itself and our place in it, which is to affirm the pattern and renew and preserve it. The horses help us. They are part of the pattern and remind us of our place in it.' (190)

The women's camp is thus truly a 'horse culture,' and for them, their difference from the fems is embodied by this deep attachment.

Though the fems do not have a similar, singular symbol on which their culture is based, they do structure their society in ways that reflect their Holdfastish origins. In contrast to the women's loosely structured, widely spread kinship ties, the fems' camp is governed by excessive hierarchy and rigid role structures patterned after the master-slave dichotomy. The fems also reject everything they consider 'marish'; in many ways their society is deliberately structured to oppose what they know of the women's culture. In general, however, the fems' society is informed by relationships of dominance and submission, a slave mentality, and a loathing of anything that resembles heterosexual sexuality. Finally, the fems readily become agents of change and adapt well to it, a trait that results from their dangerous, unpredictable lives in the Holdfast.

Charnas's two societies thus oppose each other over seemingly irre-solvable (because they appear to be based in biological processes) bi-nary oppositions. And while it is true, as Gearhart notes, that Charnas does not portray the problems among women that arise from racial (or even class) differences ('Future Visions' 307), Charnas does create her oppositions around similar social constructions.

The conflicts between Charnas's fictional societies thus parallel the tensions in feminist communities and separatist collectives during the 1970s around the issues of race (tensions that resulted in splits for sep-aratist collectives and subsequent creations of women-of-color collec-tives such as Sassafras), class, and even sexual orientation. (I do not mean to imply that class or sexual orientation is usually constructed as a biological phenomenon as is the characteristic of race. However, the te-nacity with which these social constructions cling or shape individual identities often elevates them in our society to a status similar to that of racially based constructions.) For example, recall the fierce debates on class that occurred in separatist groups such as the Furies collective, de-bates that broke up the collective despite everyone's earnest participa-tion in downward mobility. Remember, too, the arguments on sexual orientation within the lesbian community at this time (and even today) over just who was a 'real' lesbian: one who came out as a result of the feminist movement, or one who was a lesbian before the 'choice' be-came a vogue? This argument in particular implies that lesbianism em-bodies two types of women: those born to it and those who choose it as a result of their politics. And like these tensions within the separatist community, the conflicts within the societies of *Motherlines* seem to have no viable resolution.

As it did in the *Wanderground,* the utopian process of *Motherlines* neu-tralizes rather than resolves these binary oppositions. I suggest that this neutralization occurs through the medium of Alldera, her child, and, surprisingly, Daya as well. We should keep in mind that while such a process does not erase the perceived biological difference – or the so-cial constructions – of the tensions between the two groups, it does re-frame those constructions in such a way as to make the oppositions no longer signify within either camp.

Though she leaves the Riding Women to seek her own kind among the camp of the free fems, Alldera finds that she is now as ill-suited to their life as she was to that of the women. As Daya remarks, Alldera 'be-longs' in neither camp (206). Yet though she may not fully belong in either camp she is still a part of both, a fact that is unique in the experience of each group. Alldera's existence thus begins to blur the boundaries between the two groups.

The resentment Alldera earns from the free fems endangers her position in their camp, though Alldera is unaware of its implications until she is mistakenly caught in a net of intrigue and suspicion cast by Daya. Falsely accused of theft, Alldera is sentenced by Elnoa to confinement in the camp and is banned from running. Alldera both resents and disdains the sentence and attempts to escape the encampment. She is caught and severely beaten by the camp's guards, an experience that appears to break her spirit and elicits a slide into an alcohol-induced stupor (98–121).

Daya, motivated by guilt for her part in Alldera's misfortune, advises Alldera to sneak out of camp and flee to Fedeka the healer's wagon. Alldera complies, but her absence does not entirely remove all the suspicion Daya herself faces in the camp. Some fem, possibly the woman Daya had intended be charged with theft, poisons Daya's fertility douche. Extremely ill, Daya is left with Fedeka by the fems in an effort to save her life (125–30).

Daya's arrival, of course, is less than welcomed by Alldera. In fact, she briefly considers killing the unconscious Daya but refrains for the sake of Fedeka's hospitality. However, as time passes and both fems slowly recover, they cautiously become more friendly toward one another. They talk and argue about the women, Fedeka, the fems, and the fems' plan for freeing the Holdfast. Their relationship begins a new paradigm for the existence of both the women and the free fems.

Alldera eventually leaves on a self-chosen quest to capture and tame several horses stolen from the women's herds by a wild stallion. When she returns, Fedeka is dismayed at the prospect of having anything to do with the horses and demands:

'One thing I want to know now,' Fedeka said, lowering her voice. 'This old stallion, the leader of the herd – did he ever think you were another of his herd? The Mares get male horses to mate with them; weren't you afraid what the stallion might do to you?'

Alldera blinked at her, 'I didn't say I got to smell like a horse, only like myself,' she protested. 'I never gave off the right odors to rouse the stallion. I don't think a horse has any choice about mating, when the time comes. If I had smelled right, he couldn't have helped it, he'd have had to try to mount me. Since I smelled wrong, I never feared to turn my back on him. The women are right – horses may do things that look like what humans do, but the meaning is all changed.' (147)

This exchange marks the transition Alldera has made from her position of immediate revulsion over the women's matings to one that at least begins to understand the perceptions they hold. We become increasingly aware that Alldera is preparing to return to the women's camp; her feat of taming the wild horses is a major step in her attempt to comprehend the women's culture. It is also a step she takes in her personal quest to discover what she can achieve alone, and as such, this action begins to synthesize the society of the fems with that of the women. Alldera continues to improve her riding skills; even Fedeka softens toward the horses when she sees how easily they carry most of her medicinal supplies (157).

To Alldera's surprise, however, it is Daya who becomes fascinated with the horses. Alldera teaches her to ride and notes with a twinge of jealousy that Daya is a 'natural' rider while she rides only to experience the feeling of mastery it gives her (157–58). Alldera's and Daya's experiences with the horses further blur the boundaries Alldera herself has transgressed: as fems, their (even minimal) relationship with horses crosses supposedly irrevocable lines the fems themselves have drawn. Yet Alldera and Daya are isolated cases; as outcasts their 'defection' carries little meaning in the society of the fems as a whole. But their acts suggest a trend that takes shape in surprising ways as the novel progresses.

After nearly a year with Fedeka, Alldera prepares to leave for the women's camp to attend the 'coming out' ritual of her daughter. The ritual marks a child's transition from the 'childpack' to adult status in the tribe and takes place at the onset of the girl's menses. Alldera asks Daya to accompany her, in part to remind herself of her own origins (159). But Daya rightfully worries about her reception in the women's camp:

'There's what you call a family waiting for you to join it, Alldera. What would I be, among the Mares?'

'I've thought about that. You'd be my cousin Daya. As my relation, you'd be their relation.' (159)

Alldera's compromise signals the beginning of a new paradigm for both communities. As the bloodmother of the Holdfaster tent in the women's community, Alldera can claim kin to her other sharemothers

and all their kin. And as a fem, Daya can be understood as Alldera's –
and her child's – cousin and thus kin to them all, if the women accept
the relationship.

They do, however uneasily. Once Daya is accepted by the women, the
importance of her femmish origins begins to fade within the ideology
of the women. She is increasingly expected to act less like a fem and
more like a woman. Although Daya angers the women when she fails,
the fact that they expect such behavior from her at all (as they do from
Alldera) changes the antagonism between them in a way that shifts the
emphasis of conflict away from their different origins. These changes
continue to develop through the child's coming out and growth to adult
status within the tribe.

The coming out of Alldera's daughter appears in the aptly titled section 'Kindred.' All the sharemothers, save Sheel, fervently hope the
coming out goes well. Sheel is convinced it will fail. The ceremony includes a ritual bathing, a recitation of the tribe's history, the singing of
each woman's 'self-song,' and finally a naming ceremony to be per-
formed by Alldera herself. The women accomplish the first parts of the
ceremony without difficulty; Sheel herself concludes those sections by
imparting the tribe's history to the child (200).

But the naming has given Alldera great cause for concern. She
comes to the ceremony with no name for her child; even Daya's suggestions have been of little help:

'How about "Tezera"?' Daya said hopefully. 'That's a pretty name.' She listed
several others: 'Fenessa, Maja, Leesha, Tamsana.'

Alldera disapproved. 'Those are all femmish names that a master would give
a new-bought slave.'

She saw Daya's eyes widen slightly. 'She is a femmish cub, Alldera.'

'Is that what they say at the trade wagon?'

'Yes,' Daya admitted. 'They think she should have a femmish name, ending
in "a." We've all kept our slave names, in respect for our past. And she was conceived back there.'

Alldera laughed. 'A femmish name wouldn't make any difference. The
women would just drop the "a," since to them she's a woman, not a fem – unlike
ourselves, who wobble along somewhere in between.' (205)

Alldera's child remains a source of contention between the women and
the fems even to the point of her naming ceremony. Alldera herself
seems to perceive the child as a woman, not a fem, as is exemplified by
her continued refusal to give the child a Holdfast name.

Yet the name Alldera eventually chooses is not really a woman's name, either. Still pondering the decision, Alldera returns to the ceremony with no name clearly in mind. In the final stages of the ceremony, Barvaran (one of the sharemothers) says to the child:

> 'Your bloodmother has a name for you.'
>
> The child turned to Alldera.
>
> It was two days since the beginning of the coming out. Looking at her now, Alldera saw something new: the color of her hair, which hung dry and clean and fire-glossed. She saw very suddenly and strongly the color of the two men who had fucked her shortly before her flight from the Holdfast: one tawny, the other pale-skinned with thick black hair. She said the first thing that came into her head:
>
> 'You haven't got the color of either of them. Your hair is like the coat of Shayeen's sorrel mare.'
>
> She saw consternation on the women's faces.
>
> Then the child of the tent, oblivious, laughed her shining laugh and announced with her thin arms outflung, 'My name is Sorrel! I'll ride nothing but red horses all my life, so watch out for me, you who keep red horses in your herds!'
>
> 'A lucky beginning,' old Jesselee muttered. She got up and closed the tent. The naming part was over. (207)

Alldera's choice of 'Sorrel,' codified by the child herself, operates on several levels in the text to help neutralize the tensions between the two camps. Most immediately, Sorrel's name belongs neither to the fems nor to the tradition of names in the women's society, a fact that effectively at once places Sorrel within and frees her from both cultures.

More important, however, is the connection to horses that Sorrel's name gives her. As close to their horses as they are, the women do not have a tradition of naming that reflects that bond. Sorrel, born of the fems, is named in connection to the women's horses much more strongly than any woman before her. Symbolically, then, Sheel's insistence that the child can never be a woman because 'the horses won't dance with her' (150) is countered by the bond now formed between Sorrel and the horses.

Further, Sorrel's name also continues to neutralize the opposition between the fems and the ideological structures both they and the women have constructed around the horses. If Sorrel, child of fems, can be named (indeed, help name herself) in connection with the horses, then the boundaries between fems and women predicated on their ideological constructions of their relationship to the animals no longer carry the meanings they once did. That Sorrel is increasingly claimed by both the women and the fems is evident in the final moments of her naming ceremony. The ceremony closes with each sharemother singing her self-song, a ritual geared to impart the history of the individual women to the child and thereby predict her future in the tribe. When Alldera's turn comes, she yields her right to sing to the fem band that has come to trade with the women. They sing a song based on their plan, a song that tells of the hoped-for defeat of men at the hands of fems. Thus Sorrel is placed in the futures of both camps (209).

Yet despite the acceptance Sorrel finds within both groups, her ability to break the barriers between them is limited because she is seen as neither truly fem nor woman. Though she raises the potential for a new relationship between the fems and the women, she alone cannot fully negate the tensions created by the oppositional values each group holds. But her presence, as well as that of Alldera and Daya, does begin a process of neutralization that is completed by the rest of the fems themselves.

As word reaches the fem camp of Alldera's, Daya's, and now Sorrel's life among the women, several fems begin to drift into the women's camp and claim kinship with Daya and Alldera. The women are baffled and often angry at the intrusion, but the fems' claim to kin prevents the women from turning them away. When the fems' bickering, jealous, and possessive ways cause trouble in the camp, the women respond as they would to any other troublesome Motherline: they fine the Holdfaster tent a set amount of horses, clothing, or food stores. And while such fines at one time might have been greeted with derision by the fems, the fems too have begun to change their perception in such a way as to place themselves within the newly forming paradigm and thus within at least some of the values of the Riding Women.

Part of the draw to the women's camp for the fems is, ironically, the horses. Many fems over the years have grown weary of simply talking about their plan: they want to act upon it. Word of Daya's riding ability has drifted back to the fems' camp; several fems, envisioning the usefulness a horse might have in their plan, join Alldera's 'family' in hopes of learning as Daya has learned (215–16).

Yet Alldera is not pleased by the influx of fems. Whereas she once wanted to spark them into acting on their plan, she now wishes to be left in peace in the women's camp. But the fems persist, learning about horses, self-defense, and the geography of the wasteland. In the interim, the fems begin to win the respect of the women when they perform admirably against a band of vicious animals during an attack on the camp (226).

Our final realization that the old paradigms governing both camps no longer carry the cultural currency they once did comes as the fems learn, as a group, to work the horses. At first, such a phenomenon upsets women such as Sheel, who turns away because it hurts too much to see the fems subdue the horses. Slowly, however, even Sheel recognizes the changes in the fems, the women, Alldera, and herself. This recognition comes as Sheel and Sorrel watch Alldera patiently teach another group of fems about their horses. Sorrel is eager to join in the instruction, and Sheel watches with pride as Sorrel aids her mother in the explanations. As she watches, Sheel

had to admit to herself that Alldera was no longer the anxious, touchy, self-absorbed young fem who, thanks to Sheel's own error, had come to Stone Dancing [the women's camp] years ago and lived as a woman. . . .

Sheel could remember now how it had been once: thinking about correcting her original mistake and killing Alldera; rejecting that course because she would not stoop to be outlawed on account of a dirty little fem. The thoughts came back and even some of the fierce feeling, but none of it seemed to apply in the least to Alldera Holdfaster sitting over there teaching her followers about horses.

Which was strange, because plainly the thing Sheel had always feared – that the free fems would truly determine to return to the Holdfast, with unforeseeable consequences for all women – was clearly happening. As a nightmare, the idea had maddened her. Now, with the phantoms of angry imagination vanished in the face of reality, it became simply a fact of the future to be dealt with in its time. (239–40)

Sheel is saddened by the loss of her hatred but finds herself incapable of mustering the old ferocity toward Alldera or any of her kin.

With this portrayal of Sheel's grudging acceptance, Charnas completes the neutralization of the conflicts raised by the irresolvable binary oppositions constructed within the two groups. This neutralization, begun when Alldera – and later Daya – are accepted as kin within the women's camp, is furthered during Sorrel's coming out and naming ceremony. It is only completed, however, when the tensions that govern each group as a whole no longer carry the significance they once did. The fems' acceptance of the horses as useful to their own purpose functions to destabilize their vows never to have any concourse with the animals and, as such, blurs the ideology around which they negatively constructed the women's origins. Similarly, the women's recognition that they have changed and will continue to do so in response to the fems aligns them with the fems themselves, who have had to change and adapt continually to survive their unstable world. Thus change, hallmark of the fems' origins, no longer threatens the material and ideological worlds of the women. Though the two societies may never create one culture, they now exist in the world in such a way as to aid and assist each in the pursuit of their separate(?) goals, a fact that should ensure the future of both groups.

While the reviews of *Motherlines* were less enthusiastic (and certainly less numerous) from the lesbian community than were the reviews of *The Wanderground*, they nonetheless focused on the depiction of conflict between the two groups of women in the text as the crucial theme of the novel. For example, though she is quite disturbed by the use of horses in the women's reproductive cycle, Pamela Johnston in a review written for *Sinister Wisdom* finds the conflict in values a 'major theme' of the novel:

It is not so much the *presence* of this offensive material [the horse matings] in *Motherlines* that I find disturbing, but the *use* of it. It is clear that a major theme of the book is the conflict in values between the two groups of wimmin. But Charnas never finds quite the right voice or the right perspective to make the reader feel that she has not been offended. (96)

Johnston further criticizes the novel for its 'misrepresentation' of lesbian sexuality in its emphasis on penetration: 'Is Charnas confusing the pleasures of vaginal stimulation with a desire for penis-like penetration?' (96). Johnston's review thus aligns her with the inflexible position of the fems prior to the integration of their concerns with those of the Riding Women. And like the fems, Johnston conflates reproduction (via the stallions) with sexuality (the women's is explicitly lesbian). Unlike the fems, however, Johnston does not achieve a change in perception that allows her to reconceptualize the differences she finds between the women and what she feels lesbians should embody. And while we might blame Johnston's position on a failure of the text's community work (or even of the reviewer's), the fact that Johnston focuses

on, analyzes, and is willing to discuss *Motherlines*'s portrayal of difference among women is in and of itself a change for a community that
was, as we have seen, loath to claim any difference at all among women.
Other reviewers did embrace the difficult questions Charnas addressed as a necessary new step for the lesbian community. Two of the
book's most enthusiastic reviewers were, interestingly, Sally Gearhart
and Joanna Russ. In an interview for the *Lesbian Insider/Insighter/Inciter*,
Gearhart discusses the issue of the Riding Women's lives: 'I'm glad the
women's community has gotten on to *Motherlines* because it's got the
toughness maybe that is more our reality. Or at least it might be what's
happening with women in Algeria, or South America, or somewhere
where life is really much tougher than here in middle-class America'
(Klasse 7). Gearhart's comment characteristically both embraces and
pushes away the connection she wishes to make between a 'reality' of
the women's community and how that reality might be represented in
the discourse of the novel. But while she may be unsure whether it is
politically correct to claim the stark lives of the women for 'middle-class
America,' she nonetheless acknowledges that the issues at work had
more to do with women's perceptions of themselves and other women
than they did with any direct confrontation of the patriarchy. Similarly,
Joanna Russ lauds Charnas's careful descriptions of the book's unique,
if contradictory, characters and cites the depiction of conflict in the
characters' lives as 'rock-bottom political awareness if ever any existed'
("'Listen, There's a Story for You . . .'" 91).

What reviewers Johnston, Gearhart, Russ, and others such as Dorothy Allison[5] have in common is that whether or not they liked the book,
all point to *Motherlines*'s model of the interactions of different groups of
women as its central theme. And although I can find no written evidence as to how *Motherlines* might have been incorporated into the
worldview of separatists who strove to create community through collectivity, I suggest that for most of its readers, *Motherlines*'s impact was
felt most strongly in its portrayal of the cultural differences and the resulting conflicts among groups of women.[6]

In summary, then, the community work accomplished by Charnas's
Motherlines both parallels and diverges from Sally Miller Gearhart's *The
Wanderground*. In its portrayal of separatist women who struggle to survive and to improve their communities independent of male interference, *Motherlines*, like *The Wanderground,* speaks to issues found primarily within separatist collectives of the 1960s and 1970s. But

Motherlines also addresses conflicts within feminist communities experienced as opposition between groups of feminists altogether: oppositions not unlike those faced by separatist groups (such as that of the *Lavender Woman* collective) characterized by differences of race, class, or sexual orientation. And while Charnas's text does not provide a 'blueprint' by which feuding feminist factions might resolve their differences, the novel does offer new ways to think about the social constructions of differences among us that seem so impossible to negotiate.

Through her suggestion that symbols of a deeply felt experience (for example, biologically separate origins) upon which difference is constructed can be integrated into the ideologies and practice of opposing cultures, Charnas allows us to envision a world of women wherein differences such as those of race, class, or sexual orientation might not be insurmountable. Indeed, *Motherlines* suggests processes by which each culture's origins offer something necessary for the survival of the other, processes that thereby reconceptualize difference and its social constructions for separate groups of feminists. These processes, like those in *The Wanderground* and many other separatist utopias, define the community work of a genre written by, for, and in response to separatist discourse of difference as it appeared during the 1960s, 1970s, and early 1980s.

BLOODROOT FIVE

No one was home at the inn when I made my way back to Bridgeport late that afternoon, but I knew I'd find several women over at the restaurant. I packed my bags and loaded the car, making sure to set aside both my wallet and the book Joan had given me. A short time later I walked over to say goodbye to the collective.

'Dana!' a voice called as I entered the restaurant. 'Hi! How'd your last day go?'

I squinted through the semidarkness. 'Great – thanks, Dot. I got everything finished.'

'Glad to hear it! What are you up to now?'

'Just came in to say goodbye. And pay my bill.' I smiled, turning to Noel, who was seated at the cash register. 'How much do I owe you?' She figured the bill and took my check.

'Listen,' I began, hesitating. 'Before I go I want to show you something. A book you might like for the bookstore.' I handed her *Women on Women*. She glanced at the title, took in the names of the editors. 'There's a great selection of stories,' I rushed to open the front cover, 'it's even got Sapphire's "Eat." We were thrilled to publish that one in *Common Lives*. And Becky Birtha, Lee Lynch, and Willa Cather. It looks really good.' I didn't want to leave her much room for disagreement.

'Well,' Noel said, doubtfully, turning the book over in her hands several times, 'I don't know. We'll have to talk about it at the next meeting.'

'Good!' I exclaimed, sounding as enthusiastic as I could. 'I hope you'll carry it.'

'Hey!' Another voice emerged, this time from the kitchen. 'You weren't going without saying goodbye, were you?' I turned to see Lori walking from behind the counter.

'Of course not,' I smiled. 'In fact, I came in for that very reason.'

'Let us walk you out to your car, then,' she said. Dot nodded in agreement.

'I'd like that. And Noel, thanks – I hope I see you again soon.'

'Sure, no problem. Don't be a stranger.' She waved as we left the restaurant.

'Lori, Dot,' I began as we reached the car, 'thanks for everything. And when I get it all done, I'll send you a copy, okay?'

'You do that,' Lori replied. 'And have a safe trip.' We exchanged hugs and I got into the car, hoping to make western Pennsylvania by nightfall.

Separatist Discourse and the Continuing Search for Female Community

CONCLUSION

In 1983, a Ph.D. student at Purdue University wrote:

Because of [the] urge toward utopian vision in feminist critical theory, I would be willing to predict that the novels I can count today are only the first blossoming of this genre. . . .

As a matter of fact, the genre seems amazingly prolific in recent years, and there is little indication that this tendency for feminists to think about utopia is in any danger of dying out. It seems, indeed, to be simply the beginning of a major focus in feminist thinking. (Thomas 28)

When Jennice Thomas predicted the bright future for feminist utopian literature, she did not realize that the early 1980s would be the final years of this particular surge of interest in utopias to feminist authors. Indeed, after 1983 only a few separatist (or even more broadly feminist) fantasy novels were published. Though critics such as Susanna Sturgis recently noted the sudden decline in the numbers of published feminist utopias (*Memories and Visions* 2), they have been at a loss to explain the decrease.

I suggest that if we read these texts in light of the community work of separatist discourse, we might provide a plausible explanation for both the specific decline in the numbers of utopian stories and novels and the more recent influx of lesbian or separatist writings in genres unexplored by 1960s and 1970s authors. As we have seen, white women's roles in the leftist protest movements of the 1960s compelled many to agitate against oppression in their own lives. If these women were to make the Left pay attention to their concerns, however, they had to develop a theoretical analysis of sexism that challenged the primacy of class and racial oppression. Radical feminism's analysis of sexism as the primary contradiction seemed perfect for the task: bold enough to con- 179 front Marxist theories of class, sexism as the primary contradiction also differentiated radical feminists from both the liberal and socialist factions of women's liberation.

Yet radical feminism's theoretical conceptions of and writings on sexism influenced more than just the discursive exchange of ideas. These works motivated an entire segment of women to develop theories and practice of female community within radical feminism, a phenomenon that led to the popularity of separatism as an active method by which to confront sexism. I have suggested that an examination of these documents in light of their community work yields a useful understanding of the attractions these texts held for feminists and provides an example of the interactions between discourse and practice within social communities.

What we found in radical feminist theory, however, suggested that the connections between a discourse and its culture are more complex webs of interactions than they are simple, direct lines. By this I mean that the discourse of radical-feminist theory not only sparked a variety of feminist practices, it also led to new genres of literature within which women responded to and wrote new ideas for that practice. Radical-feminist theory of sexism as the primary contradiction, for example, both created concepts of the universality of women's oppression and encouraged the practice of female community as one response to that oppression. Yet that practice aided the development of a specifically separatist theory and activism that simultaneously challenged and expanded feminism's understanding of sexism in women's lives.

What emerged from debates over separatism within radical feminism, however, created another set of problems both represented in and responded to through separatist discourse. Lesbians' anger at the homophobia they found in feminist groups, women's anger at sexism in general, and the infectious zeal for revolutionary change that affected everyone encouraged debates over the political and social effectiveness of separatism as a tool both for women's self-growth and for the eradication of sexism. But these discursive debates began to divide the same women separatism was meant to unify; with such high stakes as the revolution at hand, women on all sides had little patience for those who disagreed with their views.

Women's anger and energy, as well as the discursive call to separatism, encouraged the development of another phenomenon as well. During the 1970s, women increasingly practiced their politics through the creation of separatist business and residential collectives. By this time, however, separatist ideologies of women, men, and their respective 'natures,' bantered about so easily in theory, began to impact the practice of feminist activism in ways for which few were prepared. Sexism as the primary contradiction or, more specifically, its extension to name all men the enemy created binary categories of oppositions that, while they may have made it easy to take a strong stand against sexism, also eroded the practice of female community so cherished within the visions of separatist theory.

What, then, was at stake? Creating a binary other in the figure of men compelled separatists to place all their collective conflicts outside the practice of women themselves. And while some of the opposition women faced did indeed come from external sources, much more of it came from conflicts among collective members themselves. Yet because the binary structures in separatist ideologies constructed women as unable to really hurt or oppress other women, there was no conceptual structure through which to claim responsibility for destructive behavior and thus begin the difficult process of creating coalitions among diverse groups of women. The conceptualization of such a process was, in fact, made all the more difficult through separatism's frequent refusal (mandated by the lack of complexity in any binary opposition) to fully acknowledge that women claimed different, not necessarily compatible, social identities. The visible demon 'other' in separatist ideology became the unrecognized demon within for separatist practice.

Construction of a demonic, binary other thus ironically provided the impetus toward female community and made the success of that community impossible. During the mid-1970s, then, a new genre of separatist literature – historical narratives of separatist collectives – sought to depict collective life in hopes of encouraging women to join or form collectives. But the high rate of internal discord and collective failure described in these narratives worked to produce nearly the opposite effect. And the continuation of separatist ideology of binary oppositions within these narratives, such as we have seen in Michal Brody's *Are We There Yet?* or in Joyce Cheney's *Lesbian Land,* did little to create new paradigms that might provide a more useful way to think through community conflicts.

By the late 1970s, the community work of these narratives also compelled women who had been instrumental in the creation of separatist theory and in the call for female community to revise their visions drastically. Again, the importance of practice to theory and theory to practice became very clear as women such as Sarah Hoagland or those in the Seattle collective tried to repair, through theory, the damage done to separatist visions of female community. Yet they, too, found no effective way to write separatism beyond the paradox of the patriarchy: still the unconquerable oppressor, the patriarchy was cast in these works as that which made collectives both necessary and impossible.

Because the patriarchy remained a paradoxical sign for female community even after separatists responded to collective narratives, the quest for female community was at a conceptual standstill. Unable to break through the patriarchal gates, female community nonetheless remained the only effective weapon in the battle against oppression. At this crossroads, then, the genre of separatist utopian literature served to move concepts of community beyond their ideological binds. Fantastical enough not to be limited by representations of community found in separatist theory or historical narrative, separatist utopias worked in their communities to establish new paradigms for both the quest for and shape of that community.

Because utopias in general can be read as processes that neutralize (not destroy) socially constructed binary oppositions, separatist utopias such as Gearhart's *The Wanderground* or Charnas's *Motherlines* worked to move women beyond binary conceptions of opposition into frameworks that created new paradigms for conflicts within the community itself. In short, separatist utopias created new paths for female community just when that community faced a conceptual and material dead end. And perhaps the work of separatist utopian literature is also marked by shifts in the realm of feminist thought: no longer is it feasible or helpful in feminist theory to work within the constructs of binary oppositions.

The use of binary oppositions in practice, however, proves to be more difficult to overcome. Despite the occasional (re)birth of second-generation separatist collectives such as HOWL, the collapse of collective endeavors continued throughout the 1980s. Though there is little written evidence to support my claim, I feel that the continued decline of collective success contributed directly to the decline in interest in separatist utopias as a way to create community for authors and readers alike. Whether there is some direct correlation, scholars interested in feminist utopias have noted a decline in the publication of novels and stories, as I have mentioned, and in the interest in utopian fiction by feminist readers.[1] Those few separatist fantasy novels published after 1983, such as Katherine Forrest's *Daughters of a Coral Dawn,* ceased to focus on community issues and turned increasingly to individual and couple concerns.[2] Further, I find it interesting that of all the separatist utopias written between 1960 and 1990, not one was written by a woman of color or envisioned a utopia for women of color. Such a phenomenon, I think, points to the avoidance of the genre by women who were important characters in the separatist theories that resulted in divisive conflicts within feminist communities. In other words, women who often were most affected or excluded by the ideologies in contention chose not to use the vehicle of utopian literature to convey their concerns, create coalitions, or construct their futures.

When we, as scholars, analyze the various genres of separatist discourse, it is of course interesting and challenging to apply our training in literature as we search for literary tropes, conventions, rhetorical devices, feminist themes, or representations of gender. But it is crucial to remember that our objects of study are not simply esoteric: these works had material effects on the lives of women, effects that in turn influenced the creation of other discourses as women worked through the problems of community they encountered in both theory and practice. Nor are these effects historically contained. In 1988, Sarah Hoagland and Julia Penelope cited community as one of their underlying values in the creation of *For Lesbians Only* (9); Bev Jo, Linda Strega, and Ruston in 1990 named creating community as one of the reasons they wrote *Dykes-Loving-Dykes: Dyke Separatist Politics for Lesbians Only* (1).

Thus the use of literature to aid in finding, creating, and shaping separatist community continues, though the genres within which such community work is attempted have changed. No longer the prerogative of fiction, autobiographical narrative, or even theory, the genre through which lesbian authors now present their goals for community is often what I would term the community-help text. By community-help I mean texts that identify specific problems within lesbian community and offer advice or even exercises for women to complete to overcome these problems. Books such as Sarah Hoagland's *Lesbian Ethics,* for example, are offered to the lesbian community in the following manner:

I wrote this book in the hope that it will provoke discussion which will take us beyond where we are in our understanding and actions. I will consider this book successful if it inspires lesbians to get together in something like consciousness-raising groups to discuss the suggestions here: how they might work, whether they apply in different situations, whether they are capable of helping us avoid some of the pitfalls we have faced up to now. (xiii)

Hoagland's text, then, is meant to describe a new system of values ('ethics') intended to recreate the lesbian community in a lasting way. Other recent texts such as JoAnn Loulan's *The Lesbian Erotic Dance* (Spinsters, 1990), Merilee Clunis's *Lesbian Couples* (Seal Press, 1988), and the Boston Lesbian Psychologies Collective's *Lesbian Psychologies* (University of Illinois, 1987) all approach their subjects from a nonfictional, problem-solving paradigm but do so within a framework that relates these (often) personal issues to the larger concerns of community building. By contrast, most new lesbian fiction (represented in, for example, the Womankind Book's brochure)[3] falls within the genres of love stories or detective/murder mystery novels and focuses primarily on one or two main characters.

Just as the choice of genre in the search for community over the last ten years has changed, so too the discursive debates that divide the separatist and lesbian communities have shifted. While issues of race, class, and the degree to which one should practice separatism remain as concerns within the separatist community, they are no longer at the forefront of the community's most divisive arguments. Rather, issues of sexual practice – specifically sadomasochism, pornography, and to a certain extent butch-femme history – divide the lesbian community today in ways that race, class, and separatism did during the 1970s.[4] For example, when Sarah Hoagland states that 'the norms we've absorbed from anglo-european ethical theory promote dominance and subordination through social control (what I call heterosexualism) . . . [and] thwart rather than promote the successful weaving of lesbian community' (*Lesbian Ethics* 2–3), or, conversely, when Pat Califia writes that the community 'insists on sexual uniformity and does not acknowledge any neutral differences – only crimes, sins, diseases, and mistakes' (*Macho Sluts* 9), they line up on sides of a debate that lays claim to very deep community stakes.

As a lesbian sometimes involved in community building over the last years, I have watched and participated in the debates over sexual practice. What interests me about the debates is not so much their outcome – lesbians always have made and will continue to make their sexual choices despite (sometimes because of) opposition[5] – but the divisive rhetorical processes these debates and confrontations follow and the community work they continue to do. For example, when Hoagland argues that sadomasochism is 'inconsistent with Lesbian-feminism' ('Sadism, Masochism, and Lesbian-Feminism' 153), or when the authors of *Dykes-Loving-Dykes* insist that 's&m is part of [the] Lesbian-hating influences' (Jo, Strega, and Ruston 191), they do so from ideologies of the ways women should behave in community with one another, ways that were preceded in analyses such as that of Ti-Grace Atkinson's early views on lesbianism and feminism.

Conversely, when Califia responds that feminists who support or remain silent on antiporn legislation are nothing more than hypocritical supporters of a right-wing status quo (*Macho Sluts* 23–25), she uses an argument similar to that of Radicalesbians' critique of heterosexual feminists who refused to support lesbians in the women's movement. Thus while the field of contention has changed, the underlying structures of the debate – who belongs to the community, who has chosen not to belong, who never had the right to belong in the first place, and who is able to referee these categories in general – have remained basically the same.

I do not raise the specter of the current sex debates in the lesbian community to take sides or judge the weight of the arguments but rather to point out how important the issue of female community continues to be in separatist, lesbian, and feminist circles today. Further, written discourse remains a crucial medium in the exchange and creation of ideas on community as participants continue to express their views through theoretical essays and autobiographical narrative, along with the more predominant genre of community-help literature.[6] And there is even some indication that the genre of fantasy literature will once again be utilized in the process of these debates, as is evident by the recent publication of Califia's *Doc and Fluff*.[7] Though the advent of fiction in this argument is still too recent to allow an accurate assessment of its effects, its existence further attests to the importance that literature continues to carry in the creation and growth of women's communities today.

NOTES

1 Bonnie Zimmerman's distinction between separatism and cultural feminism is quite useful: she finds separatism's primary goal to be the creation of political theory and alternative institutions designed to bring about sociopolitical change; cultural feminism, on the other hand, is characterized by its goals to define a 'uniquely female nature, vision, and artistic expression' (*The Safe Sea of Women* xiv).

2 For recent examples of the debate over cultural feminism, see Linda Alcoff, 'Cultural Feminism versus Post-Structuralism: The Identity Crisis in Feminist Theory'; Alice Echols, *Daring to Be Bad: Radical Feminism in America, 1967–1975;* Teresa de Lauretis, 'The Essence of the Triangle or, Taking the Risk of Essentialism Seriously: Feminist Theory in Italy, the U.S., and Britain'; Diana Fuss, *Essentially Speaking: Feminism, Nature, and Difference;* and Naomi Black, *Social Feminism.*

3 My use of 'community work' is only partly meant to invoke Jane Tompkins's analysis of 'cultural work,' by which she means the ways these texts 'provided men and women with a means of ordering the world they inhabited' (Tompkins xiii), though my study is indebted to her analysis of the power discourse has to shape a society's thoughts and actions. Like Tompkins, I feel these texts clearly had designs on their readers, but I argue that in the case of separatist discourse, those designs were intent on revolutionary change rather than the more liberal project of ordering, maintaining, or making changes in an extant social system. Thus while Tompkins intends the term 'cultural' to connote a nationally based movement or social ideology, I use 'community' to refer to a very historically and politically specific group that utilized its discourse to shape itself as a community so that it might revolutionize American society rather than reorganize that society on existing principles. The 'work' of the texts I will examine, then, is intended for a much smaller, more intimate audience than 187

those Tompkins scrutinizes; we are both, however, interested in the sociopolitical and material functions such texts had within their respective communities.

4 In this claim I am again indebted to Tompkins's understanding of the value a reading of community work can produce.

5 Discussion of this link has begun to appear in recent studies of lesbian communities. See, for example, chapters 9 and 10 of Lillian Faderman's *Odd Girls and Twilight Lovers.*

6 Prof. Diane Crowder (Department of French, Cornell College) has compiled a bibliography of feminist utopias that includes over eighteen separatist utopias published in English. Parts of that bibliography appear in the bibliography section of this study.

7 This reading of the function of feminist utopias is quite common in contemporary critical theory. See, for example, Frances Bartkowski, *Feminist Utopias;* Angelika Bammer, 'Visions and Re-Visions: The Utopian Impulse in Feminist Fictions'; and Jennice Gail Thomas, 'Coming Home to Mother: Feminist Utopian Visions, 1880–1980'; Lillian Faderman, *Odd Girls and Twilight Lovers;* and Sonya Andermahr, 'The Politics of Separatism and Lesbian Utopian Fiction.' For an alternative overview of utopian literature and its connection to lesbian communities, see Bonnie Zimmerman, *The Safe Sea of Women.*

CHAPTER 1: RADICAL FEMINISM AND FEMALE COMMUNITY

1 When I use phrases that imply that the radical feminist, women's liberation, or even feminist-separatist movements were first engaged in the 1960s, I do not mean to suggest that these movements or their ideas were unique to the twentieth century. The nineteenth-century feminist movements in the United States and Britain, of course, debated these theories and ideologies, as did women before them. But often to their chagrin today, activists from the 1960s recall not knowing of their predecessors' work; to them, the ideas and debates of the modern feminist movement truly were unique.

2 For an early overview of radical feminist theory, see Hester Eisenstein, *Contemporary Feminist Thought.*

3 The prowoman line stated that women were aware of the charade they played daily; that, in effect, all actions that might be conceived of as stereotypically feminine were, in reality, means of survival in the patriarchy. Thus women were always conscious of the things they did that might seem misogynist and were actually only victims (never agents) of the oppression of women. See, for example, Redstockings, *Feminist Revolution* or the original three volumes of New York Radical Women's *Notes.*

4 The glaring absence from this list – and from recent historical accounts of

radical feminism – is Cellestine Ware's *Woman Power: Transitions in American Feminism.* This work is, as far as I know, the only book written by a woman who identified herself as a black radical feminist. The book offers analyses similar to those found in Morgan's and Koedt, Levine, and Rapone's anthologies but also exhorts women of color to recognize the sexism of black men and the necessity, therefore, of radical feminism. That this book has disappeared from most modern accounts of radical feminism reflects, I think, the willingness to cast the movement as of concern only to white women, a willingness that is shared, interestingly enough, by white and African-American feminists alike.

5 The capitalization of 'Movement' reflects the combination of the various protest movements of the 1960s and 1970s. The description that follows is indebted to Echols.

6 As I have pointed out in the fourth endnote, however, many women of color chose radical feminism as the framework in which to fight for liberation. Women such as Cellestine Ware, Florynce Kennedy, Elizabeth Sutherland, Enriqueta Vasquez, Charlotte Cohen, and Anita Cornwell and groups such as the short-lived Black Feminist Organization may be less-often remembered than their white counterparts, yet they too were an integral force that shaped radical feminism. But the consensus today is that African-American feminists in particular were disillusioned by radical feminism and went on to form analyses that better incorporated theories of racial and gender difference. See, for example, Gloria Joseph's discussion 'White Promotion, Black Survival,' in Joseph and Lewis, eds., *Common Differences: Conflicts in Black and White Feminist Perspectives,* 19–42.

CHAPTER 2: BEYOND SEXUALITY

1 Despite the impact of feminism on lesbians throughout the United States, it is important to remember that many lived their lives and defined themselves with little or no reference to feminist theory or feminist organizations. This study, then, does not speak to, or for, those lives.

2 Such a definition appears to have been culturally reinforced by the Kinsey study on the prevalence of homosexual experiences among men in the United States.

3 *Vice Versa,* the only lesbian journal known to precede the *Ladder,* ran between June 1947 and February 1948. It was published privately and distributed in the Los Angeles area. The *Ladder* was published monthly and included news, public forums, letters, book reviews, fiction, poetry, and artwork.

4 For another excellent study on butch-femme visibility, see Madeleine Davis and Elizabeth Lapovsky Kennedy, 'Oral History and the Study of Sexuality in

the Lesbian Community: Buffalo, New York, 1940–1960,' or their subsequent book on that community, *Boots of Leather, Slippers of Gold.*

5 For a discussion of the general theoretical implications of this essay, see Hester Eisenstein, *Contemporary Feminist Thought,* 48–57.

6 The capitalization of 'lesbian' that Bunch and others use reflects the origins of the term in Sappho's island of Lesbos. Today, most writers do not use the capitalized form; I follow that tradition.

7 The influence of Adrienne Rich's conception of the lesbian 'continuum' found in her 'Compulsory Heterosexuality and Lesbian Existence' exemplifies the strength which the concept of the lesbian as the quintessential feminist eventually gained within the feminist movement.

8 For an explanation of Atkinson's earlier views, see chapter 1.

CHAPTER 3: LESBIAN SEPARATISM AND REVOLUTION

1 Separatist use of essentialism in theoretical works did not carry the same connotations of naiveté that they do today. In fact, separatist reliance on essentialism was meant to drive the categories of men and women farther apart as well as to represent all the rage separatists felt over the fact of women's oppression. For recent reconsiderations of the issue of essentialism, see Diana Fuss, *Essentially Speaking,* and Teresa de Lauretis, 'The Essence of the Triangle.'

2 This view of the false consciousness behind women's oppressive behaviors toward one another can be found, too, in radical-feminist works such as Firestone's *Dialectic of Sex.* The ideology is, however, far more often articulated in lesbian-separatist theory.

3 Barbara and Beverly Smith provide such an analysis in their article 'Across the Kitchen Table: A Sister-to-Sister Dialogue.'

4 For similar views from Native women, see Chrystos, 'I Don't Understand Those Who Have Turned Away from Me,' in Moraga, Anzaldúa, and Bambara, eds., *This Bridge Called My Back,* 68–70, and 'Nidishenŏk (Sisters).'

5 While I do not discuss this aspect of oppression, it is important to cite infiltration and agitation around issues of race, class, and sexual orientation by undercover FBI agents, especially after it was known that Susan Saxe (wanted for bank robbery and as an accomplice to murder) hid successfully from police in separatist land collectives. For more information on the Saxe case, see Jill Johnston, 'The Myth of Bonnies without Clydes: Lesbian Feminism and the Male Left.'

INTRODUCTION TO PART 2, NARRATIVES OF SEPARATIST COLLECTIVES

1 It is impossible to know exactly how many separatist collectives were

formed during this period: many folded before they properly began, others left no written record with which to verify their existence, several continue to thrive in quiet obscurity. From the scant written evidence, discussions with women involved in a variety of separatist collectives, and my best guess, I would cautiously estimate that at least one hundred residential collectives existed sometime between 1965 and 1980 (in some cases continue to do so) and that well over one hundred business collectives were formed. This study excludes collectives that left no written record. The experiences of those women, I think, might make a wonderful oral history project.

2 Most of these early narratives were typed on loose-leaf paper, untitled, and unpublished. A few, however, such as Juana Maria Paz's *La Luz Journal* or Womanshare Collective's *Country Lesbians* (Womanshare, 1976), were privately published and distributed through the women's community for a nominal fee. These early accounts in some ways homogenized the experience of women's collectives in that they made it possible for women to realize that collective problems were not unique to the individual groups.

CHAPTER 4: *ARE WE THERE YET?*

1 I use the term 'politics' here to refer to much more than theories of government or community organization. Lesbian-feminist politics often include a code of behavior to govern one's relations with other lesbians and – less significantly – with mainstream society. My use differs from the term 'values' in that values describe a code of personal ethics ideally held by lesbians, ethics that govern behavior not necessarily related to other people. I am thinking here of vegetarianism as a lesbian value, for example, though even that has recently developed into a political issue (i.e., the 'politics' of meat).

2 Individual differences, of course, did make their way into the pages of many collective narratives and statements. But even when they were printed, such statements were expressed as 'some felt that . . .' or 'some said . . .' and so on. To name those who disagreed with collective consensus was, as far as I can determine, a relatively rare practice.

3 The critique that lesbian feminism's avoidance of sexual issues resulted from an initial need to make lesbians acceptable to heterosexual feminists is detailed in chapter 2.

CHAPTER 5: EXCOMMUNICATING THE PATRIARCHY

1 Cheney chooses, as have many of our authors, to use alternate spellings of 'woman' and 'women.' She leaves contributors' spellings as they were submitted. Cheney's choice reflects an understanding of language as important to the

creation and shape of our perceptions of the world. Since 'woman' includes the masculine, and since the word was derived from an Anglo-Saxon term that meant the 'wife of man,' radical-feminist use of alternate spellings was in part a protest against mainstream understandings of femaleness and a reflection of the ideology that held women could recreate themselves if they followed alternative codes of language, fashion, and behavior. The same ideology often is at work in the names women choose for their collectives or themselves.

2 Cheney notes later in the introduction that she is only concerned with collectives that specifically intended to create community: 'This book is about only one segment of lesbians in the country; that is, womyn whose main focus has been to make community' (10).

3 Portions of *La Luz Journal* also can be found in Cheney.

4 Many land collectives, for example, called in outside friends to mediate collective impasses caused by divisions over social constructions of difference.

5 For an explication (and dismissal) of both positions, see Sarah Hoagland, *Lesbian Ethics*, 95.

6 For such an argument, see Anna Lee, 'The Tired Old Question of Male Children,' in Hoagland and Penelope, eds., *For Lesbians Only*, 312–15.

7 See, for example, Nancy Breeze's 'Where the Boys Aren't!!' in Hoagland and Penelope, eds., *For Lesbians Only*, 309–12.

8 Today, of course, such an analysis seems overly simplistic when viewed through the lens of Foucault's theories on the nature, effectiveness, and limitations of mainstream institutions. In an era that made connections between always-destructive male behavior and institutional oppression, however, state apparatuses clearly were seen as the culmination of oppressive power.

INTRODUCTION TO PART 3, SEPARATIST UTOPIAN LITERATURE

1 For a good discussion of the contexts and currents that influenced Marxist scholars in their perceptions of utopia and their subsequent shifts in perception during the mid-1900s, see Jean Pfaelzer's introduction in *The Utopian Novel in America, 1886–1896: The Politics of Form*.

2 For representative examples, see Natalie Rosinsky, *Feminist Futures: Contemporary Women's Speculative Fiction;* Jennice Gail Thomas, 'Coming Home to Mother: Feminist Utopian Visions, 1880–1980'; and Lee Cullen Khanna, 'Women's Worlds: New Directions in Utopian Fiction.' A comprehensive list of feminist critical theory on the genre of utopian literature appears in the bibliography.

3 Such a reading is inaccurate because it assumes that separate spaces for women or a female community were the ideals these texts envisioned. As we

have seen, however, separatism was an established practice well before any of these second-generation separatist utopias were written and thus, by definition, could not be the element that characterized these texts as utopian. Despite her dedication to the historical and material values of Marxist criticism, Angelika Bammer shares this view of separatism as the utopian gesture in these texts.

4 Recent critical interest in lesbian and gay history has begun to encourage readings that focus on connections between these utopias and lesbian communities. Bonnie Zimmerman's *The Safe Sea of Women*, for example, offers an insightful discussion on the ties between works such as *The Wanderground* and the desire to form lesbian communities. Zimmerman's reading, though, sees these novels as blueprints for an ideal community, not as processes in and of themselves. The discussion on lesbian utopian literature in Lillian Faderman's *Odd Girls and Twilight Lovers* reads these works in a similar fashion.

CHAPTER 6: WE MAY NOT BE TOGETHER ALWAYS

1 Critics tend to approach this text in four distinct ways. Frances Bartkowski's *Feminist Utopias* dismisses it because of its essentialism. Natalie Rosinsky's *Feminist Futures: Contemporary Women's Speculative Fiction* examines the text but only as it embodies literary tropes that she searches for throughout utopias; in other words, the politics of separatism are more ignored than dismissed. Jennice Gail Thomas's dissertation 'Coming Home to Mother: Feminist Utopian Visions, 1880–1980' examines *The Wanderground* and other utopian novels in order to point out the 'feminist' themes they embody, but 'feminism' is never differentially defined. The most common response, however, is exemplified by Nan Bowman Albinski's *Women's Utopias in British and American Fiction:* Gearhart's novel and separatist utopias like it are analyzed for the ways they incorporate feminist ideals of social and political life.

2 For a work that relies on essentialist constructions, see Gearhart, 'The Future – If There Is One – Is Female,' in McAllister, ed., *Reweaving the Web of Life*, 266–84. For a work that relies more heavily on theories of social construction, see Gearhart et al., 'A Kiss Does Not a Revolution Make: A Search for Ideology.'

3 In this regard Gearhart's conceptions are quite similar to French feminists' theories of women's language such as those found in Hélène Cixous's 'The Laugh of the Medusa.'

4 Gearhart may also be attempting to convey a multicultural dimension to her community through the representation of spirituality and her use of names in the text. For example, many of the rituals enacted by the women in the novel catch the rhythms of Native American poetry and religious liturgies. I also have

been told that the name 'Seja,' given to a character present in several of the novel's chapters, translates as 'sister' from a Slavic language.

5 All references to the novel are taken from Sally Miller Gearhart, *The Wanderground: Stories of the Hill Women*.

6 Because separatism could not by itself ensure the reproduction of women, separatists often were interested in theories of parthenogenesis or other reproductive methods that did not involve intercourse with men. For an exploration of those theories within the context of lesbian separatism, see Laurel Galana, 'Radical Reproduction: X without Y,' in Covina and Galana, eds., *The Lesbian Reader*, 122–37.

7 For a thorough discussion of *Wanderground's* essentialist constructions, see Zimmerman, *The Safe Sea of Women*, 147–48.

8 Alice Echols suggests that the Furies disbanded in part because no facet of the women's lives was untouched by collective structures: they shared living, sleeping, and eating spaces, clothes (including underwear), possessions, money, food, work, partners, and so on.

9 See Bonnie Zimmerman, 'Beyond Coming Out: New Lesbian Novels,' 65.

10 By 'second generation' I mean a collective begun and maintained after the initial rush to separatist collectives had waned. HOWL is very conscious of its status as a separatist collective in a postseparatist world and thus is careful to distance itself from those ideologies that created so many problems in the 1970s.

CHAPTER 7: FEMMISH OR WOMANIST?

1 For further biographical information, see Neal Wilgus, 'Interview with Suzy McKee Charnas.'

2 In the description that follows, I adhere to Charnas's choice of nouns and pronouns to describe the two groups in the novel: 'fems' are always those conceived in the Holdfast; 'women' refer to those of the Motherlines' tribes. Never does Charnas refer to a fem as a woman, even in the generic sense of the term. The title of my chapter, too, is meant to reflect Charnas's use of these terms.

3 All references to the novel are taken from Suzy McKee Charnas, *Motherlines*.

4 Though Charnas was, of course, taking sexism to its extreme in her portrayal of the Holdfast and of (apparently) heterosexual women's lives within such a system, she was shocked to receive several letters from women who said she had depicted their lives realistically (Wilgus 22–23).

5 Dorothy Allison, 'Once upon a Feminist Future,' 22.

6 Such a reading contrasts with others that concentrate on the novel's vision of separation from (or opposition to) men as its central focus. See, for example, Natalie Rosinsky, *Feminist Futures: Contemporary Women's Speculative Fiction*.

CONCLUSION: DISCOURSE AND THE SEARCH FOR COMMUNITY

1 Susanna Sturgis noted that during the early 1980s, women buying books at a feminist bookstore turned increasingly from fantasy and science fiction to romance (*Memories and Visions* 5–6).

2 Forrest's novel uses the utopian setting as a backdrop for the love story of her protagonist. Other examples include works that began to lean more toward individual problems during the late 1970s (Donna J. Young's *Retreat! As It Was!* and Rochelle Singer's *The Demeter Flower*); those that fully engage individual and couple problems as their focus (Pamela Sargeant's *The Shore of Women*); and the more ambiguous utopia of Sheri Tepper's *The Gate to Women's Country.*

3 Womankind Books is a fairly comprehensive source for what I would call lesbian popular fiction as well as for nonfictional lesbian books in print. Their brochure is available from Womankind Books, 5 Kivy St., Huntington Station, NY 11746.

4 I realize that I am using the terms 'separatist' and 'lesbian' interchangeably here. Since the mid-1970s, separatism has grown to be almost exclusively lesbian, and texts that focus on the lesbian community are nearly by default separatist. My point is that when searching for separatist concerns of community in the 1990s, one must look almost exclusively in lesbian sources.

5 I do not intend to argue that we choose our sexuality somehow free of our cultural conditioning. But the history of lesbian sexuality, at least as it has been written in the last century, indicates that harassment ranging from verbal and physical threats to imprisonment and even death has not been able to suppress lesbian sexuality in its various forms – butch/femme, lesbian-feminist, sadomasochism, and others I am unaware of – over an extended period of time.

6 I have mentioned essays written by Sarah Hoagland, the authors of *Dykes-Loving-Dykes,* and Pat Califia. See also theoretical and autobiographical accounts in *Against Sadomasochism* and the ongoing debates in various issues of *On Our Backs, Outlook,* or *Lesbian Connection.*

7 *Doc and Fluff* portrays a singularly odd relationship between the 'Angels' motorcycle gang and a lesbian-separatist rural collective whose members practice sadomasochism as a purification rite. The combination of sadomasochism and separatism is as shocking today as was Gearhart's portrayal of the relationship between the Hill women and the gentles in 1978.

BIBLIOGRAPHY

Abbot, Sidney. 'Lesbians and the Women's Movement.' In Ginny Vida, ed., *Our Right to Love*, 139–43.

Abbot, Sidney, and Barbara Love. *Sappho Was a Right-On Woman*. New York: Stein and Day, 1972.

Adair, Nancy, and Casey Adair. *Word Is Out: Stories of Some of Our Lives*. New York: New Glide, Dell, 1978.

Albinski, Nan Bowman. *Women's Utopias in British and American Fiction*. New York: Routledge, 1988.

Alcoff, Linda. 'Cultural Feminism versus Post-Structuralism: The Identity Crisis in Feminist Theory.' *Signs: Journal of Women in Culture and Society* 13/3 (spring 1988): 405–36.

Alice, Gordon, Debbie, and Mary. 'Addition to the First Printing of "Lesbian Separatism: An Amazon Analysis."' In Sarah Lucia Hoagland and Julia Penelope, eds., *For Lesbians Only*, 307–9.

———. 'Directions.' In Sarah Lucia Hoagland and Julia Penelope, eds., *For Lesbians Only*, 40–44.

———. 'Problems of Our Movement.' In Sarah Lucia Hoagland and Julia Penelope, eds., *For Lesbians Only*, 379–94.

———. 'Separatism.' In Sarah Lucia Hoagland and Julia Penelope, eds., *For Lesbians Only*, 31–40.

Allen, Jeffner. *Lesbian Philosophy: Explorations*. Palo Alto, Calif.: Institute of Lesbian Studies, 1986.

Allison, Dorothy J. 'Once upon a Feminist Future.' Review of *Wanderground* and *Motherlines*. *off our backs* 9/3 (March 1979): 22.

Andermahr, Sonya. 'The Politics of Separatism and Lesbian Utopian Fiction.' In Sally Munt, ed., *New Lesbian Criticism*, 133–52.

Anderson, Linda, ed. *Plotting Changes: Contemporary Women's Fiction*. London: Edward Arnold, 1990.

Andreadis, A. Harriette. 'The Woman's Commonwealth: Utopia in Nine-teenth-Century Texas.' In Ruby Rohrlich and Elaine H. Baruch, eds., *Women in Search of Utopia*, 86–98.

Atkinson, Ti-Grace. *Amazon Odyssey*. New York: Link Books, 1974.

Average, Salad, Beth Butler, and others. 'Sassafras: A Land in Struggle.' N.d., 2 pp. Separatist Land Space File, Lesbian Herstory Archives, New York City.

Badami, Mary Kenny. 'A Feminist Critique of Science Fiction.' *Extrapolation* 18/1 (December 1976): 6–19.

Bammer, Angelika. 'Utopian Futures and Cultural Myopia.' *Alternative Futures* 4/2–3 (spring/summer 1981): 1–15.

———. 'Visions and Re-Visions: The Utopian Impulse in Feminist Fictions.' Ph.D. dissertation, University of Wisconsin–Madison, 1982.

Barr, Marleen S., ed. *Future Females: A Critical Anthology*. Bowling Green: Bowling Green State University Popular Press, 1981.

Barr, Marleen S., and Richard Feldstein, eds. *Discontented Discourses: Feminism/ Textual Interventions/Psychoanalysis*. Urbana: University of Illinois Press, 1989.

Barr, Marleen S., and Nicholas D. Smith, eds. *Women and Utopia: Critical Inter-pretations*. Lanham, Md.: University Press of America, 1983.

Bartkowski, Frances. *Feminist Utopias*. Lincoln: University of Nebraska Press, 1989.

———. 'Toward a Feminist Eros: Readings in Feminist Utopian Fiction.' Ph.D. dissertation, University of Iowa, 1982.

Baruch, Elaine. 'A Natural and Necessary Monster: Women in Utopia.' *Alterna-tive Futures* 2 (winter 1979): 28–48.

Benhabib, Seyla, and Drucilla Cornell, eds. *Feminism as Critique*. Minneapolis: University of Minnesota Press, 1987.

Benstock, Shari, ed. *Feminist Issues in Literary Scholarship*. Bloomington: Indiana University Press, 1987.

Berson, Ginny. 'Only by Association.' *Furies* 1/5 (June–July 1972): 5–6.

Bethel, Lorraine. 'What Chou Mean We, White Girl.' *Conditions* 5 (July 1979): 86.

Birkby, Noel Phyllis, and Leslie Kanes Weisman. 'A Woman-built Environment: Constructive Fantasies.' *Quest* 2/1 (summer 1975): 7–18.

Birkby, Phyllis, Bertha Harris, Jill Johnston, Esther Newton, and Jane O'Wyatt, eds. *Amazon Expedition: A Lesbian-Feminist Anthology*. Albion, Calif.: Times Change Press, 1973.

Black, Naomi. *Social Feminism*. Ithaca: Cornell University Press, 1987.

Blanchard, Margaret, Ann Gordon, Chris Novak, and Lucky Sweeney. 'The Power of Fantasy (A Conversation).' *Women* 5/1 (1976): 14–17.

Bloodroot Collective. 'Bloodroot: Brewing Visions.' *Lesbian Ethics* 3/1 (spring 1988): 3–22.

Bristow, Joseph, ed. *Sexual Sameness: Textual Difference in Lesbian and Gay Writing.* London: Routledge, 1992.

Brody, Michal. *Are We There Yet? A Continuing History of* Lavender Woman: *A Chicago Lesbian Newspaper, 1971–1976.* Iowa City: Aunt Lute Book Co., 1985.

Brown, Elsa Barkley. 'Womanist Consciousness: Maggie Lena Walker and the Independent Order of Saint Luke.' *Signs* 14/3 (spring 1989): 610–33.

Brown, Rita Mae. 'Living with Other Women.' In Nancy Myron and Charlotte Bunch, eds., *Lesbianism and the Women's Movement,* 63–67.

———. *A Plain Brown Rapper.* Oakland, Calif.: Diana Press, 1976.

Bunch, Charlotte. 'Learning from Lesbian Separatism.' *Ms.* (November 1976): 60+.

———. 'Lesbian-Feminist Theory.' In Ginny Vida, ed., *Our Right to Love,* 180–82.

———. 'Lesbians in Revolt.' In Nancy Myron and Charlotte Bunch, eds., *Lesbianism and the Women's Movement,* 29–37.

Califia, Pat. *Doc and Fluff.* Boston: Alyson Press, 1990.

———. *Macho Sluts.* Boston: Alyson Press, 1988.

Callahan, Pat. 'Women's Future Explored.' *Spartan Daily* (San Jose State University), March 12, 1976.

Carby, Hazel V. *Reconstructing Womanhood: The Emergence of the Afro-American Woman Novelist.* New York: Oxford University Press, 1987.

Charnas, Suzy McKee. 'Dear *Frontiers:* Letters from Women Fantasy and Science Fiction Writers.' *Frontiers* 2/3 (Fall 1977): 64–68.

———. *The Furies.* New York: Tom Doherty Associates, 1994.

———. 'Interview.' *Janus* 3 (winter 1977): 40.

———. *Motherlines.* New York: Berkley-Putnam, 1978.

———. 'A Woman Appeared.' In Marleen S. Barr, ed., *Future Females,* 103–8.

Charoula. 'Dyke-Separatist Womanifesto.' *Tribad: A Lesbian Separatist Journal* 1/1 (May 1977): 1–4.

Cheney, Joyce, ed. *Lesbian Land.* Minneapolis: Word Weavers, 1985.

Chrystos. 'I Don't Understand Those Who Have Turned Away from Me.' In Cherríe Moraga, Gloria Anzaldúa, and Toni Cade Bambara, eds., *This Bridge Called My Back,* 68–70.

———. 'Nidishenŏk (Sisters).' *Maenad* (winter 1982): N.p.

Combahee River Collective. 'A Black Feminist Statement.' Reprinted in Cherríe Moraga, Gloria Anzaldúa, and Toni Cade Bambara, eds., *This Bridge Called My Back,* 210–18.

Contemporary Authors: A Bio-Bibliographic Guide to Current Writers. Various volumes. Detroit: Gale Research Co.

Cornwell, Anita. *Black Lesbian in White America.* Tallahassee, Fla.: Naiad Press, 1983.

Covina, Gina, and Laurel Galana, eds. *The Lesbian Reader.* Oakland, Calif.: Amazon Press, 1975.

Cowan, Liza. 'Separatism Symposium.' In Sarah Lucia Hoagland and Julia Penelope, eds., *For Lesbians Only,* 220–34.

Crowder, Diane G. 'Separatism and Feminist Utopian Fiction.' In Susan Wolfe and Julia Penelope, eds., *Sexual Practice, Textual Theory,* 237–50.

Daly, Mary. *Gyn/Ecology: The Metaethics of Radical Feminism.* Boston: Beacon Press, 1978.

———. *Pure Lust: Elemental Feminist Philosophy.* Boston: Beacon Press, 1984.

Darty, Trudy, and Sandee Potter, eds. *Women-Identified Women.* Palo Alto, Calif.: Mayfield Publishing Co., 1984.

Davis, Elizabeth Gould. *The First Sex.* Harmondsworth, England: Penguin Books, 1971.

Davis, Madeline, and Elizabeth Lapovsky Kennedy. *Boots of Leather, Slippers of Gold: The History of a Lesbian Community.* New York: Routledge, 1992.

———. 'Oral History and the Study of Sexuality in the Lesbian Community: Buffalo, New York, 1940–1960.' *Feminist Studies* 12/1 (spring 1986): 7–26.

Day, Phyllis J. 'Earthmother/Witchmother: Feminism and Ecology Renewed.' *Extrapolation* 23/1 (1982): 12–21.

d'Eaubonne, Françoise. *Le Féminisme ou la mort.* Paris: Pierre Horay, 1974.

de Lauretis, Teresa. 'The Essence of the Triangle or, Taking the Risk of Essentialism Seriously: Feminist Theory in Italy, the U.S., and Britain.' *Differences* 1/2 (summer 1989): 3–36.

———. *Feminist Studies/Critical Studies.* Bloomington: Indiana University Press, 1986.

———. *Technologies of Gender.* Bloomington: Indiana University Press, 1987.

Diner, Helen (Berta Ekstein-Diner). *Mothers and Amazons.* New York: Doubleday, 1973.

Dolkart, Jane, and Nancy Hartsock. 'Feminist Visions of the Future.' *Quest* 2/1 (summer 1975): 2–5.

Duberman, Martin, Martha Vicinus, and George Chauncey, Jr., eds. *Hidden from History: Reclaiming the Gay and Lesbian Past.* New York: Meridian, 1990.

Dunbar, Roxanne. 'What Is to Be Done?' *No More Fun and Games* 1 (October 1968): Unpaginated.

du Plessis, Rachel Blau. 'The Feminist Apologues of Lessing, Piercy and Russ.' *Frontiers* 4/1 (1979): 1–8.

Dykestein, Naomi. 'One More Contradiction.' In Sarah Lucia Hoagland and Julia Penelope, eds., *For Lesbians Only,* 279–81.

Echols, Alice. *Daring to Be Bad: Radical Feminism in America, 1967–1975.* Minneapolis: University of Minnesota Press, 1989.

Eisenstein, Hester. *Contemporary Feminist Thought.* Boston: G. K. Hall, 1983.

Elliot, Robert C. *The Shape of Utopia: Studies in a Literary Genre.* Chicago: University of Chicago Press, 1970.

Engels, Friedrich. *The Origin of the Family, Private Property and the State.* London: Laurence and Wishart, 1972.

Evans, Sarah. *Personal Politics.* New York: Alfred A. Knopf, 1979.

Faderman, Lillian. *Odd Girls and Twilight Lovers.* New York: Penguin Books, 1991.

Farewell, Marilyn. 'Heterosexual Plots and Lesbian Subtexts: Toward a Theory of Lesbian Narrative Space.' In Carla Jay and Joanne Glasgow, eds., *Lesbian Texts and Contexts,* 91–103.

———. 'Toward a Definition of Lesbian Literary Imagination.' *Signs: A Journal of Women in Culture and Society* 14 (autumn 1988): 100–119.

Firestone, Shulamith. *The Dialectic of Sex.* New York: William Morrow and Co., 1970.

Firestone, Shulamith, and Pam Allen, eds. *Notes from the Second Year: Women's Liberation.* New York: New York Radical Women, 1970.

Fitting, Peter. '"So We All Became Mothers": New Roles for Men in Recent Utopian Fiction.' *Science-Fiction Studies* 12 (1985): 156–83.

Fitzgerald, Karen. 'The Good Books: Writer's Choices.' *Ms.* 14/6 (December 1985): 80–81.

Forrest, Katherine V. *Daughters of a Coral Dawn.* Tallahassee, Fla.: Naiad Press, 1984.

Foster, Frances Smith. 'Octavia Butler's Black Female Future Fiction.' *Extrapolation* 23/1 (1982): 37–49.

Freedman, Estelle. 'Separatism as Strategy: Female Institution Building and American Feminism, 1870–1930.' *Feminist Studies* 5/3 (fall 1979): 512–29.

Freibert, Lucy M. 'World Views in Utopian Novels by Women.' *Journal of Popular Culture* 17/1 (1983): 49–60.

Fritz, Leah. *Dreamers and Dealers.* Boston: Beacon Press, 1979.

Frye, Marilyn. 'Some Reflections on Separatism and Power.' In Sarah Lucia Hoagland and Julia Penelope, eds., *For Lesbians Only,* 62–72.

Furie, Noel. 'Mes Amies, Les Amantes.' *Common Lives/Lesbian Lives* 20 (summer 1986): N.p. Biographical statement, p. 129.

Fuss, Diana. *Essentially Speaking: Feminism, Nature, and Difference.* New York: Routledge, 1989.

Gearhart, Sally, and Jane Gurko. 'The Sword-and-the-Vessel versus the Lake-on-the-Lake.' *Bread and Roses* 2 (spring 1980): 26–34.

Gearhart, Sally Miller. 'The Future – If There Is One – Is Female.' In Pam McAllister, ed., *Reweaving the Web of Life*, 266–84.

——. 'Future Visions, Today's Politics: Feminist Utopias in Review.' In Ruby Rohrlich and Elaine H. Baruch, eds., *Women in Search of Utopia*, 296–309.

——. 'The Spiritual Dimension: Death and Resurrection of a Hallelujah Dyke.' In Ginny Vida, ed., *Our Right to Love*, 187–93.

——. *The Wanderground: Stories of the Hill Women.* Watertown, Mass.: Persephone Press, 1978.

Gearhart, Sally Miller, Lani Silver, Sue Talbot, Rita Mae Brown, Jeanne Cordova, and Barbara McLean. 'A Kiss Does Not a Revolution Make – A Search for Ideology.' Parts 1–3. *Lesbian Tide* (June/July/August 1974): 3, 10, 12.

Gilman, Charlotte Perkins. *Herland.* New York: Pantheon, 1979.

Grahn, Judy. *Another Mother Tongue: Gay Words, Gay Worlds.* Boston: Beacon Press, 1984.

Gray, Elizabeth Dodson. 'Patriarchy as a Conceptual Trap.' *Alternative Futures* 4/2–3 (spring/summer 1981): 135–55.

Greene, Gayle, and Coppelia Kahn, eds. *Making a Difference: Feminist Literary Criticism.* New York: Methuen and Co., 1985.

Griffin, Susan. *Women and Nature: The Roaring inside Her.* New York: Harper and Row, 1978.

Gutter Dyke Collective. 'Over the Walls.' In Sarah Lucia Hoagland and Julia Penelope, eds., *For Lesbians Only*, 27–31.

Harraway, Donna J. 'A Manifesto for Cyborgs: Science, Technology and Socialist Feminism in the 1980s.' *Socialist Review* 15/80 (March/April 1985): 65–107.

Harris, Bertha. *Lover.* Plainfield, Vt.: Daughters, 1976.

Hartman, Joan E., and Ellen Messer-Davidow, eds. *(En)Gendering Knowledge: Feminists in Academe.* Knoxville: University of Tennessee Press, 1991.

Henderson, Lisa. 'Lesbian Pornography: Cultural Transgression and Sexual Demystification.' In Sally Munt, ed., *New Lesbian Criticism*, 173–91.

Hoagland, Sarah Lucia. *Lesbian Ethics.* Palo Alto, Calif.: Institute of Lesbian Studies, 1988.

——. 'Sadism, Masochism, and Lesbian-Feminism.' In Robin Ruth Linden et al., *Against Sadomasochism*, 153–63.

Hoagland, Sarah Lucia, and Julia Penelope. 'Lesbian Separatism.' A workshop given at the 14th Annual Michigan Womyn's Music Festival, August 11, 1989.

———, eds. *For Lesbians Only: A Separatist Anthology*. London: Onlywomen Press, 1988.

hooks, bell. *Ain't I a Woman: Black Women and Feminism*. Boston: South End Press, 1981.

Howard, June. 'Informal Notes toward "Marxist-Feminist" Cultural Analysis.' *Minnesota Review* 20 (spring 1983): 77–92.

HOWL. Untitled flyer, April 1986. Lesbian Herstory Archives, New York City.

Hull, Gloria T., Patricia Bell Scott, and Barbara Smith, eds. *All the Women Are White, All the Blacks Are Men, but Some of Us Are Brave*. Old Westbury, N.Y.: Feminist Press, 1982.

Jameson, Fredric. 'Introduction/Prospectus: To Reconsider the Relationship of Marxism to Utopian Thought.' *Minnesota Review* 6 (spring 1976): 53–58.

———. 'Of Islands and Trenches: Naturalization and the Production of Utopian Discourse.' *Diacritics* 7/2 (1977): 2–21.

Jay, Carla, and Joanne Glasgow, eds. *Lesbian Texts and Contexts: Radical Revisions*. New York: New York University Press, 1990.

Jo, Bev. 'Female Only.' In Sarah Lucia Hoagland and Julia Penelope, eds., *For Lesbians Only*, 74–75.

Jo, Bev, Linda Strega, and Ruston. *Dykes-Loving-Dykes: Dyke Separatist Politics for Lesbians Only*. Oakland, Calif.: Battleaxe, 1990.

Johnston, Jill. *Lesbian Nation: The Feminist Solution*. New York: Simon and Schuster, 1973.

———. 'The Myth of Bonnies without Clydes: Lesbian Feminism and the Male Left.' *Village Voice*, April 28, 1975, 14.

Johnston, Pamela C. 'How Lesbians Read Literature: A Constructive Criticism.' *Sinister Wisdom* 15: 94–98.

Jones, Libby Falk, and Sarah Webster Goodwin, eds. *Feminism, Utopia, and Narrative*. Knoxville: University of Tennessee Press, 1990.

Joseph, Gloria I. 'White Promotion, Black Survival.' In Gloria I. Joseph and Jill Lewis, eds., *Common Differences*, 19–42.

Joseph, Gloria I., and Jill Lewis, eds. *Common Differences: Conflicts in Black and White Feminist Perspectives*. Boston: South End Press, 1986.

Kane, Eileen. 'A Comparative Study of the Women's Movement: Part 1.' *Tribad: A Lesbian Separatist Newsjournal* 1/1 (May 1977): 5–8.

Kaufman, Felix. 'Nonreproductive Male/Female Differences: Some Philosophical Implications and Cultural Consequences.' *Alternative Futures* 4/2–3 (spring/summer 1981): 36–46.

Khanna, Lee Cullen. 'Women's Worlds: New Directions in Utopian Fiction.' *Alternative Futures* 4/2–3 (spring/summer 1981): 57–59.

Kim, Alison. 'Pacific/Asian Lesbians and the Printed Word: Building Community through Writing.' Unpublished manuscript, June 11, 1987. Lesbian Herstory Archives, New York City.

King, Katie. 'Audre Lorde's Lacquered Layerings: The Lesbian Bar as a Site of Literary Production.' In Sally Munt, ed., *New Lesbian Criticism*, 51–74.

Klasse, Leila. 'Interview with Sally Gearhart.' *Lesbian Insider/Insighter/Inciter* 2 (August 1980): 7+.

Klein, Yvonne M. 'Myth and Community in Recent Lesbian Autobiographical Fiction.' In Carla Jay and Joanne Glasgow, eds., *Lesbian Texts and Contexts*, 330–38.

Knight, Isabel. 'The Feminist Scholar and the Future of Gender.' *Alternative Futures* 4/2–3 (spring/summer 1981): 17–35.

Koedt, Anne, Ellen Levine, and Anita Rapone, eds. *Notes from the Third Year: Women's Liberation*. New York: New York Radical Women, 1971.

———, eds. *Radical Feminism*. New York: Quadrangle, New York Times Book Co., 1973.

Koolish, Lynda. 'Country Women: The Feminists of Albion Ridge.' *Mother Jones* (April 1978): 23–32.

Kreps, Bonnie. 'Radical Feminism 1.' In Anne Koedt, Ellen Levine, and Anita Rapone, eds., *Radical Feminism*, 234–39.

Kuhn, Annette, and AnnMarie Wolpe, eds. *Feminism and Materialism: Women and the Modes of Production*. London: Routledge and Kegan Paul, 1977.

Kumar, Krishan. 'Primitivism in Feminist Utopias.' *Alternative Futures* 4/2–3 (spring/summer 1981): 61–66.

Lee, Anna. 'A Black Separatist.' In Sarah Lucia Hoagland and Julia Penelope, eds., *For Lesbians Only*, 83–92.

Lefanu, Sarah. *Feminism and Science Fiction*. Bloomington: Indiana University Press, 1988.

Lesbian Lifespace Journal. Drafts of a May 1973 lesbian-separatist newsletter. Lesbian Herstory Archives, New York City.

Lesh, Cheri. 'Women of Wander.' *Lesbian Tide* 9/4 (January/February 1980): 16–17.

Lewis, Jill. 'Sexual Division of Power: Motivations of the Women's Liberation Movement.' In Gloria I. Joseph and Jill Lewis, eds., *Common Differences*, 43–71.

Lewis, Reina. 'The Death of the Author and the Resurrection of the Dyke.' In Sally Munt, ed., *New Lesbian Criticism*, 17–32.

Lewis, Sasha G. *Sunday's Women: Lesbian Life Today.* Boston: Beacon Press, 1979.

Lilly, Mark. *Lesbian and Gay Writing: An Anthology of Cultural Essays.* Philadelphia: Temple University Press, 1990.

Linden, Robin Ruth, Darlene R. Pagano, Diana E. H. Russell, and Susan Leigh Star, eds. *Against Sadomasochism: A Radical Feminist Analysis.* East Palo Alto, Calif.: Frog in the Well, 1982.

Lorde, Audre. 'Man Child: A Black Lesbian Feminist's Response.' *Conditions* 4 (1979): 30–36.

Madsen, Catherine. '*The Wanderground,* a Review.' *Conditions* 7 (1981): 134–39.

Maggiore, Dolores J. *Lesbianism: An Annotated Bibliography and Guide to the Literature, 1976–1986.* Metuchen, N.J.: Scarecrow Press, 1988.

Malloy, Rue. 'Understanding Separatism.' *Plexus* (May 1980): 5.

Marcus, Eric. 'What a Riot!' *10 Percent* 2/8 (June 1994): 48–53, 78–82.

Marin, Louis. 'Thesis on Ideology and Utopia.' *Minnesota Review* 6 (spring 1976): 71–75.

McAllister, Pam, ed. *Reweaving the Web of Life: Feminism and Non-Violence.* Philadelphia: New Society Publishers, 1982.

Mellor, Anne K. 'On Feminist Utopias.' *Women's Studies* 9 (1982): 241–62.

Miller, Margaret. 'The Ideal Woman in Two Feminist Science-Fiction Utopias.' *Science-Fiction Studies* 10 (1983): 191–98.

Moi, Toril. *Sexual/Textual Politics.* New York: Methuen and Co., 1985.

Molloy, Alice. *In Other Words: Notes on the Politics and Morale of Survival.* Oakland, Calif.: Women's Press Collective, 1973.

Moraga, Cherríe, Gloria Anzaldúa, and Toni Cade Bambara, eds. *This Bridge Called My Back: Writings by Radical Women of Color.* New York: Kitchen Table Women-of-Color Press, 1981.

Morgan, Robin, ed. *Sisterhood Is Powerful: An Anthology of Writings from the Women's Liberation Movement.* New York: Random House, 1970.

Munt, Sally, ed. *New Lesbian Criticism: Literary and Cultural Readings.* New York: Columbia University Press, 1992.

Myron, Nancy. 'Class Beginnings.' *Furies* 1/3 (March/April 1972): 2–3.

Myron, Nancy, and Charlotte Bunch, eds. *Lesbianism and the Women's Movement.* Baltimore: Diana Press, 1975.

Native American Solidarity Committee (NASC). 'Separatism and Racism.' *Out and About* (August 1977): 13–14.

Nestle, Joan. *A Restricted Country.* Ithaca, N.Y.: Firebrand Books, 1987.

Newton, Judith, and Deborah Rosenfelt, eds. *Feminist Criticism and Social Change.* New York: Methuen, 1985.

Notes from the First Year: Women's Liberation. New York: New York Radical Women, 1968.

Ozark Wimmin on the Land. 'Women on Land.' 1976. Lesbian Herstory Archives, New York City.

Palmer, Paulina. 'Contemporary Lesbian Feminist Fiction: Texts for Every Woman.' In Linda Anderson, ed., *Plotting Changes*, 42–62.

Patai, Daphne. 'When Women Rule: Defamiliarization in the Sex-Role Reversal Utopia.' *Extrapolation* 23/1 (1982): 56–69.

Paz, Juana Maria. *La Luz Journal.* Fayetteville, Ark.: Paz Press, 1980.

Pearson, Carol. 'Women's Fantasies and Feminist Utopias.' *Frontiers* 2/3 (1977): 50–61.

Penelope, Julia. 'And Now for the Hard Questions.' *Sinister Wisdom* (1980): N.p.

———. 'Imagining Our Future: Vision and Revision.' *Sinister Wisdom* 11 (Fall 1979): 71–73.

Pfaelzer, Jean. *The Utopian Novel in America, 1886–1896: The Politics of Form.* Pittsburgh: University of Pittsburgh Press, 1984.

Phelan, Shane. *Identity Politics: Lesbian Feminism and the Limits of Community.* Philadelphia: Temple University Press, 1989.

Rabine, Leslie. 'Essentialism and Its Contexts: Saint Simonian and Post-Structuralist Feminists.' *Differences* 1/2 (summer 1989): 105–23.

Radicalesbians. 'Woman Identified Woman.' In Anne Koedt, Ellen Levine, and Anita Rapone, eds., *Radical Feminism*, 240–45. Originally published in *Notes from the Third Year*, 1971.

Radical Feminists #28. 'On Separatism.' Unpublished position paper, May 1972. Lesbian Herstory Archives, New York City.

Raymond, Janice. *The Transsexual Empire.* Boston: Beacon Press, 1979.

Redstockings, eds. *Feminist Revolution.* New York: Random House, 1978.

Redwomon. 'Freedom.' In Sarah Lucia Hoagland and Julia Penelope, eds., *For Lesbians Only*, 76–83.

Rich, Adrienne. 'Compulsory Heterosexuality and Lesbian Existence.' *Signs: A Journal of Women in Culture and Society* 5/4 (1980): 631–60.

———. '"It's the Lesbian in Us . . ."' In *On Lies, Secrets, and Silence: Selected Prose 1966–1978.* New York: W. W. Norton and Co., 1979, 199–202.

———. 'Notes for a Magazine: What Does Separatism Mean?' *Sinister Wisdom* 18 (fall 1981): 83–91.

———. *Of Woman Born: Motherhood as Experience and Institution.* New York: W. W. Norton, 1976.

Rich, Cynthia. 'Interview with Women from Persephone Press.' *Sinister Wisdom* (spring 1980): 81–86.

Roberts, Lou. 'Review of *The Wanderground.*' *Frontiers* 5/1 (1980): 54–55.

Robinson, Lillian S. *Sex, Class and Culture.* Bloomington: Indiana University Press, 1978.

Rohrlich, Ruby, and Elaine H. Baruch, eds. *Women in Search of Utopia: Mavericks and Mythmakers.* New York: Shocken Books, 1984.

Roof, Judith. *A Lure of Knowledge: Lesbian Sexuality and Theory.* New York: Columbia University Press, 1991.

———. 'The Match in the Crocus: Representations of Lesbian Sexuality.' In Marleen S. Barr and Richard Feldstein, eds., *Discontented Discourses,* 100–116.

Rosenfeld, Marthe. 'Language and the Vision of a Lesbian-Feminist Utopia in Wittig's *Les Guérillères.*' *Frontiers* 6/1 (1981): 6–9.

Rosinsky, Natalie M. *Feminist Futures: Contemporary Women's Speculative Fiction.* Ann Arbor, Mich.: UMI Research Press, 1984.

Rowbotham, Sheila. *Woman's Consciousness, Man's World.* Harmondsworth, England: Penguin, 1973.

Russ, Joanna. '*Amor Vincit Foeminam:* The Battle of the Sexes in Science Fiction.' *Science-Fiction Studies* 7 (1980): 2–15.

———. *The Female Man.* New York: Bantam, 1975.

———. '"Listen, There's a Story For You . . ." A Review of *Retreat! As It Was!*' *Sinister Wisdom* 12 (winter 1980): 89–92.

Sargent, Lyman Tower. 'Utopia – The Problem of Definition.' *Extrapolation* 16/1 (December 1974): 137–48.

———. 'Women in Utopia.' *Comparative Literature Studies* 10 (December 1973): 302–16.

Scott, Joan W. 'Gender: A Useful Category of Historical Analysis.' *American History Review* 91/5 (1986): 1053–75.

'Separatism . . . Overdose?!' *Lesbian Connection* 2/3: 8–9.

Singer, Rochelle. *The Demeter Flower.* New York: St. Martin's Press, 1980.

Singer, Shelley [Rochelle?]. 'One Woman's Viewpoint.' *Advocate* (n.d.): N.p. Lesbian Herstory Archives, New York City.

SJS [Susanna J. Sturgis?]. 'Let's Be Reasonable – Let's Demand the Impossible [a review of *The Demeter Flower*].' *off our backs* 11/2 (February 1981): 20+.

Slusser, George E., Colin Greenland, and Erik S. Rabkin, eds. *Storm Warnings: Science Fiction Confronts the Future.* Carbondale: Southern Illinois University Press, 1987.

Slusser, George E., Eric S. Rabkin, and Robert Scholes, eds. *Coordinates: Placing Science Fiction and Fantasy.* Carbondale: Southern Illinois University Press, 1983.

Small, Margaret. 'Lesbians and the Class Position of Women.' In Nancy Myron and Charlotte Bunch, eds., *Lesbianism and the Women's Movement,* 49–61.

Smith, Barbara, and Beverly Smith. 'Across the Kitchen Table: A Sister-to-Sister Dialogue.' Reprinted in Cherríe Moraga, Gloria Anzaldúa, and Toni Cade Bambara, eds., *This Bridge Called My Back,* 113–27.

Somay, Bulent. 'Towards an Open-Ended Utopia.' *Science-Fiction Studies* 2 (1984): 25–38.

Spelman, Elizabeth V. *The Inessential Woman: Problems of Exclusion in Feminist Thought.* Boston: Beacon Press, 1988.

Spinster, Sidney. 'The Evolution of Lesbian Separatist Consciousness.' In Sarah Lucia Hoagland and Julia Penelope, eds., *For Lesbians Only,* 97–121.

Spiral Wimmin's Land Cooperative. Collective statement, n.d. Lesbian Herstory Archives, New York City.

Stenson, Linnea. 'From Isolation to Diversity: Self and Communities in Twentieth-Century Lesbian Novels.' In Susan Wolfe and Julia Penelope, eds., *Sexual Practice, Textual Theory,* 208–25.

Stone, Merlin. *Ancient Mirrors of Womanhood: Our Goddess and Heroine Heritage.* New York: New Sibylline Books, 1979.

Sturgis, Susanna J. 'Discovering the Wanderground: An Interview with Sally Gearhart.' *off our backs* 10/1 (January 1980): 24–25+.

———. *Memories and Visions: Women's Fantasy and Science Fiction.* Freedom, Calif.: Crossing Press, 1989.

———. '*Retreat! As It Was!* [a review].' *off our backs* 10/4 (April 1980): 19.

———. 'Transcript of an Interview with Sally Miller Gearhart.' Unedited version of the *off our backs* interview, November 1979. Lesbian Herstory Archives, New York City.

Suvin, Darko. 'Defining the Literary Genre of Utopia: Some Historical Semantics, Some Genealogy, a Proposal and a Plea.' *Studies in the Literary Imagination* 6/2 (fall 1973): 121–45.

———. '"Utopian" and "Scientific": Two Attributes for Socialism from Engels.' *Minnesota Review* 6 (spring 1976): 59–70.

Thomas, Jennice Gail. 'Coming Home to Mother: Feminist Utopian Visions, 1880–1980.' Ph.D. dissertation, Purdue University, 1983.

Tompkins, Jane. *Sensational Designs: The Cultural Work of American Fiction, 1790–1860.* New York: Oxford University Press, 1985.

Vance, Carole S., ed. *Pleasure and Danger: Exploring Female Sexuality.* Boston: Routledge and Kegan Paul, 1984.

Vida, Ginny, ed. *Our Right to Love: A Lesbian Resource Book.* Englewood Cliffs, N.J.: Prentice Hall, 1978.

Wagar, W. Warren. 'Utopian Studies and Utopian Thought: Definitions and Horizons.' *Extrapolation* 19/1 (December 1977): 4–12.

Ware, Cellestine. *Woman Power: Transitions in American Feminism.* N.p.: Tower Publications, 1970.

Washington, Cynthia. 'We Started from Different Ends of the Spectrum.' *Southern Exposure* 4 (Winter 1977): 15–16.

Weedon, Chris. *Feminist Practice and Post-Structuralist Theory.* New York: Basil Blackwell, 1987.

Weir, Lorna. 'A Talking Bush [review of *The Wanderground*].' *Body Politic* 62 (April 1980): 36.

Weitz, Rose. 'From Accommodation to Rebellion: The Politicization of Lesbianism.' In Trudy Darty and Sandee Potter, eds., *Women-Identified Women,* 233–48.

Weston, Kathleen M., and Lisa B. Rofel. 'Sexuality, Class, and Conflict in a Lesbian Workplace.' *Signs: A Journal of Women in Culture and Society* 9/4 (summer 1984): 623–46.

Whatling, Clare. 'Reading Awry: Joan Nestle and the Recontextualization of Heterosexuality.' In Joseph Bristow, ed., *Sexual Sameness,* 210–26.

Wilgus, Neal. 'Interview with Suzy McKee Charnas.' *Algol* (winter 1978–79): 21–25.

Willis, Ellen. 'Sister under the Skin? Confronting Race and Sex.' *Village Voice Literary Supplement* 8 (June 1982): N.p.

Wolf, Deborah G. *The Lesbian Community.* Berkeley: University of California Press, 1979.

Wolfe, Gary. *Science Fiction Dialogues.* Chicago: Academy Press, 1982.

Wolfe, Susan, and Julia Penelope, eds. *Sexual Practice, Textual Theory: Lesbian Cultural Criticism.* Cambridge, Mass.: Blackwell, 1993.

Wolfman, Brunetta R. 'Black First, Female Second.' In *Black Separatism and Social Reality: Rhetoric and Reason.* New York: Pergamon Press, 1977.

Women's Commune. 'Mind Bogglers.' *off our backs* 1/9–10 (July 1973): 13.

Yates, Gayle Graham. *What Women Want.* Cambridge, Mass.: Harvard University Press, 1975.

Young, Donna J. *Retreat! As It Was!* Weatherbuty Lake, Mo.: Naiad Press, 1979.

Zimmerman, Bonnie. 'Beyond Coming Out: New Lesbian Novels.' *Ms.* 13 (June 1985): 65.

———. 'Lesbians Like This and That: Some Notes on Lesbian Criticism for the Nineties.' In Sally Munt, ed., *New Lesbian Criticism,* 1–15.

———. *The Safe Sea of Women.* Boston: Beacon Press, 1990.

———. 'Seeing, Reading, Knowing: The Lesbian Appropriation of Literature.' In Joan E. Hartman and Ellen Messer–Davidow, eds., *(En)Gendering Knowledge,* 85–99.

SEPARATIST UTOPIAS AVAILABLE IN ENGLISH
(Dates in parentheses indicate approximate year text was written, if significantly different from publication date.)
Arnold, June. *The Cook and the Carpenter.* Plainfield, Vt.: Daughters, 1973.
Bradley, Marion Zimmer. *The Ruins of Isis.* New York: Avon, 1978.
———. *The Shattered Chain.* New York: Daw, 1976.
Broner, E. M. *A Weave of Women.* New York: Holt, Rinehart and Winston, 1978.
Charnas, Suzy McKee. *Motherlines.* New York: Berkley-Putnam, 1978.
Elgin, Suzette Haden. *The Judas Rose.* New York: Daw, 1987.
———. *Native Tongue.* New York: Daw, 1984.
Forrest, Katherine V. *Daughters of a Coral Dawn.* Tallahassee, Fla.: Naiad, 1984.
Gearhart, Sally Miller. *The Wanderground: Stories of the Hill Women.* Watertown, Mass.: Persephone Press, 1978.
Gilman, Charlotte Perkins. *Herland.* New York: Pantheon, 1979 (1915).
Hossain, Rokeya. *Sultana's Dream.* Feminist Press, 1988 (1902).
Lane, Mary E. Bradley. *Mizora: A Prophecy.* New York: Gregg, 1975 (1881).
Mushroom, Merril. *Daughters of Khaton.* Denver: Lace Publications, 1987 (1977).
Russ, Joanna. *The Female Man.* New York: Bantam, 1975.
———. 'When It Changed.' In *The Zanzibar Cat.* Sauk City, Wis.: Arkham House, 1972.
Sargeant, Pamela. *The Shore of Women.* New York: Bantam, 1986.
Scott, Sarah. *Millenium Hall.* London: Virago Press, 1986 (1762).
Sheldon, Racoona [Alice Sheldon]. 'Your Faces, O My Sisters.' In Vondra McIntyre, and Susan Anderson, eds., *Aurora beyond Equality.* Greenwich, Conn.: Fawcett, 1976.
Singer, Rochelle. *The Demeter Flower.* New York: St. Martin's, 1980.
Slonczewski, Joan. *A Door into Ocean.* New York: Avon, 1986.
Tepper, Sheri. *The Gate to Women's Country.* New York: Doubleday, 1988.
Tiptree, James Jr. [Alice Sheldon]. 'Houston, Houston, Do You Read?' In Vondra McIntyre and Susan Anderson, eds., *Aurora beyond Equality.* Greenwich, Conn.: Fawcett, 1976.
Wittig, Monique. *Across the Acheron.* London: Peter Ownen, 1987.
———. *Les Guérillères.* New York: Avon, 1971.
———. *The Lesbian Body.* New York: Avon, 1976.
Young, Donna J. *Retreat! As It Was!* Weatherbuty Lake, Mo.: Naiad Press, 1979.

INDEX

DATE DUE

APR 2 8 2000			
GAYLORD			PRINTED IN U.S.A.